Forging Ideal Muslim Subjects

LEXINGTON STUDIES IN CLASSICAL AND MODERN ISLAMIC THOUGHT

Hussam S. Timani

This series will explore and examine a vast literature on understudied strands in Islamic thought. The series topics include, but not limited to, Qur'an and hadith studies, classical theological and philosophical doctrines, the human knowledge, law and tradition, law and legal reforms, tradition and renewal, Salafi thought, piety movements, neo-traditionalism, neo-liberalism, neo-reformism, neo-Islamism, cultural pluralism, and liberal and ethical humanism. Additional subjects for consideration would be trends in contemporary Islamic thought such as democracy, justice, secularism, globalization, international relations, Islam and the West, and feminism. The volumes in the series would examine, historicize, and analyze Muslim intellectual responses to the various trends of Islamic thought that have been understudied in Western scholarship. This series would make an important and timely literature available to the English reader.

While the series encompasses both classical and modern Islamic thought, a special emphasis will be put on modern and contemporary Islamic reformist thought. In light of radicalism and the rise of violence in the Islamic world today, the expectations of reformist thought in Muslim societies are running high. What are the programs that qualify as reformist, what are the qualities an Islamic reformist is expected to demonstrate, and what exactly makes for Islamic reformist thinking? There are two strands of Muslim reformers in the Islamic world today: those who refer to themselves as Islamic reformers (they are out to reinterpret the Islamic tradition to make it compatible with the current age) and those who are described as reformist but claim that they are not out to reform Islam, but rather only to interpret it in an "Islamically correct" manner. To date, far too little attention has been devoted to the thought of the thinkers in both groups. The volumes in this series would examine contemporary reformist thought as well as its reception in both the Islamic world and the West.

Titles in the Series

Forging Ideal Muslim Subjects: Discursive Practices, Subject Formation, & Muslim Ethics, by Faraz Masood Sheikh
Decoding the Egalitarianism of the Qur'an: Retrieving Lost Voices on Gender, by Abla Hasan

Forging Ideal Muslim Subjects

Discursive Practices, Subject Formation, & Muslim Ethics

Faraz Masood Sheikh

LEXINGTON BOOKS
Lanham • Boulder • New York • London

Published by Lexington Books
An imprint of The Rowman & Littlefield Publishing Group, Inc.
4501 Forbes Boulevard, Suite 200, Lanham, Maryland 20706
www.rowman.com

6 Tinworth Street, London SE11 5AL, United Kingdom

Copyright © 2020 by The Rowman & Littlefield Publishing Group, Inc.

Nursi, Bediuzzaman Said. *Living the Quran with Joy and Purpose: Selections on Tawhid from Said Nursi's Epistle of Light* (forthcoming). Translated with introduction and notes by Yamina Bouguenaya and Isra Yazicioglu. Gorgias Press, 2020.

Nursi, Bediuzzaman Said. *The Letters: From the Risale-i Nur Collection.* Translated by Sukran Vahide. Istanbul: Sozler Nesriyat, 1994.

Nursi, Bediuzzaman Said. *The Flashes: From the Risale-i Nur Collection.* Translated by Sukran Vahide. Istanbul: Sozler Nesriyat, 1995.

Nursi, Bediuzzaman Said. *The Words: From the Risale-i Nur Collection.* Translated by Sukran Vahide. Istanbul: Sozler Nesriyat, 2004.

All rights reserved. No part of this book may be reproduced in any form or by any electronic or mechanical means, including information storage and retrieval systems, without written permission from the publisher, except by a reviewer who may quote passages in a review.

British Library Cataloguing in Publication Information Available

Library of Congress Cataloging-in-Publication Data

ISBN: 978-1-7936-2012-5 (cloth : alk. paper)
ISBN: 978-1-7936-2014-9 (pbk : alk. paper)
ISBN: 978-1-7936-2013-2 (electronic)

∞™ The paper used in this publication meets the minimum requirements of American National Standard for Information Sciences Permanence of Paper for Printed Library Materials, ANSI/NISO Z39.48-1992.

Contents

Acknowledgments	vii
Notes on Transliteration	xi
Introduction: Narrating Ideal Muslim Subjectivities in a Foucauldian Register	1
1 Muhasibian Religious Subjectivity and the Travails of Sincerity	31
2 Living with Vulnerabilities: Muhasibian Moral Subjectivity and Self-Care	63
3 Belief Perspectives and the Nursian Religious Subject	99
4 Nursian Believer as Moral Subject	135
Conclusion: Forging Ideal Subjectivities Everyday Over a Lifetime	159
Bibliography	171
Index	177
About the Author	185

Acknowledgments

I have had good teachers and caring mentors: Aaron Stalnaker, Richard Miller, Kevin Jaques, Constance Furey, Nazif Shahrani, John Walbridge, Shaul Magid, David Vishanoff and Zainab Istrabadi. Thank you! Their scholarship, guidance and encouragement were crucial for the conception and execution of this project. My colleagues at the religious studies department at William & Mary have been exceptionally collegial, supportive and intellectually engaging. My conversations with them have helped me think more deeply and clearly about the aims and arguments of this book. Thank you! I thank Shahzad, Muhammad Hasan, Elijah Reynolds and Munir Jibril for their generous and prompt help with translating and deciphering Muhasibi's dense Arabic prose over the past many years. My editors at Lexington, Michael Gibson and Mikayla Mislak, have been a pleasure to work with: thorough, professional, prompt and collegial. Thank you! I wish to thank Gorgias Press for giving me permission to cite from their forthcoming title, *Selections on Tawhid from Said Nursi*, by Yamina Bougenaya and Isra Yazicioglu. I also wish to thank Sukran Vahide and Söz Basım Yayın for giving me permission to use excerpts from Vahide's English translation of Nursi's works, the *Words*, *Letters*, and *Flashes*.

My deep and sincere appreciation is due to Dr. Ali Mermer and Dr. Yamina Bougenaya. They introduced me to the writings of Said Nursi. They have had an anchoring effect on my intellectual and spiritual life. I am truly grateful to them for helping me notice and understand aspects of Nursi's methodology and thought that would otherwise have certainly escaped my attention. They have been intellectual and spiritual role models. Over the years, I have had the privilege of keeping company with a circle of intellectually honest, affectionate and thoughtful friends through weekly discussion circles. I thank them all for generously sharing their wisdom, hospitality, comradery and humanity with me. My ongoing conversations with them have helped shaped some of the ideas presented in this book. The list of friends is long and I mention just a few names that come to my forgetful and aging mind: Andrea Dziubek, Omer Tatari, Maha Nour, Asma Mermer, Elijah Reynolds, Yusuf Osmanlioglu, Birkan Tunc, Zafer Ozdemir, Muhammed Alan, Aysenur Guc, Hatice Beyza, Aalia Khidr and several others.

I want to thank my family and my wife's family for their unfailing support and love. For their affection and hospitality, I thank my in-laws: Osman and Selma Yazicioglu, Latife and Shahin, Ridvan and Benan. They welcomed me into their hearts and homes and prayed incessantly for my success and well-being. My loving and adorable nephews and nieces, Ryva, Ehaab, Zaynah and Raeha, brought immense joy into my life during years of cheerless isolation that was often demanded by this book. Not a small part of the emotional energy needed to write this book came from a desire to make them proud of their absentee uncle. Thank you! To my beloved brothers, my best friends and my pillars of support, for whom my smallest successes have always been cause for great joy and celebration, Asim and Samir and their families. I offer to all of them my love and sincere thanks. A large extended family on both sides, mine and Isra's, have helped us in indescribable ways and I thank them all for their good wishes and support from the bottom of my heart. A special mention for my late paternal uncle, Naseem Ullah Sheikh. He would have been overjoyed and especially proud had he lived to see the publication of this book.

I have met few people who are as silently and constantly self-giving, loving, well-meaning and generous than the people who have made me feel loved and supported in whatever I have chosen to do in life: my dearly beloved mother (Ammi ji), Ghazala Aqdas Butt and my dearly beloved father (Abbu ji), Masood Javed Sheikh. Thank you. You have taught me how to love and feel loved. You have modelled what it means to live for others and find the highest of life's meanings and joys in so doing. This book is a small token of my appreciation for instilling the love of truth, justice and meaning in me. God bless you in all worlds.

A heartfelt but woefully inadequate thank you to my kind, ever supportive, loving partner, Isra. I could not have written this book without her, her immense love, support and countless daily sacrifices and kindnesses. She gave of herself and her life to this project, repeatedly read drafts of each chapter and gave extensive and insightful suggestions throughout. Had I not the worry that my words might be misinterpreted, I would have said that we wrote this book together.

Finally, a note of appreciation and thanks to my beloved son, my *jan* (sweetheart), Isa. Isa Omer Sheikh, a rambunctious fifth grader at the time of this book's completion. He kept reminding me that a beautiful life-after-book awaits and encouraged me to get off Facebook and focus on the writing. I started writing it when he was four years old and finished when he was ten. Over these years, he sacrificed much precious time that he wanted to spend with me, sometimes with resignation, at others with protest but always with love. I cannot say if the book you now hold in your hands, or see on your screens, was worth all the sacrifices he made. All I know is that Isa's love and support (and occasional impatience) have all been gifts for me and I shall always cherish them. Thank you, Isa! I am done bruh! If it is any consolation for the many named and unnamed teachers, mentors, friends and family members who have helped me think about and develop the ideas and questions I grapple with in the pages that follow, let me end by the customary confession that all the shortcomings and mistakes that remain are mine alone.

Notes on Transliteration

In the transliteration of Arabic, I have made the following exceptions in this book:

1. 'ayn and hamza are represented with a regular quote mark, (as ' and ' respectively) instead of a ring quote.
2. In order to make the book easier to read for nonspecialists, I have often skipped elongation marks from words or names within the body of the text, except for text titles. Thus, for instance, I have used "Muhasibi" instead of Muḥasibī. I also used "Quran" instead of "Qur'ān." For several terms that entered into English usage and are listed in Oxford Concise Dictionary, I have also skipped diacritics, such as "*sharia*" instead of "*sharī'a*." (The references and bibliographical entries contain full diacritics.)

In discussing Said Nursi, who mostly wrote in Ottoman Turkish, I give the Arabic transliteration for the terms originating in Arabic in brackets. When I occasionally refer to Turkish renderings Nursi used, I prefaced it with "Tk."

Introduction

Narrating Ideal Muslim Subjectivities in a Foucauldian Register

This book is about the nature and formation of *ideal Muslim subjectivity*. What makes a person an ideal Muslim? What form should an ideal, religiously informed Muslim consciousness and ethical life take? What values ought a committed Muslim to live by? What thoughts and worries ought they nurture or disparage and why? Which commitments ought to anchor and guide their interpretations of themselves, society and the universe? Which perspectives and standpoints ought they inhabit, which sensibilities ought they cultivate and by what means should they forge such standpoints and sensibilities? In this book, I explore answers to these questions through the lens of two important and understudied Muslim thinkers, the ninth-century moral pedagogue, al-Harith b. Asad al-Muhasibi (d. 856) and the twentieth-century Kurdish Quran scholar, Bediuzzaman Said Nursi (d. 1960).

The questions I have posed above are broad and general, but we should not expect the answers to be generic. It cannot be gainsaid that Islam is an internally differentiated, contested and diverse religious and moral tradition. It has not been lived by people in a single, uniform way. What makes Islamic tradition diverse is not only the diversity of the languages, ethnicities, nationalities and cultures affiliated with it. It is also the case that there have always been disagreements within the tradition about how basic tenets of the faith are to be understood and elaborated, what philosophical and ethical implications ought to be drawn from them and, basically, how people ought to live their lives as authentic Muslims. It is common knowledge among scholars today that Islam, as a discursive tradition, has several (often but not always competing and irreconcilable) sub-traditions.[1] Therefore, we should expect statements by Muslim thinkers about the nature and formation of ideal Muslim subjectivity to differ, coalesce, converge and diverge in multiple, layered ways and along various axes.[2] Needless to say, this book should not be read as offering the most authentic, *sui generis* account of being an ideal Muslim. Focusing on two thinkers, Muhasibi and Nursi, signals that the book is about *accounts* of ideal Muslim subjectivity and not an account of *the* ideal Muslim subject. I examine Muhasibi's and Nursi's accounts with due attention to their context and to their particular conceptual vocabularies.[3] Though interest in Muslim subjectivities is not very old among academics, several scholars have offered accounts of ideal Muslim subjectivity through the lens of Islamic law, mysticism, philosophy and anthropology over the past two decades.[4]

The two most commonly elaborated accounts of being an ideal Muslim have been the *juridical* and *mystical* ones. This book adds to these because it shows that in Muhasibi's and Nursi's case, the ideal Muslim subject is more than a person who can perfectly observe legal obligations and rituals; and also someone different and more than a person who loses his ego-self and bears a mystical love for God. All too often, scholars have interpreted Muslim religious and ethical life in terms of Islamic law (*sharia* and/or *fiqh*).[5] I think this overemphasis on law as an index for Muslim ethical life can give the impression that Muslim ethical life is marked by an obsession with rules about the minutiae of life. No matter how noble some Muslims may feel this notion of an ethical life can be, many Muslims and outsiders are bound to feel that Muslim ethics, as dogged concern for rules, is at best inaccessible and unintelligible to them and, at worst, a shallow and parochial vision of a morally excellent life. Others have argued that the ethical core of Muslim religious life is a mystical or Sufi one, a way of life that seeks to overcome one's lower self and that ends with communion and finally union with the Divine. This too has left some wondering how a self-absorbed quest for friendship or union with the divine (the Sufi masters are called friends of God or *awliya* in the Islamic tradition) ought to manifest morally in the everyday consciousness and life of an average Muslim and how it ought to shape intersubjective relations.[6] In my view, it is possible to offer accounts of Muslim subjectivity that do not neatly fit the juridical or Sufi frameworks, even as they share certain features with them. It is important to shine some light on these other, rich and textured accounts of Muslim subjectivity that, while retaining a place for the legal and the mystical, are not easily reducible to either of these frameworks. Muhasibian and Nursian accounts of ideal subjectivity are, I hope to show in this book, good examples of such accounts. They give us insights into Muslim thinking about what it means to be a Muslim beyond inhabiting a strictly legal or mystical form of life. But in order to properly reconstruct such accounts, we need some new conceptual tools, categories and methods. The bulk of this chapter is dedicated to a discussion of such tools, categories and methods. The reader will likely notice that these theoretical tools and categories (and scholarship from which I draw them) reappear explicitly in the rest of the book only occasionally and in a somewhat scattered way even as they remain relevant and operative in the background. A more sustained, explicit engagement with theory and method throughout the book would make for a more cumbersome and less accessible, theory-heavy read.

Before I move forward, let me provide a quick overview of what is to come in this chapter. First, I briefly introduce Muhasibi and Nursi, restricting my remarks to the bare essentials as this book is neither a historical study of their lives and works nor an exhaustive study of their vast and rich teachings. There is much that Muhasibi and Nursi speak about that I do not discuss in this book. In my short introduction to their lives, I indicate how, prima facie (because a fuller answer would have to await the end of the analysis), both thinkers present accounts of ideal subjectivity that juridical and mystical approaches do not fully capture. A significant portion of this chapter will then be devoted to explaining the theoretical and conceptual apparatus that undergirds and guides my interpretation of Muhasibi's and Nursi's writings in the subsequent chapters. I discuss these conceptual, methodological and terminological issues here and do not repeatedly bring them up in the subsequent chapters, where I simply present the outcomes of using these methodological and conceptual tools. The latter remain relevant throughout but remain in the background. The goal of the book is not to engage with Foucault or other theorists in a sustained way but to use the latter's insights and methods to reconstruct, as richly and fully as possible within the limited space available, Muhasibian and Nursian accounts of ideal Muslim consciousness and subjectivity.

MUHASIBI AND NURSI: MOVING BEYOND JURIDICAL AND MYSTICAL MODELS

From what we can gather based on scant historical information about the man, Muhasibi was born in Basra sometime in the late eighth century, probably around 781 CE.[7] His family moved to the newly established Abbasid capital, Baghdad, presumably attracted by the many economic and educational opportunities it offered its new inhabitants, while Muhasibi was still a young boy.[8] He spent most of his life in Baghdad and most likely, died there in 857 CE with a brief interlude in Kufa, where he was forced to flee because of persecution by his traditionist detractors in Baghdad.[9] Scholars have noted that we have little to no reliable historical information about Muhasibi's life.[10] A handful of biographical anecdotes in Arabic biographical dictionaries present an image of a man trained in multiple religious sciences, a person of exemplary scrupulosity, with a deep concern for inward piety and a robust appetite for theological discussion.[11] Gavin Picken, one of only two scholars to have written a full-length manuscript in English about Muhasibi, opines that one of Muhasibi's main goals was "the correction of the misplaced notion that being detached from the world in a spiritual sense or to refrain from sin requires that one remain secluded from society."[12] Muhasibi's alleged repudiation by the leading *hadith* scholar of his time, Ahmad b. Hanbal (d. 855 CE), also gives us the impression that Muhasibi's teachings were too radical and nontraditional.[13] Muhasibi wrote in a context when, it seems, different approaches to understanding and practicing Islam were yet to crystallize and find acceptance. Muhasibi's contemporaries seem to be zealously committed to their own nascent paths, chastising all other paths or schools of thought as dangerously corrupting and condemnable innovations. In his works, Muhasibi cautions against such self-righteous, conceited and arrogant contempt toward those that one does not agree with.

Muhasibi's writings show that he was concerned about arrogance and self-righteousness of all kinds: he criticizes the Mutazilites for thinking they alone are on the right path, the Sufis and ascetics for thinking their practices are the most excellent, the traditionalists for thinking that the pursuit of traditions (reports about Prophet Muhammad's words and actions) was more important than living by the principles and values exemplified in those traditions. He had a problem with the legal-minded externalists, but he was also suspicious of easy-going claims to spiritual progress, inner purity and nearness to God. His dissatisfaction with complacency in piety leads him to focus considerable attention on moral psychology. His works show a keen interest in revealing the hidden dangers in all modes of piety, no matter how apparently meritorious, while also insisting that one must nevertheless struggle to properly fulfill God's rights.[14] In so doing, he seems to have emphasized, in a way that had not been customary in Muslim thought, a highly self-reflective and discursive way of being Muslim, a way of being that was psychologically attuned, at every moment, to the ways in which a person, no matter how "spiritually advanced" or "knowledgeable," could get religiously and morally compromised. For this book, I have drawn from a range of his extant works, focusing on discourses that allow me to best illuminate his account of the nature and formation of ideal Muslim subjectivity.

In contrast to Muhasibi, much more is known about Bediuzzaman Said Nursi, as he lived relatively recently (1877–1960). Over the past two decades, there have been several comprehensive but general studies of his life and works.[15] Nursi was born in eastern Anatolia, which was part of the Ottoman Empire, and died in 1960 in Urfa in what had become the modern, democratic Turkish republic. This means that as a young man, educated in the religious sciences, he saw the collapse of the Ottoman empire and lived to see the rise of the secular Turkish republic. Scholars often divide his life into three distinct phases, the Old Said, the New Said and the Third Said. The interested reader can get a good overview of Nursi's main intellectual and spiritual interests in each of these phases of his life by reading Sukran Vahide's detailed biographical account.[16] Suffice to note here that as a thoughtful, pious, religiously trained and highly intelligent man, Nursi saw that materialist and naturalist philosophies were making deep inroads into Turkish society and psyche and he saw these ideologies as a grave threat to belief in God and religious commitment more generally. He spent the early years of his adult life as a traditional religious scholar, taking interest in political reform, social issues, the survival of the caliphate and encouraging a combination of contemporary and Islamic education through a new kind of university/medrese that he envisioned. A series of events led to his change of heart: his attention turned away from social and political issues and became razor focused on what we can generally call *belief* matters. He became, in his own words, "New Said," who realized that the foundations of belief in God were so weak among Muslims that no other matter deserved greater attention. He became more inward as well during this time. He set about writing what would become his main work, the *Risale-i Nur* (henceforth *Risale*), which is roughly a six thousand page, unconventional, non-linear commentary on the Quran. The aim of the *Risale*, which Nursi indicates in the book itself, was to help his contemporaries develop a strong, Quranically inspired and rationally defensible belief in God, against atheistic and naturalist philosophies coming from the geographical West. Toward the final years of his life, he again took some cursory interest in politics and seems to have supported the democratic party, constitutionalism and democratic government, as "the lesser of two evils."[17]

One important point to know about Nursi's background is that he was persecuted, imprisoned and exiled by the Turkish Republic on one or another pretext throughout his mature years. Much of the *Risale* was written under conditions of exile and imprisonment. Nursi did not write in the company of scholars, as a head of some religious institution or as an employee of any institution or government. His ideas, we can assume, are not tainted by concerns about his livelihood, status in society, popularity and impact (in terms of radical social or political change). By the same token, they have not come about as a result of robust and challenging conversations among one's scholarly peers. Nursi's aim was to speak to as wide an audience as possible. This explains Nursi's use of simple, yet rich, metaphors and parables to convey complex theological and ethical reasonings and ideals. He sought deep transformations in people's attitudes, that of commoners' as well as the attitude of the scholarly elite, toward the Quran and toward belief matters. It seems to me that he was offering nothing less than a completely new way of being a Muslim in a world where religious claims could not retain their appeal without the warrant of reason and rationality. He thought that the path he was showing would be more fully understood and could materialize more fully at some distant time in the future. In that sense, his teachings are an act of hope and a bold act of imagination, modelling a way for Muslims to engage with the Quran in a deeply personal and rational way. In this book, I mostly focus on the writings and thoughts of the New Said. The Quran became the centerpiece of Nursi's life as New Said. Nursi offers some theoretical reflection on hermeneutics in his earlier writings, but in most cases he simply applies his method and lets the reader figure out which principles of interpretation have allowed him to confirm Quranic truths and draw life-changing lessons and insights from Quranic verses that, at first glance, might seem distant and irrelevant for an average person's daily struggles and problems. His approach privileged reflection on Quranic verses, a direct engagement with the Quran as God's living word, subject to the reader's affirmation. Thus, reflection on everyday life experiences through the lens of Quranic verses, affirming thereby the truth claims of the text, itself emerges as a basic practice and a form of life that Nursi wanted to promote. He presented himself as a student of the Quran and encouraged studentship of the Quran as the foundation for an ideal Muslim religious and moral life. What this studentship meant in practice and how it was supposed to form ideal subjects, we shall see in chapters 3 and 4 of this book.

Muhasibi and Nursi have generally appeared to scholars as too enigmatic (and sometimes too simplistic) to merit serious critical analysis of their teachings and pedagogical projects. I think part of the problem lies with the broad and unsuitable categories of analysis scholars have typically used to approach their writings, categories such as law, mysticism/Sufism and asceticism. It is not nuanced and precise enough, for instance, to find Muhasibi's mention of love of God or his counsels about the need to purify the *nafs* (recalcitrant soul) and conclude that he was a mystic or Sufi, recommending a mystical piety as the ideal way of being Muslim in the world.[18] Nor should we take his use of a discourse about renunciation of one or another bodily pleasure to be a sign of his ascetic disposition.[19] Such observations are trite and perhaps ethicists can actually help historians of Islam move beyond simplistic classificatory interpretations (i.e., interpretations that seek out the slightest indications in a thinker's writings that would help us classify them in one or another group, school, genre and so on). Many rich and insightful discourses written by Muslims are read simply so that they could be filed in the correct slot in the proverbial filing cabinet. In Muhasibi's and Nursi's case, we have few serious studies in a Western language that critically and ethically examine their writings. Approached without a novel and creative interpretive framework, their writings would continue to present a conundrum and yield puzzling interpretations.

On the one hand, scholars tell us that Muhasibi is a mystic and a proto-Sufi.[20] They cite Muhasibi's endorsement of knowledge of God, gnosis, attention to the conditions of the heart and love of God as evidence of Muhasibi's credentials as a proto-Sufi thinker.[21] On the other hand, we also read that Muhasibi is not truly mystical because he does not espouse ideas such as being intoxicated with divine love, union with the divine or extraordinary mystical experiences.[22] Then we read that Muhasibi is basically an ascetic and a renunciant but are also informed that he expects human beings to be fully engaged in the world and does not think shunning material goods is, on its own, a desirable ideal.[23] Rather, he simply wants people to inwardly realize that everything in the world is transitory and he wants them to avoid unlawful consumption of food and property.[24] It puts a strain on the term *ascetic* to extend it to include an attitude that does not take the shunning of material goods as an important or central requirement of piety. Now we do sometimes find Muhasibi talking about divine love and we do often find him recommending renunciation and presenting as models, knowledgeable scholars who wept on account of the responsibility they felt toward God, but then he also criticizes those who cry a lot to give the appearance of piety. Muhasibi's simultaneous incorporation of these ideas into his overall discourses only seems odd to us because our frameworks of analysis (mysticism/Sufism and asceticism) make us focus only on the content of his writings without adequate attention to the ways those concepts are situated and *deployed* in his discourses and the *practical work* that these ideas ought to do for the person who would engage with them.

Nursi's writings suffer a similar fate in the hands of scholars who approach him through the lens of Islamic mysticism. We find references to Nursi as a Sufi thinker on account of his use of Sufi ontology and epistemology.[25] And then we find others who note that Nursi presented his *Risale* as an alternative, new form of piety, founded on a personal, existential and pragmatic reading of the Quranic verses.[26] I think it would be a mistake to interpret Nursi as a Sufi thinker because this would obscure his novel contributions to Islamic thought.[27] Nursi himself is explicit that his way, the way of the *Risale* is not a Sufi path, even as he stops well short of disparaging Sufis or Sufism and makes it clear that he thinks Sufis were, and are, people of truth. Again, I think the desire to classify Nursi's writings as one or another *type* of Islamic discourse based on the presence or absence of technical terminology or explicit statements alone, fails to examine how he invokes concepts within larger discourses and for what practical and self-formative purposes. Thus, both Muhasibi and Nursi, each in his own way, would be ideal candidates for the present book, which explores the relations between practical reflection, and other discursive practices, and the formation of religious and moral subjectivity.

Both Muhasibi and Nursi write at a time when, in quite different ways, they think "business as usual" is no longer viable in terms of being a Muslim. They both see themselves offering new possibilities of being Muslim because they feel deeply dissatisfied with, and worried about the inadequacies of, the contemporary (each for their own time) understandings of the meaning of being Muslim in the world. Both are quite exceptional in their interest in the predicament and lifeways of the common person even as the rigors (psychological and intellectual) they seem to demand from an ideal subject gives one the impression that their target might be a select few, the spiritual elites. They are both interested in psychological matters and their teachings betray a sense of urgency about teaching the common person how to think about the religious life, and how to exist as a religious being in a complex and mysterious world.

Another important reason for my interest in Muhasibi and Nursi, one that only became clearer after I had already made some headway into their works, is their sense of a deep, salutary and interminable connection between the tragic and the beautiful. Both seem to me to be opposed to what we might call cheap optimism or easy triumphalism in religious and moral matters. Muhasibi teaches that the good (*khayr*) is quite often, and often indistinguishably, mixed with the bad (*sharr*) and it is not at all easy for a person to be able to distinguish between the two. Hence, for instance, a person might know pride to be wrong but when he gets angry with a sinful or disobedient person, he may erroneously imagine his anger to be pious, "for God's sake," and hence not a matter of pride.[28] Similarly, Nursi teaches that the beauty of this world comes into view not by looking away from the maladies and tragedies of existence but by refusing to look away from them and instead engaging with them with a perspective that yields insights and meanings that elevate the human being from this lowly and miserable position.[29] They are thinkers who envision a religious subject that repeatedly registers the tragic but without affirming it as the final word on existence and without suggesting that one reaches a psychological state of mind where one no longer feels the pain and heartache that accompanies the apprehension of life's many tragedies. They insist that one contemplates the tragic, deeply and with the help of divine guidance, without keeping oneself at an ironic distance from it. For our times, when slogans like "look at the bright side of life" ring hollow in the face of human tragedies—political, psychological, cultural, social and environmental catastrophes of unprecedented scale—Muhasibi and Nursi offer us conceptions of an ideal Muslim subject who can engage with these challenges. They do not recommend that the pathological and the tragic is something that can be fully overcome or rendered insignificant or irrelevant. Their discourses are enigmatic and ambivalent because they try to authentically track, rather than eliminate or downplay, the vicissitudes and surprises of lived human existence.

Before I more fully discuss the approach I take to Muhasibi and Nursi in this book, let me comment a bit more on existing approaches to Muslim subjectivity and their prima facie inadequacies as interpretive frameworks for studying Muhasibian and Nursian accounts. As I indicated earlier, we can identify two major overlapping models of piety and moral agency that scholars of Islam think best describe ideal ways of being Muslim in the world. One is a *mystical model* and the other a *juridical model*. Scholars have shown that an ideal Muslim, religiously and ethically, is either predominantly a mystical lover of the divine or else predominantly a law-abiding, rule-following, obedient, legal subject. As a mystic, his goal is intimate knowledge of God and, ultimately, self-loss and union with the divine. As a legal subject, he is an ideal subject insofar as he obeys more (or all) of the positive, religious laws rather than less of them. Let's look at each model a bit more closely through examples from contemporary scholarship. Let me be clear that what I present below are examples of, and not representatives of, the mystical and legal models of Muslim subjectivity. There is immense richness and diversity within what I am reductively, but self-consciously, labeling mystical and legal models of Muslim subjectivity. Yet, regardless of this diversity, certain key assumptions and features that I highlight in the examples below, suffice to warrant a new, different approach to reconstructing Muhasibian and Nursian accounts of ideal Muslim consciousness and moral subjectivity.

Ideal Muslim Subject as Juridical Subject

Some scholars argue that being an ideal ethical Muslim means that one follows, in letter and spirit, the dictates of Islamic law.[30] To be sure, the Islamic juridical tradition is extremely rich, complex and sophisticated. But when we are told that Muslim ethics, once all is said and done, is primarily about following the law, we are left to assume that being Muslim, in a lived, ethical sense, is to be a person who dutifully and unquestioningly obeys religiously-derived (through the *fiqh*-process), rules of practical conduct. For our purposes, Wael Hallaq's work on Muslim moral subjectivity can serve as an example, though not a representative, of studies that adopt a *legal* or juridical approach to Muslim religio-moral subjectivity because he makes the point in strong and clear terms.[31]

Hallaq makes the remarkable claim that the distinction between the legal and the moral is a nineteenth-century European invention and that in the Islamic tradition, "morality-cum-law possess a teleology whose very fulfillment is their own raison d'etre."[32] He asserts that the legal subject was simply assumed to have already been a well-formed *moral* subject for otherwise the latter would not have bothered with the law. Morality in an Islamic sense, Hallaq argues, "traces its sources in large measure to the performative force of the five pillars" of Islam, namely, the faith declaration (*shahāda*), prayer, fasting, alms-giving and the pilgrimage. It would require too much space to analyze all of Hallaq's sophisticated arguments in defense of his claim so one short example would have to suffice. Regarding what Hallaq understands to be the legal-moral practice of faith declaration, "I witness there is no deity but God and that Muhammad is His messenger," he makes the following observation: "There is no more to do about it than to require its *physical pronouncement* provided it is done with full intention. The rest is hidden in the cerebral and emotive world of the believer."[33] This, dare I say, is a somewhat trite claim but quite understandable given Hallaq's belief that the moral subject, as a fully-formed, stable *entity*, already in possession of a desire to obey the law, predates the performance of religious-legal duties. He mentions "with full intention" in passing but in the end brushes aside "cerebral and emotive" matters as "hidden" and thus irrelevant to the *production* of the moral subject. In Hallaq's view, one simply cannot be performing a bodily action as a legal duty without already being a fully formed moral subject, a person who already loves performing the duty: "It would be meaningless to attempt the fulfillment of a religious obligation if the performer dislikes the performance—if, that is, the intention is caught up in the emotive web of reluctance and resentment."[34] Such a framework is unsuitable for analyzing Muhasibi because Muhasibi thinks most all performances of legal obligations are marked by some deep, inner reluctance to perform them and it is precisely in continuously and watchfully reflecting about and negotiating the emotive web of reluctance that a person attains ideal subjectivity. In sum, an account of the Muslim religious subject as, if you may, a Hallaqian juridical subject is not adequate for capturing or articulating Muhasibi's account of the same.

Nursi, too, does not think that the physical performance of juridical and ritual duties is the epitome of an already-formed, ideal subjectivity. This is not to say that Nursi does not give importance to the performance of legal obligations. Yet, his intellectual output, as we shall see later, is dedicated to quite a different goal—the dynamic and repeated cultivation of a belief perspective on existence. Because scholars like Hallaq assume that the legal code is a set of intelligible, normative prescriptions and proscriptions for *already* existing moral subjects, they do not allow us to even raise, let alone answer, the kinds of questions that I have raised above, namely, what kinds of intellectual exercises and practices do people use to make themselves into ideal subjects?[35] How are religious and moral subjects, people who may come to see themselves under obligation, formed in the first place? Would an account of mystical subjectivity be adequate or suitable here? I think not.

Ideal Muslim Subject as Mystical Subject

On a typical account of a mystical-ascetic subject, the ideal Muslim subject starts life as a novice, who then travels a spiritual path, often under the spiritual tutelage of a master or guide or Shaykh, then passes through many stations, gradually increasing in his realization of divine reality, until finally he loses himself (rather, his contingent self) in God as the only Real. This journey is sometimes described as comprising the twin processes of *fanā fillah* or annihilation and self-loss in God, followed by *baqā billah*, subsistence with/in God.[36] Most accounts of Muslim subject as mystical subject converge when it comes to the idea of a gradual cultivation of *perfection*, a stage-wise progress along a path that ends, mystically, with the spiritually advanced subject losing itself in God's being.[37] Take, for instance, the recent work of scholar of Islamic mysticism and Islamic philisophy, Cyrus Zargar. Zargar helpfully notes that *tawhid* or God's oneness is not simply a foundational doctrine or creed for Sufi thinkers but a quality of the self, a state of being that one arrives at. Zargar's observation comes as part of his analysis of a classical Sufi work by the famous Muslim mystic al-Attar, titled *The Language of the Birds*. In this poetic story, the birds set out to find a king only to discover in the end that they, all of them together, are the reflections of the king. The poem is beautiful and the metaphors layered, and Zargar does an outstanding job of distilling not only Attar's conception of self-perfection but also the ideals of excellence and perfection espoused by classical Islamic mystical and philosophical thinkers alike. In Zargar's analysis, the ideal of self-perfection through self-loss, and the metaphor of the heart as a polished mirror reflecting God, persists as common themes among Muslim mystics and philosophers. Yet it is hardly self-evident how an average person would translate, for instance, the birds finding themselves to be reflections of the king, to human beings and their relationship with God. What would it mean, emotionally, practically and psychologically, for a person to see himself, and all other beings, as nothing but reflections of God? Looking at *tawhid* as a discursive practice, as I do in this book when I analyze Nursi, rather than a doctrine or a supra-sensual, elite mystical state of the self, gives us a clearer picture of the psychological and ethical work that a tawhidic perspective ought to do for a subject that might consciously adopt such a perspective. In Nursi, the idea of being a mirror to God is not best described as mystical or metaphysical state but instead pedagogical, psychological and, insofar as it is part of a discursive mode of a self's relation to itself and others, ethical. It should be admitted that many aspects of Muhasibi's and Nursi's thought make it compelling to see them as Sufi thinkers. But I think if we do so, and I frankly grant that it is possible to do so, we stand to lose the ability to recover the more detailed, discursive and nuanced conception of ideal religious and moral subjectivity that I think they espouse.

In short, neither the juridical model nor the mystical model seems suitable for reconstructing Muhasibi's and Nursi's accounts of ideal subjectivity.[38] How then shall we approach Muhasibi and Nursi if we want to find out how they thought about the meaning of, and the practice for becoming, ideal Muslim subjects? It is time to turn our attention to seemingly tedious but indispensable matters of theory and method and discuss the categories, conceptual apparatus and terms of art that undergird my approach to these thinkers in the subsequent chapters.

CONCEPTUAL APPARATUS: THEORY, METHOD AND KEY TERMS OF ART

The present book *describes* Muhasibi's and Nursi's accounts of ideal subjectivity, using *concepts* drawn from comparative religious ethics, and *evaluates* these accounts for their moral merits and demerits whenever such an evaluation stands to illuminate an ethical concern or problem we wrestle with today. In structuring the analysis this way, this book accomplishes three goals, all of which are important for any study in religious ethics. I take guidance from Richard Miller's threefold typology of scholarship in religious ethics here. He notes that religious ethics scholarship falls into three broad categories, *descriptive*, *evaluative* and *conceptual* and good scholarship in the area ought to keep all three aspects in view.[39] One may be able to describe, as anthropologists of ethics tend to do, without much evaluation and one may engage in conceptual work, as moral philosophers often do, without much thick description. It is possible and desirable, Miller argues, to engage in two or more of these styles of scholarship simultaneously as long as the scholar alerts the reader when they are engaged in description and when they have moved to conceptual and evaluative modes of interpretation. The descriptive aspects of this book are most prominent when I quote directly from Muhasibi and Nursi and explain their ideas on their own terms. The conceptual mode of interpretation is dominant in the book and it will be too tedious to alert the reader every single time I engage in conceptual analysis. One clue I can offer as an aid is that whenever I discuss something in terms of *discursive practices* or in terms of forming or transforming *subjectivity*, I am engaging in conceptual analysis. I generally flag whenever I am about to launch into evaluative/comparative analysis and often it takes the form of a discussion about how the descriptive and conceptual analyses might speak to us today. In other words, the comparative and evaluative aspects come to the fore when I compare and evaluate the contemporary relevance of their accounts of ideal subjectivity. To bring them into our conversations, with the risks that such a move always carries, is a methodological choice that this book makes.

There is an important lesson that this book learns from Thomas Lewis's *Why Philosophy Matters for the Study of Religion—and Vice Versa*. In the past two decades, there has been a decisive move toward a focus on the *body* and processes of *embodiment* in the study of subjectivity in religious studies.[40] There are many who celebrate the movement away from ideas, interpretations and reasoning (theological and philosophical) in the study of religion, and by extension in religious ethics, toward a focus on the body, embodied practices and living communities in which these bodies and practices thrive today. In some way, the focus on living, embodied communities is salutary. But there is also a less salutary side to the story. Lewis is right to observe that one reason for the movement away from the philosophical and intellectual aspects of subjectivity has been the widely shared (and problematic) assumption among scholars of religion that religion is "reason's other."[41] Lewis observes that many scholars typically believe that religions are a matter of faith and thus not subject to, or beholden to, reasoned argument. He raises the important point that,

> In accepting this picture and portraying theology as antithetical to reasoned inquiry, adamant secularists unwittingly join forces with anti-intellectual adherents of religious traditions in supporting the idea that we cannot engage religious ideas constructively. . . . The public discourse about religion that results is remarkably uninformed and uncritical.[42]

Lewis accepts that some adherents of a tradition may claim that their beliefs and ideas are not subject to rational examination and rational inquiry but this attitude would, Lewis notes, remove such people from the realm of rational and critical academic discourse.[43] Now this may work for studies that do not wish to take the voices of the subjects they study on board. But insofar religious ethics is an inherently evaluative enterprise and seeks to engage critically with ideas, albeit religious ones, ethicists must resist the problematic assumption that religious and theological discourses are, ipso facto, arational or irrational. We should allow the subjects the ability to espouse reasons for their positions and actions and we should not only describe but also evaluate their discourses.

Subjectivity, Internalizations, and Externalizations

Muslim subjectivity is analyzed along two axes in this book: *religious subjectivity* and *moral subjectivity*. The distinction is primarily a heuristic one, and I make it to isolate inner religious commitments and standpoints from external expressions of those psychic standpoints. The external expressions are the manifest form of life, ideally consistent with inner psychic standpoints and commitments. In other words, by making this distinction, I heuristically disassemble each thinker's ideal subject, their proverbial humpty dumpty, into religious and moral spheres only to better understand what the subject is made up of and how it puts itself together, with the help of the king's men—namely, religious discourses.

Beyond heuristics, there is also theoretical warrant and inspiration for this distinction, which Richard Miller has succinctly articulated in his important essay about the cultural turn in religious ethics.[44] Miller makes the important observation that human beings are "culture-absorbing" and "culture-producing" creatures at the same time.[45] They absorb and "appropriate the values passed along by parental and other authorities, pedagogical practices, and cultural processes," a process Miller calls *internalization*.[46] Simultaneously, the individual "fashions something in the cultural world according to the drives of his or her psyche."[47] Miller refers to this process as an *externalization* of one's psychic states. He uses these schemes to underscore the connection between individual psyche and culture as a collectivity and to stress why religious ethicists ought to study culture as part of their vocation. I agree with Miller and I use his distinction between the psyche and culture for organizing my analysis of Muhasibi and Nursi along these two axes, the religious-psychic dimension that focuses on *ideal standpoints* of the subject and the *ethical-cultural dimension* that focuses on how these standpoints shape and manifest in relations with others and the world. I thus construe a person's emotional responses and interactions with others, which flow from psychic states and look to objects and experiences outside of the psyche itself, as referring to the person's moral or ethical subjectivity. These responses and interactions manifest as a form of life that includes more than just the individual psyche and, in that sense, they become ethical-cultural artifacts.[48] The ideal standpoints, curatorially and not exhaustively speaking, that a religious individual's psyche ought to engender, I refer to as *ideal religious subjectivity* or sometimes just *religious subjectivity* in this book. And the manner and mode in which one's psychic states ought, and ought not, to be consciously and reflectively expressed in everyday lived life and relationships with others, I refer to as *ideal moral subjectivity* or simply moral subjectivity.

Perhaps the reader has been wondering what exactly I may mean by the *ideal subject*: *whose* subjectivity are we talking about? Who exactly are we referring to when we speak about the ideal Muhasibian or Nursian subject? Did such ideal Muslims actually exist during Muhasibi's and Nursi's times? Let me briefly address these legitimate concerns.

In the primary sense, the ideal subject I speak of in this book is the subject of the text—the addressee of the thinker in the text, their interlocutor, as they advise him to perceive, feel, interpret, think and act in particular ways should they want to attain particular religious and ethical ideals. In my analysis, I analyze what a person would be like *if* they could fully become the person that the thinker wants them to become. That is to say, this book addresses the question of Muslim anthropology philosophically and imaginatively similar to how Jonathan Lear, in his book *Radical Hope*, imagines what an excellent way of life *might look like* if the culture within which certain excellences had meaning, was to be destroyed.

Lear's book is about the American tribe, Crow Nation and, more specifically the story of how the Crow chief modelled an excellent, courageous way of living, even when the tribe's social and cultural life was destroyed. I mention Lear's book not for its themes but for the way he frames his inquiry. Lear describes his work as a study in *philosophical anthropology* that studies the possibilities of being human *if* something had happened. Lear reports the words of Crow Nation chief, Plenty Coups: "When the buffalo went away the hearts of my people fell to the ground and they could not lift them up again. After this nothing happened."[49] Lear observes that we know that is not what *actually* happened. All things did not cease despite the devastation. Things did happen after the buffalo went away. But Lear interprets the chief's words as providing an opportunity for general ethical reflection about moral psychology and anthropology when the social context necessary for gauging human excellence disappears. Lear's question is: How should one live in relation to a radical and peculiar human possibility, in Crow Nation's case, the possibility of radical and total cultural devastation?[50] How to create a new life and new excellences worth aiming at? I think Lear's framework is suggestive as a methodological strategy for studying philosophical-ethical (and theological) anthropology. I want to argue that Muhasibi and Nursi are narrating an ideal subject that they feel does not yet exist or, when it does, faces imminent threat and devastation. They write and teach because they feel a new form of subjectivity needs to be created and sustained. In this book, I read their discourses as the means by which new forms of psychic and ethical lives can be created *if* those reading them were to be shaped by those discourses. Lear's study raises questions about the psychological changes and resources that would be required to create new forms of religious and ethical life.[51] These are relevant considerations for the present book as well. While Lear presents virtue and excellence in a purely social register, my sources (i.e., Muhasibi and Nursi) ground socially relevant moral excellences to a theological vision of the self and the world. Having said that, and perhaps contrary to what we might expect, the theological aspect does not shelter the person from the vulnerabilities that attend social life. Instead, the theological angle intensifies and multiplies these vulnerabilities and makes them components of *discursive practices* of subjectivation.

The ideal subjects I analyze in this book are, firstly, the interlocutors or addressees of the authors, in the texts. They are ideal insofar as we can imagine what they would be like if they actually lived like Muhasibi and Nursi think an ideal subject would live if he were to truly be conscious about its commitments and their meanings. In construing the ideal subject as the subject of the text in this way, I take guidance from scholar of Jewish ethics, Jonathan Schofer, who studies rabbinic didactic texts not too far removed in form from the Muslim texts I analyze in this book. For Schofer's study, the ideal Jewish subject is the addressee of the text even when the text uses a third person pronoun to describe some state of affairs. The addressee is an ideal subject insofar as he is expected to replace the second or third person pronouns of the text with himself as he reads or hears the text. The text may instruct, "He should say, 'Woe is me, perhaps retribution will come upon me today.'" Here the third-person pronoun "he" is the place where the reader can shift the utterance to, "I should say to myself, 'Woe to me. . . .'" The *subject* delineates a rich and messy terrain, characterizing the self as it speaks, experiences, knows, chooses and acts.[52] The ideal subject is the reader willing and able to enact and inhabit the relationships between ideas and subjectivity and consciousness idealized by the discourse.

This study does not make historical and empirical claims that Muhasibi's and Nursi's writings actually transformed people into the ideal subjects implied and portrayed in their texts. Yet, I think it is safe to assume that at least some people must have seriously tried, and perhaps some may have succeeded to some extent, in being formed by the teachings in the way that these teachings sought to form them. Those unnamed and unknown individuals are included as referents for the term ideal subject as used in this book.

Finally, Muhasibi's and Nursi's accounts of ideal subjectivity are self-directed. They themselves wanted, we can easily say when we see them addressing themselves along with others, to be the kinds of ideal subjects they exalt and uphold in their teachings. Thus, the addressee of the thinker in the text, a person referred to, with a second or third person pronoun in the text, any serious reader/listener of the text (and this could include us as well as the immediate historical contemporaries of these thinkers) and the thinker's own self—all these connotations are carried by the term *subject* as used in this book.

A brief comment also needs to be made about my choice of the terms *subject* and *subjectivity* instead of possible alternative such as *self* and *selfhood*. I have made a difficult but deliberate choice to use subject/subjectivity based on three main considerations. First, there is general agreement in the field of Comparative Religious Ethics that the term *self* carries significant conceptual baggage and, as Schofer puts it, "tends to be associated with Enlightenment formulations that present selfhood as bounded, individual and autonomous."[53] Such a term does not capture the way Muhasibi and Nursi refer to individuals as slaves of God (*'abd*) or as the canvass of intersubjective experiences and sometimes as a sort of a nonentity, substantively or ontologically speaking. Whereas, Schofer's definition of *subject* as "a specific form that the self can take" seems quite apt for interrogating Muhasibian and Nursian accounts of ideal consciousness. Adopting Schofer's formulation, I take the subject to be a stance or *standpoint* of the "I" rather than a particular substantive part or aspect of the "I." In this book, the subject then is not a substance or entity within the human being, separate from the self but a "standpoint of the self," where the self's true nature or essence is only important insofar as one is thinking about a particular psychic standpoint. Echoing Miller's internalization/externalization scheme mentioned above, Schofer interprets rabbinic teachings as instruction through which the self "forms itself as a subject through chosen and cultivated relations of subordination to external authorities along with the *internalization* of certain discourses."[54] As we shall see, Muhasibi and Nursi do not speak about the ideal Muslim as a substance or thing. Rather, they are after particular psychic standpoints and perspectives that they think are ideal for a person, the "I," to inwardly inhabit and then externalize in its relations with others. The terms *subject* and *subjectivity* then are better-suited than *self* and *selfhood* for interrogating Muhasibi's and Nursi's teachings about ideal ways of being Muslim.[55]

SUBJECTIVATION, HABITUS, AND THE FOUCAULDIAN REGISTER

In comparative religious ethics and moral philosophy, there has been a surge of interest in the relationship between discourse and self-cultivation, especially since the publication of G. Anscombe's seminal essay "Modern Moral Philosophy" and later Alasdair Macintyre's magisterial work, *After Virtue*.[56] The work of French sociologist and philosopher, Michel Foucault, especially his later work on *technologies of the self* has also lent support to a general revival of virtue ethics and what has been called ethical formation.[57]

Foucault isolates a "distinct stratum of analysis" in the study of ethics that other philosophers overlook.[58] In Foucault's view, moral philosophers (and we may include scholars of theological ethics, jurisprudence and mysticism here) have been predominantly concerned with the intelligible content, concepts and the system of thought those concepts spawn, in the works of thinkers they study. Moral philosophers often study the principles, discourses and rules according to which positive or negative moral valuations might be arrived at and assigned to human beings and their actions within particular cultural and historical settings. Sociologists and anthropologists, on the other hand, typically focus on the actual, empirically observable behaviors, communities and institutions. They focus on the lived everyday lives of actual individuals and communities, their actual choices and practices and the forces that drive or guide the same. Their enterprise is primarily descriptive and documentary. In Foucault's view, both approaches are useful and necessary but they are both blind to the ways that, Foucault came to realize, individuals, as embodied, linguistic and intellectual-emotional agents relate themselves with the normative codes, narratives and stories of their tradition and make themselves the kinds of agents that those norms and codes uphold as ideal, pure, virtuous or excellent. In Davidson's view, Foucault, in his later work, wanted to shift the emphasis from the unseen forces to which people are unselfconsciously subjected, toward analyzing "how the individual is supposed to constitute himself as a moral subject of his own actions without, however, denying the importance of either the moral code or actual behavior."[59] Thus, one of Foucault's most basic contribution to the study of ethics is to conceive of "ethics as a study of the self's relationship to itself."[60] In Foucault's own words:

> Analyzing the experience of sexuality, I became more and more aware that there are in all societies, I think, in all societies whatever they are, techniques which permit individuals to effect, by their own means, a certain number of operations on their bodies, on their souls and on their own thoughts, on their own conduct, and this in a manner so as to transform themselves, modify themselves, and to attain a certain state of perfection, of happiness, of purity, of supernatural power, and so on. Let us call this kind of technique, a technique or technology of the self.[61]

Foucault tells us that these technologies of the self and the "forms of understanding that a subject creates about himself" through these technologies ought to be the distinctive subject matter of ethics, an analytical approach distinct from both moral philosophy and anthropology.[62] This was a simple yet radical proposal and one that, as Davidson pointed out some years ago, ethicists have been slow to adopt but which they are ill-advised to ignore. The study of Muslim ethics has hitherto struggled to engage Foucault's simple yet elegant conception of ethics seriously or build on Foucault's suggestive proposal about the subject matter of ethical inquiry. In this book, I hope to construe Muhasibian and Nursian teachings in a Foucauldian register. A few scholars of Islam, especially anthropologists of Islam, have taken guidance from Foucault's ideas but, in my view, have sadly missed a key aspect of his proposal, the aspect that accommodates a person's reflective agency and moral subjectivity in the processes of their own formation. In this book, the term *moral subjectivity* evokes the idea that a human being has the ability and freedom to reflect about, understand and, if needed, choose to consciously revise (or not) their deepest commitments, including their conception of themselves as agents.[63]

Saba Mahmood is perhaps the most well-known anthropologist of Islam to have examined Muslim subjectivity from a decidedly Foucauldian-via-Asad perspective. Mahmood was inspired by the work of Talal Asad. In his seminal essay, *The Idea of an Anthropology of Islam*, Asad offered not only a scathing critique of how anthropologists and sociologists of his time framed the study of Muslim anthropology and Islam but also offered a positive proposal for its proper study.[64] His proposal has enjoyed widespread support among scholars of Islam. Asad famously proposed that if one wanted to write an anthropology of Islam, one ought to start by thinking of Islam as a *discursive tradition*. It is worth quoting Asad here:

> An Islamic discursive tradition is simply a tradition of Muslim discourse that addresses itself to conceptions of the Islamic past and future, with reference to

a particular Islamic practice in the present. Clearly, not everything that Muslims say and do belongs to an Islamic discursive tradition. Nor is an Islamic tradition in this sense necessarily imitative of what was done in the past. For even where traditional practices appear to the anthropologist to be imitative of what has gone before, it will be the practitioners' conceptions of what is *apt performance*, and of how the past is related to present practices, that will be crucial for tradition, not the apparent repetition of an old form.[65]

Asad clearly asserts that not everything that Muslims say and do belongs to the Islamic discursive tradition. And he gives a prominent place to an individual "practitioner's *conception* of *apt performance*" as the subject matter of an anthropology of Islam. But he offers little guidance about how a researcher would distinguish between those performances and practices that ought to count as part of the Islamic discursive tradition and those that ought to be excluded. What it means to be Muslim then, after all is said and done, is whatever Muslims already do. Just a few lines down the page, Asad offers a clue by saying that any practice that is "authorized by the discursive tradition" and taught to Muslims by other Muslims is to be recognized as a part of those "instituted practices" into which "Muslims are inducted *as* Muslims."[66] The "established practices of unlettered Muslims," Asad stresses, are those practices that are *authorized* by the discursive tradition and a discursive tradition consists of those practices whose *apt performance* concerns even an unlettered practitioner.[67] Asad's emphases on practices, aptness of performance and lay practitioners are unmistakable. Also unmistakable is the connection between aptness of a practice and the practice's authorization by the discursive tradition. A practice is authorized by the tradition and the tradition is constituted by the practices of lay Muslims. In drawing this circle, Asad turns down the volume on his idea of an individual's *conception* of a given practice, their particular (mis)interpretation of it and any ambiguities and tensions that might make apt performance, and the determination of its aptness, itself a discursive exercise. At the risk of oversimplification, I want to suggest that in Asad's account, the process of Muslim self-fashioning is guided so tightly by the power of authorized discourses and the authority of tradition that there is little to no room left for the fuller Foucauldian notion of technologies of the self (i.e., for the idea that an individual, "by his own means," forms himself or herself into a subject). It seems to me that the work of self-formation, in Asad's account, is actually done by authorized discourses of the tradition not self-reflective interpretive agents.

Saba Mahmood produced a groundbreaking study of a contemporary Muslim women's mosque movement in Egypt in which, I think, she amplified both Asad's emphases and his omissions. While she offered a nuanced and rich account of the way the women in the piety movement fashioned themselves into religious and moral subjects, her focus, resonant with Asad's emphasis noted above, was the cultivation of virtues through *repeti-*

tive bodily practices, with little prominence assigned to acts of reflection by subjects themselves about their interpretive choices.[68] This leads Mahmood to inadvertently de-intellectualize the subjectivity of the women she studies; the "view of virtue as relying on repetitive, bodily, external practices blocks her from understanding and adequately representing the value of reasoning to her informants themselves."[69] What matters for us is not whether the women Mahmood studied, in fact, valued reasoning. Mahmood might have argued that they did not do so in the way her critics, unfairly, expect them to because of their modern, Protestant, secular biases. What is important is that she found or privileged the vocabulary of bodily practices and habitual actions as *adequate* for describing the religious and *moral subjectivity* of the women in the Egyptian mosque movement. There is little dispute that the women Mahmood studied were religious subjects. But in what ways were they also *moral* subjects, it is not as clear. Recent scholarship in anthropology of ethics helps us identify the issue.

Some within the fraternity of anthropologists recognize the potential for a misreading of Foucault on the issue of moral agency. Anthropologist of ethics, James Faubion, for instance, cautions against reading Foucault's view of ethical *askesis* or moral self-cultivation as merely a process of slave-like subjection to authoritative norms. His remarks are worth quoting at length,

> Nietzsche's satire of the triumph of the ascetic *ressentiment* of the slave and the commoner over the robust self-affirmation of the ancient aristocracy fades in Foucault into a more balanced assessment of a civic aristocracy's own pursuit of disciplined *asujettissement*—not "subjugation," as the term is usually glossed, but instead "subjectivation," a condition that, precisely because it falls short of the actual enslavement, falls within the ethical domain. It is anthropologically imperative and in good accord with Foucault's precedent not to conceive of the subject position within a mechanical model whose variables are finite and definite and whose systematic transformation are strictly determinable.[70]

Foucault's approach provides an understanding of "habitus" as an "analytical space for attention to the subject's capacity to change itself."[71] Thus, Foucault's notion of habituation as a process of subjective self-formation is different than Bourdieu's and includes more than mere slave-like repetition of prescribed bodily practices and reproduction of the habitus. There is indeterminacy and therefore real agency. And this indeterminacy and the analytical space for a subject's capacity to transform and change its "subject positions" makes Foucault's idea of *subjectivation*, and not mere subjection, useful for the present inquiry.

Both Muhasibi and Nursi thought that embodying the norms prescribed by tradition was neither a seamless nor an exclusively corporeal goal. In their view, human projects of self-making always aim at a moving target. Individuals have to constantly work, intellectually and deliberatively, to attain certain subject positions or *standpoints* in response to ever-changing, everyday life situations, including their changing inner worlds. In their accounts, the processes of subjectivation, processes of forging a Muslim religious and ethical consciousness, include persistent self-questioning, deliberation, self-examination, reinterpretation, recollection, reimagination and other cognitive and intellectual exercises and these processes, as well as the products of these processes, always remain fluid, fragile and subject to revision. Foucault's idea of "technologies of the self," understood in a capacious way, is an apt lens through which we can study Muhasibi's and Nursi's understanding of the nature and formation of ideal Muslim subjectivities.

RELIGIOUS DISCOURSES AS DISCURSIVE PRACTICES

One common feature of the various studies of Muslim subjectivity briefly discussed above that needs to be revisited, is their somewhat simplistic and static conception of religious discourses as repositories of religious thought and intelligible content. Scholars of Islamic law analyze Islamic legal discourses as repositories of legal opinions and reasonings. Scholars of Islamic mysticism take mystical writings to be repositories of Islamic mystical thought. Scholars of Islamic theology study Islamic theological sources as repositories of Muslim discussions about God, His attributes, the status of human power and responsibility in relation to God's power and so on. Scholars have generally taken these textual sources as more-or-less stable, encrusting collections of ideas and debates, records of archaic religious deliberations of Muslim intellectuals and scholarly elites of various persuasions and classes. If we were to put in terms of the various ways scholars can study the history of ideas, the most common way of dealing with Muslim ideas has been to engage in what Richard Rorty would call Islamic or Muslim intellectual history. But intellectual history is not the only way to study past texts and it is not necessary for a historical approach to treat these sources as nothing more than growing repositories of diverse and contested ideas.[72] An alternative, offered by Foucault, is to treat them as *technologies of the self*, which can be interchangeably rendered as *intellectual or spiritual exercises* or, as I often refer to them in this book, *discursive practices*. We need to briefly turn to Pierre Hadot, to help clarify what I mean by the term discourse in this book.

French historian of philosophy, Hadot distinguishes between two senses of the word *discourse* in ancient philosophy and, relatedly, draws a distinction between two senses in which we may use the English term *theoretical*. Hadot observes that on the one hand, discourse can be considered "abstractly, in its formal structure, in its intelligible content."[73] This is the sense I indicated above when I said Muslim materials are treated as repositories or collections of ideas with intelligible content about topics loosely tied together as genres or specialized bodies of knowledge. It is in this sense that scholars of Islam have typically construed textual sources of the Islamic tradition, such as Islamic theology (*kalam*), Islamic jurisprudence (*usul al fiqh*), Sufism (*tasawwuf*) and others. Hadot notes that there is a second meaning of the term discourse, "insofar as it is addressed to a disciple or to oneself, that is to say, the discourse linked to an existential context, to concrete praxis, discourse that is actually *spiritual exercise*."[74] Relatedly, Hadot notes that while in one sense, theoretical is the opposite of practical, in another sense, "the theoretical life is not pure abstraction, but a life of the intellect, which, no doubt, can use a theoretical discourse, but nonetheless remains a life and a praxis."[75] It is these spiritual exercises *as* intellectual and affective praxis that I refer to as *discursive practices* in this book. Hadot, of course was concerned with ancient philosophy as a praxis whose goal, he argues, was the production of lasting effects in the soul and whose goal was a transformation of one's total personality. Philosophical discourse was a pedagogy and a psychagogy, not abstract theory. There seems to me no reason why the same should not be presumed of Muhasibian and Nursian religious discourses, given their self-avowedly pedagogical projects, unless of course, we take religion to be "reason's other" and restrict *intellectual* exercises to nonreligious "rational" philosophical discourses. But, as I indicated earlier, I do not subscribe to such a position and do not, *a priori*, assume that religious discourses are void of rationality or are effective simply because of an arational, embodied subjection to their authority. Moreover, the discourses of Muhasibi and Nursi reveal their obvious pedagogical, psychagogical and self-formative intent as soon as one starts to read them without a priori conceptions about religion and the nature of religious discourse.

Discursive practices in this book denote the deliberate, voluntary intellectual and emotional exercises that a person consciously undertakes and performs, through timely engagement with ideas, concepts, metaphors, teachings, rules of life, scriptural summons, interpretations, maxims—in short, all kinds of intelligible religious ideas expressed in language, be they legal, theological, mystical, historical, "scientific" or metaphorical/literary, in order to affect a change in their subjective standpoint. The aim of these discursive practices is engendering in oneself certain desirable psychic states and sensibilities, and to give a particular, ideal form to one's lived, moral-cultural interactions. Crucially then, what scholars of Islam typically call theology, or mysticism or Islamic jurisprudence is treated in this book, as a matter of conceptual redefinition by adopting a Foucauldian approach, as sets of discursive practices that a person engages in order to forge an ideal Muslim consciousness and moral subjectivity. In this sense, discursive practices in this book can also be understood as forms of avowals.[76] Avowals, as I understand them, are a matter of practical reflection. By avowing something, I am "attesting to my commitment to respect the implications of what I declare that I believe or desire."[77] Avowals include the kinds of reflections in which a person addresses himself about the kind of being he should be. Such avowals are not a matter of knowledge but of commitment, a desire or hope, to attain an end. Thus, as we shall see, sometimes Muhasibian and Nursian subjects engage in discursive practices by avowing what they desire themselves to be. In this book, these avowals are not to be taken as statements of knowledge (knowledge of Islamic doctrine or Islamic law and so on) that a person may gain through learning or experience or ad hoc expressions of wishes that one does not desire to seriously pursue. Rather, they should be understood as a practice, "taking a stand about how we propose to conduct ourselves in the future,"[78] as a means to transforming one's standpoints in line with one's avowed ideals.

At this point, it might be helpful for the reader to also know about an important concept that Foucault turned to, in his last series of lectures, after his encounter with the Islamic revolution of Iran in 1978. Behrooz Ghamari-Tabrizi has recently argued that what made Foucault turn to the "care of the self" in his final years and what made him think that not only the elite (as was the case in Athenian Stoicism according to Foucault) but the common person could also engage in self-formation and technologies of the self, was his experience with the Islamic revolution and a certain political spirituality he witnessed in the actions of the revolutionaries. He noticed that people spoke truth fearlessly and, in the act, "became capable of truth." Foucault thus interpreted the Greek concept of *parrhesia* as a moral virtue, a way of caring for the self by admitting the truth about oneself, to oneself and, in the process, becoming the kind of person who is capable of truth.[79] In a sense, to use Foucault's ideas about technologies of the self to interpret and understand Muslim spiritual action and self-production, as I do in this book, is not as novel as it might seem—the idea was formulated, if we believe Tabrizi, by Foucault himself precisely to make sense of Muslim spiritual action. Muhasibi and Nursi were not political revolutionaries but, in their own way, they saw that the subject, the person capable of truth, needed to form himself as an act of self-care. Their teachings are the discourses with which they thought the common person could forge himself against powerful and corrupting ideas (from within in Muhasibi's case and from without in Nursi's case) that threaten his integrity and his capacity for truth. The acts of spirituality, acts of self-care and self-formation, that took a political dimension in the Iranian revolution in Foucault's view, are still resonant with the nonpolitical (but no less difficult and fearless) acts of constant and *reflective self-scrutiny* and *practices of belief* that could produce, in Muhasibi's and Nursi's teachings respectively, ideal Muslim subjects.

Finally, a brief self-reflexive note about what I think I am doing, as a religious ethicist, as I reconstruct accounts of ideal Muslim subjectivity in this book. The present work is motivated both by an acknowledgment of the challenges presented to scholars of religion by global political and cultural realities as well as an academic interest in documenting and evaluating accounts of Muslim subjectivity. This latter interest has been inspired by the cultural and anthropological turns in religious ethics and a real efflorescence in Muslim virtue ethics and the study of Muslim subjectivity.[80] In terms of our scholarly responsibility toward larger global realities, I find myself in substantial agreement with prominent religious ethicist, William Schweiker. Schweiker argues that the aim of religious ethics should be, "to aid in the articulation and reconstruction of religious outlooks in order that they might serve their own most humane expression."[81] He argues that religious ethicists should not ignore questions about how a given tradition can be best lived in our own times. He writes:

> How will the religions be lived? Nothing but moral timidity could convince a scholar that her or his job is to ride the Zeitgeist without care about global realities. Either intellectuals work with others to help to direct global forces in ways that combat ignorance through knowledge and injustice through responsible freedom or they embrace a remorseless cynicism about the power of ideas in human life, as cowardly as it is vacuous. So despite the different forms scholarly labor can and must take in religious ethics, if one is interested in moral inquiry with and about religious resources, the present challenge is to aid the articulation and reflexive, humane reconstruction of traditions.[82]

I think that such humane reconstruction is possible without sliding into uncritical apologetics, advocacy or confessionalism. It is my hope that the accounts I present in this book are either themselves a form of such humane reconstruction or at least motivate other religious ethicists working with Muslim sources to engage in the work of reconstruction, with the awareness that their work, whether they intend for it or not, could affect how the tradition is lived.

Having introduced the scope and key methodological assumptions that undergird this study, I now turn to Muhasibi and Nursi in the following chapters. In the next two chapters, I attend to Muhasibi's account of the ideal Muslim subject, first qua religious subject (chapter 1) and second qua moral subject and social being (chapter 2). Then, I turn to Nursi's accounts of the same, respectively in chapters 3 and 4. In the last chapter, I reflect about the ways in which their accounts, reconstructed through attention to discursive practices as described above, can help us raise new questions about what it could mean to be religious and ethical subjects in our times, both in the general sense and in the specific sense of *being* Muslim.

Introduction

NOTES

1. For arguments in favor of thinking about Islam as a contested, discursive tradition, see Talal Asad, "The Idea of an Anthropology of Islam," *Qui Parle* 17, no. 2 (2009): 1–30; Shahab Ahmad, *What is Islam? The Importance of Being Islamic* (Princeton, NJ: Princeton University Press, 2015). An accessible, brief survey of the internal contestations within the tradition since its inception can be found in Martin Nguyen, *Modern Muslim Theology: Engaging God and the World with Faith and Imagination* (Lanham, MD: Rowman & Littlefield Publishers, 2018).

2. Thomas Lewis, *Why Philosophy Matters for the Study of Religion—and Vice Versa* (Oxford: Oxford University Press, 2015), 136. Presenting my book as Muhasibian and Nursian accounts of ideal subjectivity instead of using broad languages such as "ideal subjectivity in the Islamic tradition," I am following religious ethicist, Thomas Lewis's important rejoinder about using *tradition* as a unit of analysis in religious ethics. He notes that even as certain core beliefs and motifs might be distinguishing marks of a religious tradition, adherents of those traditions may still hold radically different views on the specific questions that a study seeks to answer. In such a case, to analyze the matter at hand by invoking the category of tradition would reinforce the notion that the differences between the way people understand and live out their religious commitments are somehow less important than certain general features that some adherents take to be the core of their tradition. Thus, if we structure a study in religious ethics with tradition as our unit of analysis, we risk losing sight of the ideas and accounts that were specific to particular thinkers and their contexts and potentially different from accounts of other thinkers in the same tradition. The best approach for this study, then, is to not take traditions to be "discrete and coherent entities."

3. I take this language of "vocabulary" from Aaron Stalnaker's important work, one of the pioneering studies in third-wave comparative religious ethics (CRE) scholarship. CRE is a loosely connected set of conversations by which this book is inspired which it hopes to contribute, as a new way of studying Muslim ethics. See Aaron Stalnaker, *Overcoming Our Evil: Human Nature and Spiritual Exercises in Xunzi and Augustine* (Washington, DC: Georgetown University Press, 2007). For a discussion of third-wave CRE scholarship as a new body of scholarly work with its specific foci and methodologies, see Elizabeth Bucar and Aaron Stalnaker, eds., *Religious Ethics in a Time of Globalism: Shaping a Third Wave of Comparative Analysis* (New York: Palgrave, 2012). For a collection of seminal essays that comprise, at least partially if not fully, the field of comparative religious ethics, see the immense and valuable four-volume work *Comparative Religious Ethics: The Major Works*. Edited by Charles Matthewes, Matthew Puffer and Mark Storslee (New York: Routledge, 2015).

4. For a discussion of why it should be possible to interrogate religious sources with a view to their discussions of concepts, such as subjectivity, that do not have equivalent terms in those sources, see Bryan Van Norden, "Virtue Ethics and Confucianism," In *Comparative Approaches to Chinese Philosophy*, ed. Bo Mou (London: Ashgate Publishing, 2003), 99–121.

5. Kevin Reinhart, "Islamic Law as Islamic ethics," *Journal of Religious Ethics* 11, no. 2 (1983): 186–203. Earlier scholars underscored that Islamic legal thought evaluated actions as "recommended" and "discouraged," and saw this as suggesting that the law was ethical. See Frederick Carney, "Some Aspects of Islamic Ethics," *The Journal of Religion* 63, no. 2 (1983): 159–174.

6. For a broad and a bit ambitious attempt to interpret the core of Islamic mystical piety as an other-regarding morality see Paul Heck, "Mysticism as Morality: The Case of Sufism," *Journal of Religious Ethics* 34, no. 2 (2006): 253–286. Muhasibi and Nursi do not feature in his insightful but quite general account.

7. Abu ʿAbd al-Raḥmān al-Sulamī, *Kitāb ṭabaqāt al-ṣūfiyya*, ed. Johannes Pedersen (Leiden: E. J. Brill, 1960), 49.

8. Gavin Picken, *Spiritual Purification in Islam: The Life and Works of al-Muḥāsibī* (New York: Routledge Press, 2011), 49.

9. Louis Massignon says the following: "In 232/846, he was obliged to stop teaching by blindly reactionary Sunnis who forbade any recourse to theological speculation (*kalām*), even in the case of those who, like al-Muḥāsibī, used the Mutazilites' own logical and dialectical methods only to fight them." Louis Massignon, *Essays on the Origins of the Technical Lan-*

guage of Islamic Mysticism, trans. Benjamin Clark (Notre Dame, IN: University of Notre Dame Press, 1997), 161.

10. *Encyclopedia of Islam*, 2nd ed., s. v. "al-Muḥāsibī"; Picken, *Spiritual Purification*, 46; Margaret Smith, *An Early Mystic of Baghdad: A Study of the Life and Teaching of Ḥārith b. Asad al-Muḥāsibī* (London: Sheldon Press, 1935), 6; Massignon, *Essays*, 161. While other scholars try to build a biography out of scattered and hagiographic entries in Sufi biographical dictionaries, Massignon is perhaps the most forthright when he confesses: "Nothing about his life is known except his teachings." For a discussion of Muhasibi as a Sunni theologian and associate of Ibn Kullab, see Josef van Ess, *Die Gedankenwelt Des Ḥārith al-Muḥāsibī* (Bonn: Selbstverlag des Orientalischen Seminars der Universität Bonn, 1961).

11. Those who think of him as a theologian place him in the company of Ibn Kullab, a proto-Ash'ari thinker. See Harith Bin Ramli, "The Predecessors of Asharism: Ibn Kullāb, al-Muhāsibī and al-Qalānisī" in *The Oxford Handbook of Islamic Theology*, ed. Sabine Schmidtke (Oxford University Press, 2016), 215–224. For a discussion of difficulties of taking biographical dictionaries as historical sources, see Michael Cooperson. *Classical Arabic Biography: The Heirs of the Prophets in the Age of al-Ma'mūn* (New York: Cambridge University Press, 2000).

12. Picken, *Spiritual Purification*, 55.

13. Detailed discussion of Ibn Hanbal's ambivalent repudiation of Muhasibi is found in Gavin Picken, "Ibn Hanbal and al-Muḥāsibī: A Study of Early Conflicting Scholarly Methodologies" 55, no. 3–4 (July 2008), 337–361.

14. See Picken, *Spiritual Purification*, 46–66.

15. See, for instance, Şükran Vahide, *Islam in Modern Turkey: An Intellectual Biography of Bediuzzaman Said Nursi* (Albany: State University of New York Press, 2005); Vahide, "Toward an Intellectual Biography of Said Nursi," In *Islam at the Crossroads: On the Life and Thought of Bediuzzaman Said Nursi*, ed. Ibrahim M Abu-Rabi (Albany: State University of New York Press, 2003); Adnan Aslan, "Said Nursi" in *The Biographical Encyclopedia of Islamic Philosophy*, ed. Oliver Leaman (London-New York: Thoemmes Continuum, 2006), 167–172; Colin Turner, *The Qur'an Revealed: A Critical Analysis of Said Nursi's Epistles of Light* (Berlin: Gerlach Press, 2013).

16. Vahide's *Islam in Modern Turkey* is arranged according to the three phases of Nursi's life as generally understood.

17. Vahide, *Islam in Modern Turkey*, 306.

18. Picken analyzes the concept of *tazkiya al-nafs* in Muhasibi's writings and is led to the puzzling conclusion that Muhasibi rarely talks about purification of the soul and when he does, "on each occasion the phrase is used in an exclusively negative context . . . to indicate self-praise, this being considered a blameworthy quality." Picken, *Spiritual Purification*, 168. Picken then rightly concludes that we cannot think about Muhasibi as a Sufi even though he uses many concepts and ideas that we typically associate with Sufi and mystical piety. For a different view, see Şahin Filiz, The Founder of the Muḥāsaba School of Sufism: Al-Ḥārith ibn Asad al-Muḥāsibī," *Islamic Studies* 45 (2006): 59–81.

19. For a treatment of Muhasibi as an ascetic, L. Librande, "Islam and Conservation: The Theologian-Ascetic al-Muḥāsibī," *Arabica* 30 (1983): 125–146.

20. Cyrus Zargar, *The Polished Mirror: Storytelling and the Pursuit of Virtue in Islamic Philosophy and Sufism* (London, England: Oneworld Academic, 2017), 179; Ahmet Karamustafa, *Sufism: The Formative Period* (Berkeley: University of California Press, 2007), 2.

21. Margaret Smith, *An Early Mystic of Baghdad: A Study of the Life and Teaching of Ḥārith b. Asad al-Muḥāsibī* (London: Sheldon Press, 1935), 222–252.

22. Gavin Picken, *Spiritual Purification in Islam: The Life and Works of al-Muḥāsibī* (New York: Routledge Press, 2011), 218.

23. Zargar, *The Polished Mirror*, 181; Karamustafa, *Sufism*, 2.

24. Zargar, *The Polished Mirror*, 181. Michael Sells notes that in contrast to al-Qushayri, a central 11th century mystical figure who "integrated the concept of inclination into a poetics of extraordinary experience, al-Muḥāsibī was more concerned with the inclinations (*khaṭarāt*) of everyday experience." Sells's observation supports my contention that Muhasibi is best understood not as a mystic or as proposing a mystical ideal. Michael Sells, *Early Islamic Mysticism: Sufi, Quran, Mi'rāj, Poetic and Theological Writings* (New York: Paulist Press, 1995), 176.

25. Alan Godlas, "A Religiological Analysis of Nursi's View of Sufism Expressed in the 'Nine Allusions' (*Telvihât-ı Tis'a*) of the Risale-i Nur," *Islam and Christian-Muslim Relations* 19, no. 1 (2008), 39–52.
26. See, for instance, Yamina Mermer and Isra Yazicioglu, "Said Nursi's Qur'anic Hermeneutics," in *The Companion to Said Nursi Studies*, eds. Ian Markham and Z. Sayilgan (Eugene, OR: Pickwick Publications, 2017), 55–56. Also see Sukran Vahide, "A Survey of the Main Spiritual Themes of the Risale-i Nur," in *Spiritual Dimensions of Bediuzzaman Nursi's Risale-i Nur*, ed. Ibrahim M. Abu-Rabi (New York: SUNY Press, 2008), 2–3.
27. Mustafa Tuna, "At the Vanguard of Contemporary Muslim Thought: Reading Said Nursi into the Islamic Tradition," *Journal of Islamic Studies* 28, no. 3 (September 2017), 311–340. Nursi himself both endorses the Sufi path to some degree, see Nursi, *The Letters: From the Risale-i Nur Collection*, trans. Sukran Vahide (Istanbul: Sozler Nesriyat, 1994), 519–535. But then he also notes that it has dangers and that the path of the *Risale-i Nur* is easier, better and not the same as a Sufi path (Nursi, *Letters*, 536).
28. Muhasibi, *Kitāb al-Ri'āya li ḥuqūq Allāh*, ed. Margaret Smith (London: Luzac & Co., 1940), 263.
29. The dialectic between weakness and strength, need and assistance, poverty and compassion and so on, is an important one for Nursi and, as we shall see, for ideal Nursian subjectivity. For a general discussion of the importance of the themes of weakness and poverty, see Vahide, "A Survey," 9–11.
30. Kevin Reinhart, "Islamic Law," 186–203; Mariam Al-Attar, *Islamic Ethics: Divine Command Theory in Arabo-Islamic Thought* (New York: Routledge Press, 2010); John Kelsay, "Islam and the Study of Ethics," *Method and Theory in the Study of Religion* 24, no. 4–5 (2012): 357–370; John Kelsay, "Islamic Law and Ethics," *The Journal of Religious Ethics* 22, no. 1 (1994): 93–99.
31. Wael Hallaq, *The Impossible State: Islamic, Politics and Modernity's Moral Predicament* (Columbia University Press, 2013), 110–138. I have selected Hallaq also because he explicitly uses Foucault and Foucauldian language of "technologies of the self" and "moral subject" to talk about Islamic legal discourse.
32. Hallaq, *The Impossible State*, 112.
33. Hallaq, *The Impossible State*, 120, italics added.
34. Hallaq, *The Impossible* State, 121.
35. These exercises can also be called strategies. See Lisa Sowle Cahill, "Gender and Strategies of Goodness: New Testament and Ethics," *The Journal of Religion* 80, no. 3 (2000) 442–460.
36. For a concise recent analysis of these concepts from an ethical angle, see Zargar, *The Polished Mirror*, 243–244. Ibn Arabi's mystical anthropology is complex but it seems that he is suggesting that the lover of God (the human) is obliterated in the beloved (God) and that human being, *qua ideal subject*, is the outward form of the undifferentiated names of God. See William Chittick, *The Sufi Path of Knowledge: Ibn al-Arabi's Metaphysics of Imagination* (Albany, NY:State University of New York Press, 1989), 113–115.
37. Zargar reaches this conclusion for all the ten thinkers, five philosophers and five Sufis, from medieval Muslim thought. A similar picture of a gradualist, perfectionist subjectivity is presented by Sara Sviri, "The Self and its Transformation in Sufism: With Special Reference to Early Literature," in *Self and Self-Transformation in the History of Religions*, eds. David Shulman and Guy Stroumsa (New York: Oxford University Press, 2002), 195–215. Ebrahim Moosa emphasizes the gradual movement toward perfection, understood as union with the divine. Moosa tells us: "Ghazali believed that the body and psyche ought to be subjected to repeated disciplinary practices until virtues become naturalized within the self." There is a *gradual* process of attaining *perfection* that "culminates in *mystical* unveilings and divine intuitions in the subject." Ebrahim Moosa, *Ghazālī and the Poetics of Imagination* (Chapel Hill, The University of North Carolina Press, 2006), 260.
38. This does not mean that Muhasibi did not make significant contributions to different fields of inquiry in early Muslim tradition. For a comparative analysis of his sophisticated theory of abrogation, see Christopher Melchert, "Quranic Abrogation across the Ninth Century:

Shāfi'ī, Abū 'Ubayd, Muḥāsibī, And Ibn Qutaybah," In *Studies In Islamic Legal Theory*, ed. Bernard G. Weiss (Leiden: Brill, 2002), 75–98.

39. Richard Miller, *Friends and Other Strangers: Studies in Religion, Ethics and Culture* (Columbia Press, 2018), 104.

40. For an excellent survey of how the role of the body has changed in religious studies scholarship over the last four decades, see Constance Furey, "Body, Society and Subjectivity in Religious Studies," *Journal of the American Academy of Religion* 80 (March 2012): 7–33. For Furey's marvelous study of relational subjectivity that moves the focus away from the bodily subject as a mere abstraction to the subjects formed and transformed thorough intimate relationships, see Constance Furey, *Poetic Relations: Intimacy and Faith in the English Reformation* (University of Chicago Press, 2017).

41. Lewis, *Why Philosophy Matters*, 53.

42. Lewis, *Why Philosophy Matters*, 53.

43. Lewis, *Why Philosophy Matters*, 60–61.

44. Richard Miller, "On Making a Cultural Turn in Religious Ethics," *Journal of Religious Ethics* 33 (2005) 3: 39–74.

45. Miller, "On Making a Cultural Turn," 54.

46. Miller, "On Making a Cultural Turn," 55.

47. Miller, "On Making a Cultural Turn," 55.

48. Miller, "On Making a Cultural Turn," 57.

49. Jonathan Lear, *Radical Hope: Ethics in the Face of Cultural Devastation* (Cambridge, MA: Harvard University Press, 2008), 3.

50. Lear, *Radical Hope*, 4–8.

51. See Judith Baker, "Vulnerabilities of Morality," *Canadian Journal of Philosophy* 141, no. 38 (2008), 141–160.

52. Jonathan Schofer, *The Making of a Sage: A Study in Rabbinic Ethics* (Madison: University of Wisconsin Press, 2005), 16–17. Also see Jonathan Schofer, "Ethical Formation and Subjection," *Numen* 59, vol. 1 (2012): 1–31.

53. Schofer, *Making of a Sage*, 15.

54. Schofer, *Making of a Sage*, 15. For an in-depth terminological discussion of the pros and cons of choosing between the terms self, person and subject, also see Stalnaker, *Overcoming Our Evil*, 34–38.

55. Moosa defines subjectivity somewhat broadly, and in terms of substance and not standpoints in his study of Ghazali. He says, "subjectivity is always an individual substance like the soul, self, or person," a "pre-given substance in which human experiences are rooted." Moosa, *Poetics*, 223. This construal of subjectivity, as we shall see in the book, would not work well for understanding Muhasibian and Nursian accounts of ideal subjectivity. Muhasibi is said to have been an intellectual forerunner of Ghazali. See Margaret Smith, "The forerunner of al-Ghazālī," *The Journal of the Royal Asiatic Society of Great Britain and Ireland* (January, 1936): 65–78.

56. Alasdair Macintyre, *After Virtue: A Study in Moral Theory* (Notre Dame, IN: University of Notre Dame Press, 1984). This book was definitive in making virtue ethics fashionable among academic ethicists. However, the scholar credited with first questioning the relevance of an obligation-based ethic in the modern age and pointing instead toward virtue ethics and moral psychology is G. E. M. Anscombe. See G. E. M. Anscombe, "Modern Moral Philosophy," *Philosophy* 33, no. 124 (1958): 1–19. For an important work of comparative ethics that compares Christian and Confucian accounts of virtue see Lee H. Yearley, *Mencius and Aquinas: Theories of Virtue and Conceptions of Courage* (Albany: State University of New York Press, 1990).

57. Given the complexity and widely differing understandings of Foucault's writings, I restrict myself to one of Foucault's most astute modern commentators, Arnold Davidson, who distills Foucault's distinct contribution to the study of ethics. See Arnold I. Davidson, "Archeology, Genealogy, Ethics," in *Foucault: A Critical Reader*, ed. David C. Hoy (New York: Basil Blackwell, 1986), 221–234. To be clear, I am not so much "applying" Foucault to Muhasibi and Nursi as drawing on his construal of ethics to look anew at their discourses, which are often straightjacketed into one or another discipline of Islamic tradition, be it *kalām* (speculative

theology) or *taṣawwuf* (Sufism). Foucault's insights about ethical formation helps me release them from the iron grip of native, insider categories that scholars of Islam generally bring to bear on their materials. In this sense, this study is subversive and refuses to yield that the only way to "correctly" interpret these thinkers is to use insider, *Islamic* categories. This book is not a study of Foucault or of all the ways he could be illuminating for the study of Islam, Muslim ethics and culture. For an example of this latter kind of scholarship, see Behrooz Ghamari-Tabrizi, *Foucault in Iran Islamic Revolution after the Enlightenment* (University of Minnesota Press, 2016).

58. Davidson, "Archeology," 228.
59. Davidson, "Archeology," 228.
60. Davidson, "Archeology," 228.
61. Michel Foucault, "About the Beginnings of the Hermeneutics of the Self: Two lectures at Dartmouth," *Political Theory* 21, no. 2 (1993): 203.
62. Foucault, "About the Beginnings," 203.
63. In other words, a moral subject cannot simply be an automaton. For a short discussion of moral subjectivity see Miller, *Friends and Other*, 36. For a longer philosophical discussion see Harry G. Frankfurt, "Freedom of the Will and the Concept of a Person," *The Journal of Philosophy* 68, no. 1 (1971): 6–7.
64. For a view of ritual and cultural practices that Asad argued against, see Clifford Geertz, "Religion as a Cultural System." In *The Interpretation of Cultures: Selected Essays*, ed. Clifford Geertz, 87–125. Fontana Press, 1993.
65. Asad, "Anthropology of Islam," 14–15.
66. Asad, "Anthropology of Islam," 14–15.
67. Asad, "Anthropology of Islam," 14–15.
68. Saba Mahmood, *Politics of Piety: The Islamic Revival and the Feminist Subject* (Princeton: Princeton University Press, 2005), 137. Mahmood uses the phrase "inhabiting the norms" to describe the agency of her subjects. See Elizabeth Bucar's critique of Mahmood in Elizabeth Bucar, "Dianomy: Understanding Religious Women's Moral Agency as Creative Conformity," *Journal of the American Academy of Religion*, 78 (2010) 3:662–686. Given Mahmood's popularity and stature in the study of Islam, it is likely that the unfortunate shortcomings of her construal of Aristotle and Foucault, as indicated briefly here, will continue to be replicated and amplified in the field for the foreseeable future. For a recent example of a reliance on Mahmood and construing Islamic ethics as simply habitual bodily compliance with legal religious norms, see Junaid Qadri, "Moral Habituation in the Law: Rethinking the Ethics of the *Sharī'a*," *Islamic Law and Society* 26 (2019) 3:191–226.
69. Miller, *Friends and Other*, 318.
70. James Faubion, *An Anthropology of Ethics* (Cambridge: Cambridge University Press, 2011), 44–45. He contrasts Foucault's stance with Bourdieu's approach: "Though subjectivation is a process of the formation of a habitus (among other things), it is not and should not be enclosed within the broader theoretical problematic and theoretical apparatus within which Bourdieu encloses the habitus in *The Outline of a Theory of Practice*." (Ibid., 45).
71. Faubion, *An Anthropology*, 46.
72. Richard Rorty, "The Historiography of Philosophy: Four Genres," In *Philosophy in History: Essays on the Historiography of Philosophy*, ed. Richard Rorty, J. B. Schneewind and Quentin Skinner (New York: Cambridge University Press, 1984), 49–75. In order not to further prolong an already lengthy introduction, I decided to confine Rorty's remarks on the four genres to this footnote. The four genres Rorty identifies are (i) Rational reconstruction, (ii) Historical reconstruction, (iii) *Geistesgeschichte* or canon-formation and (iv) Intellectual history. He says, "*Rational reconstructions* are necessary to help us present-day philosophers think through our problems. *Historical reconstructions* are needed to remind us that these problems are historical products, by demonstrating that they were invisible to our ancestors." (Ibid., 68, italics added)
73. Pierre Hadot, *Philosophy as a Way of Life: Spiritual Exercises from Socrates to Foucault* (New York: Blackwell, 1995), 26.
74. Hadot, *Philosophy as a Way*, 26. "Spiritual exercises" is Hadot's term for what Foucault called "technologies of the self," though it is more capacious because it includes not only

discourses with recognizably moral content, explicit or implicit, but also those discourses that appear to us, not related to morality, such as physics and biology.

75. Hadot, *Philosophy as a Way*, 26. A handful of scholars have attempted to use Hadot as a resource for interpreting Muslim materials. For a short but suggestive essay from the field of Islamic philosophy, see Sajjad H. Rizvi, "Philosophy as a way of life in the world of Islam: Applying Hadot to the study of Mullā Ṣadrā Shīrāzī (d. 1635)," *Bulletin of the School of Oriental and African Studies* 75, no. 1 (2012): 33–45.

76. Charles Larmore, *The Practices of the Self*, trans. Sharon Bowman (Chicago: University of Chicago Press, 2010), 114.

77. Larmore, *Practices*, 128–129.

78. Larmore, *Practices*, 128–129.

79. Ghamari-Tabrizi, *Foucault in Iran*, 181.

80. In addition to works I have already mentioned, I have in mind works such as Charles Hirschkind, *The Ethical Soundscape: Cassette Sermons and Islamic Counterpublics* (New York: Columbia University Press, 2006); Elizabeth Bucar, *Creative Conformity: The Feminist Politics of U.S. Catholic and Iranian Shi'i Women* (Washington DC: Georgetown University Press, 2011); Anna Gade, *Perfection Makes Practice: Learning, Emotion, and the Recited Quran in Indonesia* (Honolulu: University of Hawaii Press, 2004). Interest in Muslim moral anthropology can be traced to Asad's seminal essay ("Anthropology of Islam," 1–30), which was originally published in 1986 for the Occasional Paper Series, sponsored by the Center for Contemporary Arab Studies at Georgetown University.

81. William Schweiker, "On The Future Of Religious Ethics: Keeping Religious Ethics, Religious and Ethical," *Journal of the American Academy of Religion* 74 (2006) 1: 137.

82. Schweiker, "The Future of Religious Ethics," 137.

Chapter One

Muhasibian Religious Subjectivity and the Travails of Sincerity

It was the American philosopher and psychologist William James who said, "when a religion has become an orthodoxy, its day of inwardness is over: the spring is dry."[1] If James is right, then Muhasibi must be understood to be writing at a time when Islam was not yet an orthodoxy. Inwardness, as we shall see, is the hallmark of a Muhasibian subject, not as a stage along a path but the proper mode of being religious throughout life. The subject's inwardness is not the result of a disinterest in the world or a disavowal of outward actions but a keen awareness that the health and goodness of the outward act is incomplete, even thwarted, if a subject's inner states are compromised. At the center of Muhasibi's account of ideal religious subjectivity, are the twin concepts of rights (*huquq*)[2] and obligations (*wājibāt* or *fara'id*).

The ideal subject is the one who properly observes the rights of God. The question we should thus ask is: What kinds of standpoints and sensibilities allow God's rights to be properly fulfilled and how might a subject achieve those standpoints? In Muhasibi's teachings, the ideal religious subject is not assumed to exist simply on account of his general desire or intention to obey God's commands, even as concern for what God approves and disapproves ought to be significant for him. The subject, however, emerges and sustains its ideal subjectivity through a dynamic engagement in specific religious discourses, and by inhabiting certain standpoints toward itself and the world. This chapter describes some key discursive practices and standpoints that help us understand the nature and formation of an ideal Muhasibian religious subject.

SELF-SUBJECTION: THE FIRST RIGHT OF GOD

For Muhasibi, the first act of will that inaugurates a person's religious life qua religious subject is an avowal, telling oneself a particular truth about oneself, locating oneself as a slave or bondsmen in relation to a Lord or Master, God. The avowal involves several interesting features and it is important to quote Muhasibi at length:

> First and foremost, know that you are indeed a slave ruled over by a Lord. There is no salvation for you except with *taqwa* (consciousness or awareness) of your Master and Lord and there is no perdition for you upon attaining it. So then, remember and reflect why you were created and for what purpose you were placed in this transient world. Then, you would understand that indeed you are not created by way of sport and you are not left to your own devices.[3] Indeed, you were created and placed in this transient abode of trials and tests so that you either obey God or disobey Him, so that you are transferred from this abode to either eternal blessings or eternal torture. If you understand that you are a subjected slave, then you would think about why you were created, why things happen to you and you would understand that you are headed either toward eternal torture or toward eternal reward. This is the first thing that is incumbent upon you to begin with, because the first thing necessary for the righteousness of your *nafs*, without which there is no righteousness for it, the first of the observances of God's rights, is that you know that you are a subjected slave. If you understand this, you would realize that there is no escape for a subjected slave except through obedience to his Lord and Master.[4]

Three things are worthy of note in this paragraph. First, a subject's life as a religious being ought to be tied to their considerations about the *purpose* of their existence. The subject is asked to wonder about the transient and tumultuous nature of their life in this world and avow that their life is not to be spent, contrary to what may have seemed to them prior to this discursive intervention, seeking ease and fleeting pleasures. Instead, they ought to assign purpose to their life by avowing that it has one of two ultimate ends— eternal bliss or eternal torture. Honest reflection about life's transience and its many tribulations should lead them to such a conclusion. They ought not only to accept that their life has a purpose but also that this purpose is the attainment of permanent, lasting bliss, and therefore, the avoidance of eternal torture. In a subject's mind, there should not be any finally neutral outcomes, no reason to imagine they can simply be indifferent toward an unknown future and hence toward their own past and present, to which their future they should see as tightly linked. Second, the person is to feel that should they fail to avow the attainment of eternal bliss and avoidance of eternal punishment as the purpose of their life, their life would have no real purpose or meaning.

Other meanings they may be tempted to give their life would be, in the subject's mind, unsatisfactory and without divine warrant.

The subject is asked to make an existential choice about the meaning of their life at the outset, between being a religious subject or else someone given over to purposeless play and amusement. The reference in the passage to life not being mere sport and play and the series of questions that the subject is encouraged to ask himself, "Why were you put on this earth?" and "Why do things happen to you?" show that the ideal subject ought to question the meaning of their life and commit to one of two possibilities—as an opportunity for attaining eternal bliss or living a grueling yet trivial life, focused on transient goals that lead to eternal perdition on account of unfulfilled rights of God. The third idea in the passage worth noting is that the subject must see his goal of salvation as tied to fulfilling God's rights through taking up obedience as a mode of fulfilling his life's purpose. It is not sufficient that the subject acknowledge a Creator or that he has a Master, God. He must feel obliged to discover and fulfill this Master's rights as a matter of fulfilling the purpose of his life. Now what makes the idea of obedience to God and fulfilling His rights interesting in Muhasibi's teachings, is the way he elaborates how those rights would be, and just as often may not be, properly fulfilled.[5]

SUGGESTIONS AND CONSTANT SELF-EXAMINATION

The ideal religious subject is not simply subject to rules of outward conduct. For Muhasibi, the primary mode of fulfilling God's rights is the performance of certain inner duties. Crucially, these inner duties are to be performed by the subject while avowing that his *nafs* is naturally averse to their performance. The subject must understand that great, constant and painstaking effort would be needed to produce acquiescence in the psyche about obeying God internally. For Muhasibi, God has rights that pertain to actions of the body and those that pertain to actions of the heart. He says, "All the rights of God concerning the bodily members are this: doing what God made incumbent or obligatory and abandoning or omitting to do what God dislikes. Then there is the observance of God's rights related to occurrence of suggestions to the hearts (*'inda al-khaṭarāt al-qulūb*), suggestions that are callers to all that is good and bad."[6]

In order to fulfill God's rights inwardly, the subject needs to discern the source and nature of the suggestions that strike his heart, quite like waterdrops strike the ground, suddenly and constantly, when it rains. They can be good, for instance the heart may be struck by a suggestion to help a person in need. They can also be vicious, for instance the heart can be struck by a suggestion to boast about helping a person in need. Among the most dangerous suggestions that can occur to the heart, Muhasibi counts hypocrisy or showing-off (*al-riya*),[7] conceit (*al-'ujb*),[8] delusion (*al-ghirra*),[9] pride (*al-kibr*),[10] and envy (*al-ḥasad*).[11] The ideal subject must discern the source of each suggestion and respond appropriately to it in a timely fashion in order to properly fulfill God's rights. When the heart embraces vicious suggestions, it fails to fulfill internal obligations to God properly and all external actions that are accompanied with such internal states cannot be counted among obedient actions. Because Muhasibi makes the ideal subject answerable to God for every single suggestion that may occur to the heart, the ideal subject must conceptualize itself as a dynamic being, subject to the relentless assault of suggestions, always fending off vicious suggestions in order to fulfill God's rights properly. We may ask: Is it not possible that the ideal subject would eventually overcome these vices, once and for all, and attain some sort of a virtuous or moral character? While we do find Muhasibi saying that rejecting suggestions can become easier for the heart with experience, he does not think it is possible to attain a virtuous moral character. Moreover, as we shall see later in the chapter, good habits pose serious religious dangers of their own. Muhasibi teaches that the *nafs* has certain dispositions and *faculties*, placed in it by God that simply cannot be permanently disabled or made nonfunctional. In response to a question about the difficulty of keeping one's intentions pure, Muhasibi responds,

> The servants of God are commanded to struggle against their desires. They have not been commanded that there be no faculty of the self (*gharīza fī al-nafs*)[12] that may call them to follow their appetites. They are not commanded to get rid of all the whisperings of Satan that he presents in their inner hearts. Rather, God gave humans rational faculties and bestowed on them awareness and knowledge that are established through their rational faculties. They are tested with their faculties. He made Satan provoke human beings through their faculties, reminding them of the things they desire. God then commanded that the servants struggle against the calls of these faculties, and against those things which Satan makes desirable and that are agreeable for the faculties of the *nafs*, with their rational faculties, which God fortified with awareness and knowledge. Nothing other than this is expected from the slaves. They do not have the power to do more and it is not expected of them. There are some who are stronger than others in this and they are those who engage in strenuous struggle, until the *nafs* is weakened in its calls, without changing their nature.[13] It incites less than it incited before and the incitements are weaker than they were in the beginning. The duty of the slave of God is to struggle and reject the desires of the *nafs*. It is not his responsibility to transform his nature so that it becomes like the nature of an angel. His duty is only to reject what his nature calls him to.[14]

The *nafs* has a particular, innate aspect. This innate aspect is the source of suggestions to follow one's desires and appetites, at the expense of fulfilling

God's rights.[15] Interestingly, the urge to become pure, immune from vicious suggestions, is both impossible and irrelevant for the ideal subject. Muhasibi's anthropology thus makes constant watchfulness and self-scrutiny an abiding psychic and moral imperative for an ideal subject.[16] But let us go further and ask: What other psychic states would accompany constant watchfulness of this sort? It is not difficult to imagine that such a subject would experience persistent anxiety and vulnerability: one's status as slave of God is constantly threatened and can be compromised if one fails to respond properly to even a single suggestion. Such a subject could hardly be complacent about whatever obedient actions one does manage to perform. Such psychic concerns would produce a deflationary effect on one's self-confidence and one's sense of what is possible for one to practically achieve by way of piety or goodness more generally. When failure is possible and imminent in this way and one's highest attainment is persistent effort and struggle, it is difficult to imagine a Muhasibian subject thinking he is ever a perfect or perfectly obedient slave of God.[17] It is a somber picture. On the bright side though, they would be free from the psychological pressures of perfectionism (to be the perfect student, to be the perfect parent, the perfect employee and so on) that many of us today can readily relate with (and frankly, can do without). Muhasibi does not require that the ideal subject develop a perfect or virtuous moral character, a kind of angelic virtuosity.[18] Spiritual or moral sainthood is clearly not the ideal Muhasibi recommends.

The process of rejecting the invitations and enticements of the *nafs* involves constant reflection about the movements and actions of the heart (*'amal al-qulub*) as well as bodily actions (*'amal al-jawarih*). This unrelenting self-examination (*muhasaba*) that Muhasibi prescribes, earned him the moniker *Muhasibi*, which translates to "the one who constantly takes (oneself) to account." A Muhasibian religious subject is not constituted by the bodily reproduction of norms, through performance of rituals or external compliance with rules, even though, as we shall see, imitation of prophetic example (*sunna*) has an important place within Muhasibi's larger program of subject formation. This is important to emphasize because, as noted in the introduction, not a few contemporary studies of anthropology of Islam give primary importance to *habitus* and bodily practices, as the most essential feature of ideal Muslim religio-moral subjectivity.[19] Muhasibi's account of ideal Muslim subjectivity, we can safely say, diverges decisively from what we get from contemporary anthropologists of Islam.

Now we could argue that Muhasibian lowers the bar significantly on ideal religious subjectivity. His teachings can take away both the optimism and motivation to become a better person, a person who is not troubled by unethical thoughts and sinful temptations. We could say that Muhasibi is asking the subject to passively resign to a somewhat anemic moral ideal. In response, Muhasibi would probably argue that his is a savvier assessment of the deeply conflicted and self-centered orientation of a human psyche that is asked to obey God by giving up at least some of its cherished pleasures, chief among them the desire to be praised and esteemed by others. Be that as it may, I think it would be a mistake to think that Muhasibi is letting the subject off the hook too easily. The ideal subject may not get busy becoming morally or religiously perfect, but must remain constantly watchful and worried: one must struggle to constantly empower the heart against the *nafs*. Whatever ease comes from a rejection of a perfectionist ethics is more than compensated for by the inescapable burdens of constant watchfulness and self-scrutiny that an ideal subject must bear without complaint. Far from being some sort of Marxian opium, religion (and being religious) for a Muhasibian subject is a voluntarily undertaken, grueling and courageous hike up a steep and slippery slope.

One key psychic activity that characterizes the ideal subject is the mental act of discriminating between those suggestions that call him to do good and those that do not. The subject has recourse to three intellectual resources for making the distinction: knowledge (*al-'ilm*), the use of reason (*al-'aql*) and deliberation before acting (*al-tathabbut*).[20] Knowledge here is the knowledge of the Quran and *sunna*, understood as knowledge of everything that God likes/approves and dislikes/disapproves in both inward and outward human actions. To use one's reason is to ascertain if a given suggestion, and the actions that would flow from it if the suggestion was accepted, is beneficial or harmful in terms of one's worldly and otherworldly well-being. According to Muhasibi, deliberation before acting is "the restraining of the *nafs* prior to action and foregoing haste in action i.e., being patient and deliberate before performing an action."[21] Thus, there is no respite for an ideal subject from constant intellectual work, self-scrutiny and patient deliberation prior to every action, despite the consolation that they do not have to become angels.[22] And yet, they cannot be successful in their inner deliberations without help from outside. This help arrives as knowledge that is God's guidance, in the form of the Quran and prophetic example. After acknowledging that one has a Lord and that one owes Him rights that need difficult, inward fulfillment, the next step for the subject is to desire guidance from God about how His rights are to be fulfilled. The efficacy and success of this guidance depends crucially, however, on another of the subject's own psychic standpoint—a standpoint Muhasibi describes as excellent or proper listening.

PROPER LISTENING

Before one can fulfill God's rights properly, the ideal subject would need to inhabit a particular way of listening to the religious discourse that elaborates what those rights are and how they are properly fulfilled. An ideal subject must abide by an ethics of listening as they inquire about the rights of God. Muhasibi begins his text by presenting the subject as someone who has asked about how he could fulfill God's rights. Muhasibi responds to the questioner by counseling them to first exhibit proper or excellent listening (*husn al-istimā*).[23] So what exactly comprises proper listening? Proper listening is a transition from being a speaking self to being a listening self. One turns down the volume on the chatter of one's *nafs*. But it is more than an inner silence. It is a set of inner conditions that help the person affirm the truth of what they hear and do everything in their power to benefit from the same. The key features of proper listening are, (i) that one's heart witnesses what is said, (ii) that one's thinking capacities are present and at work (*hudur al-'aql*), (iii) that one's bodily members are at rest (to minimize distraction), (iv) that one is not distracted by sights and sounds other than God's guidance, (v) that one resolves to act on what one hears and understands, (vi) that one stops talking about other things, and (vii) that one desires to understand.[24] The person is to realize and avow that to sincerely ask a question about God's rights is to simultaneously express the intention to reflectively understand the answer and be willing to act on whatever one actually understands.

One interesting implication of a subject's internalization of these ideas about proper listening is that by doing so, the subject strengthens the feeling that, if they find themselves unable to understand the answers given, they would be responsible for the lapse and cannot put the blame on the quality of the answer or answerer. The answer's rationality or intelligibility is pushed to the background. Instead, the ideal subject would locate the source of their incomplete or deficient comprehension in their failure to listen properly. The ideal subject's initial focus, once he asks someone to guide him about how he may fulfill God's rights, is his own state of being, not how that answerer may mislead or fail to benefit him. To aim for proper listening is to take responsibility for one's understanding of what is said and for translating that understanding into action.

REPENTANCE: FEELING FAVORED AS DISCURSIVE PRACTICE

An ideal Muhasibian subject ought to feel deeply remorseful about their sinful past, a past that they ought to now see as filled with failures of fulfilling God's rights. This remorse about one's past dereliction of duty when combined with a resolve to fulfill one's obligations to God in the future is *tawba* or repentance.[25] For Muhasibi, there are many types of penitents just as there are many different levels at which people fulfill God's rights. These different types of people vary in how aware they are of their past sins, how mindful they are about the suggestions to which they are subject, how much they know about the content of God's rights, how easy it is for them to fulfill those rights and how vigorously they desire or try to fulfill them. But all the various types of penitents share some basic psychological worries occasioned by their desire to repent. I want to focus on those elements of Muhasibi's teachings that I think are designed to help address these psychological worries through specific discursive practices.

In my view, Muhasibi's discourses seem designed to help a penitent address at least two main worries: first, given a penitent's sinful past when, the penitent must recall, he had found pleasure in sin and had persisted in sin for some time before repenting, how can he realistically feel that it is now his desire to fulfill God's rights? It is an "old habits die hard" sort of worry that can cause despair about one's ability to do right in the present and the future based on one's awareness of one's sinful past. After all, Muhasibi urges the subject to continuously bring his sinful past to mind and realize how long he has neglected to fulfill God's rights without realizing the gravity of this omission.[26] And second, there is the opposite "It is easy for me" sort of a concern that Muhasibi thinks should be seen as a precursor to full blown conceit and complacent overconfidence. The penitent might be tempted to attribute their change of heart to their own strength of will and thus incline toward placing their trust in their own *nafs*.[27] They may imagine that their *nafs* is quite responsive and compliant, well under their volitional control and willingness to obey God. But this good opinion of their *nafs*, a *nafs* that had hitherto kept them well-pleased with their sinful ways, is a dangerous mistake in Muhasibi's view, as it adds to the *nafs* virtuous tendencies that an ideal subject should not imagine the *nafs* to have. The self-exaltation is dangerous for religious subjectivity for two reasons: (i) it obviates the need to put one's trust in God and seek His help and (ii) increases the subject's chances of falling into his old sinful ways again.[28] For Muhasibi, repentance is a good deed and all good deeds (including the act of repentance) bring serious threats to ideal subjectivity in their wake, in the form of suggestions to conceit and pride.[29] Paradoxically, the commission of a good deed ought to make the doer of good, worry and not rejoice. He should not consider it his achievement.[30] The feeling of repentance therefore ought to set off a series of reflective, discursive practices through which the subject can respond to threats posed, paradoxically, by their newfound desire to fulfill God's rights. The discursive practices that Muhasibi recommends in order to address the two worries I have just noted can be described as follows.

The person is to think about their inclination to repent, as God's favor to them and thus a sign of God's desire to save them on the day of judgment. One is to feel and avow that God has befriended one by making one, against the liking of one's *nafs*, remorseful and repentant. Describing the subject's condition, Muhasibi says that, "hope is stirred in them that they are, in God's decree, a friend of their Lord" and the moment of realization of their disobedience, he says, "is the moment of the establishment of their friendship with

God."[31] The ideal subject, through this thought exercise, interprets their remorse as an indication that, "God is cleansing them from sin before their meeting with Him."[32] So the ideal subject uses the moment of realization of their past sins and the emergent desire to fulfill God's rights as God's desire to save them from punishment on the day of judgment. The ideal subject takes God's active and, from his new perspective, *demonstrated* interest in one's salvation as grounds for feeling they have been unmerited and unaware, recipients of God's bounteous help and favor. The subject should now feel a psychologically justified hope—a capacity to trust that God would, despite any continuing lapses and failings, cause them to repent for the same in the future.

Things can go horribly wrong for the subject even as he resolves to make it right with God. He may start to think obedience is within his reach and easy. The subject reminds himself of the consequences of such a move:

> When the slave resolved to establish all the rights of God, after their awareness of them, with this there is a deception from the *nafs* and the enemy. They make it seem to them that they would attain the observance of God's rights, which they resolved upon, with their own reason and their own strength (*bi-'aqlihi wa quwwatihi*). *But then this person is unable to overcome their sinful desires because they forget to put their trust in their Lord* [emphasis added].[33]

What should the ideal subject do at such a time? Muhasibi prescribes bringing to mind, as a discursive practice, the notion of God's power and favor in relation to one's changed disposition.

> If they were an intelligent slave (*fa in kāna 'abdan 'āqilan*) they would return at such times to the weakness of their *nafs* and remembrance of the power of his Lord. They would petition to their Lord for its assistance for the observance of its rights and would utter a moaning cry to it with a heart that is petitioning and cautiously fearful "I forget if you do not remind me and I am weak if you do not strengthen me and I am impatient if you do not make me patient," . . . by this they cut off hope in their *nafs* and direct all their hopes toward their Maker and Master. Then they find God near, answering, bestowing favor, giving blessings and bounties.[34]

A discourse about God's unmerited assistance and favor rescues the subject from placing his trust in himself. It addresses his worry that he may not be able to, given his past, obey God upon his own strength in the future. Muhasibi describes an ideal subject's standpoint and the discursive practice that would produce it, in the following way:

> But if (in their view) God warned them and awakened them, they would know that it was because of a bestowal of God upon them and their *nafs* had no part in it. They resolved upon something against the *nafs*'s love and it did not look

> at repentance except reluctantly and because of the constraint of fear of punishment. *Then [they would think]: How can repentance be from the nafs when it is against its liking and it did not look at it except with compulsion, dislike and disdain? How can that from which it desisted and it did not want, be from it? . . . Indeed, the one who caused it to repent and made it desire obedience against its liking is its God and its Maker and the Exalted.* Praise is due to God and thanking it is obligatory. Trust becomes easy for the slave and it also becomes easy for them to have a good opinion (*husn al-dhann*) about God in terms of what is to come because of what they have seen of the traces of gracious bestowal and preferential favor. Thus trusting and relying upon God, who bestows favors in this manner, becomes easy [emphasis added].[35]

From being a sinful person deserving of God's wrath and punishment, the ideal subject comes to inhabit a state where they are now psychically inclined to thank God for a favor they have received, in the form of a resolve to obey Him, and respond by having a good opinion about God and feeling encouraged about their prospects as observers of God's rights in the future. But for Muhasibi, having a good opinion about God does not preclude a continuing fear of His wrath. An ideal subject's engagement with discourses about God's promise of reward and threats of punishment are also formative of ideal subjectivity. Let us see how.

DIVINE REWARD AND PUNISHMENT

Muhasibi often speaks about God's promise of reward and threat of punishment (*al-wa'd wa al-wa'īd*) in his works and it is quite central to his conception of ideal subjectivity.[36] Perhaps, not surprisingly, an ideal Muhasibian subject engages in a willful and deliberate cultivation of fear (*takhwīf*).[37] They actively try to "make themselves afraid" by imagining how painful and unbearable God's punishment would be on the day of judgment. To our minds, this would seem like a psychologically unhealthy and even depressing thing to do.[38] Why would Muhasibi recommend such a mental activity to people? I think he does so because of two kinds of sensibilities or psychic commitments that he thinks ideal subjects should have.

First, ideal subjects ought to experience God not as a distant creator but as an active force in their lives, someone who exercises direct power over their choices. How can they achieve such a state of mind? Muhasibi thinks that just like masters in this world want their workers to perform certain tasks in return for a wage and just like they punish them for not performing the assigned task properly, God ought to be experienced as a Lord who rewards and punishes good and bad behavior respectively. This would allow subjects to think about God in each of their actions and allow Him to affect their everyday choices. God would become present to subjects as an authority whose opinion matters for them. He says,

> It is well-known among the people of this world that one does not see a worker among the workers of the world, nor a merchant among the merchants of the world, for whom the fatigue or labor and earning sustenance is light or easy except when he hopes for his wage (*al-ajr*). Also, the builders and others, their pleasure in fatigue comes from the sweetness of the wage. Indeed, labor is a severe pain for him and leisure is agreeable to him but he preferred fatigue to rest or leisure since he hoped for the wage. If his wage was small but the employer was expected to pay in full, then when the laborer thinks of the meagerness of the wage, the work becomes burdensome but if he remembered that the employer would pay in full to him and according to his labor, the work becomes light or easy for him. If the wage was great and he was not secure from the injustice or oppression of the employer, whenever he remembers anything that scared him of the employer's injustice (i.e., that he may not pay), the work becomes burdensome. If he remembered the abundant wage and that the just employer would pay in full, the work would be light for him. If the wage was great and the employer paid in full, the work would be light for him and he would not find any burden on his heart and his action is easy to do or light on the heart. There is no employer from whom one can expect more good than from God and no wage greater than the Garden or Paradise.[39]

Muhasibi's vision of God as a powerful Master is shaped by his particular experience of the world and the environment he was in, an environment in which, it seems, was simply accepted as par for the course that a powerful superior commands authority on the basis of their ability to bestow rewards and administer punishments to those under their charge. God's promises of reward and threats of punishment can be understood as an extension, by analogy, of familiar social norms that governed relations between agents with asymmetric power in society, to a subject's relationship with God. The extended analogy between real world experience of laborious work and its compensation and the compensation that one may expect from God indicates as such.

Second, as we have already discussed above, an ideal subject takes it as given that despite any joys that could come from performing the duties owed to God, obedience to a superior, in this case God, is fundamentally detestable and burdensome for the *nafs*. The *nafs*, for Muhasibi and hence for the ideal subject, must be conceived as averse to fulfilling God's rights because the fulfillment of these rights is understood to necessitate the giving up of worldly pleasures that are deeply loved by the *nafs*. Psychologically, the subject must be able to feel that he is coercing his *nafs* into doing something it detests doing. This is the theological anthropology, a picture of a self at war with itself in the service of a higher power, that justifies a desire to deliberately cultivate fear of God. An ideal subject engages himself in the following discourse as justifying God's threats of punishment and as a means for enabling himself to cultivate fear of God,

The works to which God commanded them and to which He summoned them are more difficult for the heart and for the bodily members than their pleasurable opposites. And these commandments are disliked by nature and are burdensome for the *nafs*. And about this God says, "It may be that they hate a thing while it is good for you and perhaps you love a thing and it is bad for you" [Qur'an, 2:216]. And the most truthful one [Prophet Muhammad] said, "The Garden is surrounded by the hateful and he informed us that the veil with which the Garden is surrounded, it is the action which is disliked by the *nafs*."[40] Then he said that the one who made their *nafs* bear or carry these hateful things, they entered the Garden by the mercy of God . . . God knew about the slave before it created them: that if their nature is to love what agrees with them and what is against their nature is hateful to them . . . God knew that such a person will not abandon what their *nafs* desired intensely except that God makes for them painful torture or punishment.[41]

Thus, since the subject reminds himself that the *nafs* is created to hate obedience to God, he finds promises of rewards and threats of punishment to be excellent psychological aids, provided as favors by a God who knows well their inner aversion to obedience and their inner love for worldly pleasures. Ideal Muhasibian subjects do not then feel indignant about God's threats of punishment.[42] Interestingly, and on the contrary, they interpret a discourse about God's promises and threats not for what the latter connotes about God (as wrathful or as a deity who incentivizes piety) but as useful intellectual tools against their recalcitrant-by-design *nafs*. The unformed subject, so to speak, is attracted toward ease and comfort. Instead of seeing one's disposition to pursue the agreeable and to dislike the disagreeable as either a temporary psychic lapse or as an acceptable, natural disposition, one should see it as undesirable, yet deeply (and divinely) ingrained aspects of the human psyche that is meant to strive for God's acceptance. This aspect of one's psyche can be best cognized and known to oneself through engaging the properly uncomfortable recollection of God's threats of punishment, balanced by hope for his just rewards.[43] In addition to thinking about divine reward and punishment, the ideal subject also relies on the practice of contemplating death, in particular its unannounced suddenness, as a means for attaining a standpoint that would be conducive to fulfilling God's rights.

CONTEMPLATING DEATH: SUBVERTING ONE'S SENSE OF DEATH'S PREDICTABILITY

One of the things that concerns Muhasibi about a person's success in fulfilling God's rights is the issue of postponement or *al-taswif*.[44] Muhasibi is concerned that people tend to feel they have plenty of time to fulfill God's rights at some later time. They tend to thus postpone repentance and continue in their heedless and sinful ways even when they may be intellectually aware that what they are doing is disapproved or forbidden by God. Procrastination is as real a problem for Muhasibian religious subjects as it is for us today in our personal and professional lives. We have so much that needs our immediate attention that things we recognize as important but difficult are nevertheless postponed when their postponement does not carry any immediate negative consequences and when we feel we can do them later. It is in recognition of the psychological appeal of postponement, and as a way to address it, that the ideal Muhasibian subject ought to contemplate the sudden onset of death and focus on their weak, decaying and vulnerable bodies by bringing to mind the ruined bodies and abodes of the deceased.[45]

The main reason a person pays scant attention to fulfilling God's rights and resists repenting for his negligence, in Muhasibi's view, is that their passions drive them to seek pleasures in the things of this world. This indulgence causes their worldly hopes and aspirations to be, idiomatically speaking, elongated or lengthened. The limitations of their bodies and the world's transience are forgotten in pursuit of goals that, in order to be pleasurable, would need one's body to be young and healthy (and obviously alive). By lengthening of hopes, Muhasibi means that people tend to make extensive, time-consuming plans for things they want to achieve in this world and spend the bulk of their time and energy in the present moment, worrying about achieving those goals. The cries and creaks of their dying bodies and aching souls (aching on account of death and transience of everything around them) fail to make an impact on their minds. They do not dissuade him from trying to extract abiding pleasure from transient beings and projects. Interestingly, the ideal subject is not asked to eliminate her hopes and aspirations altogether but instead redirect them toward eternal, never-ending rewards and pleasures, available to humans in a realm, after bodily death here, where bodily frailty and decay would no longer limit pleasures and enjoyments. Thus Muhasibi talks about the contemplation of death not so much to cultivate a nihilistic despair about the impending loss of life but to encourage a sense of balance and commensurability between the strength/length of one's hopes and the possibilities of their realization in the inhospitable conditions of this world and the weak and decaying nature of one's body and its capacities (with which human beings obtain the pleasures of this world). One is to reflect about the kind of existence that would be needed for human hopes to find perfect and lasting gratification.[46] One's focus ought not be death itself as a painful tragedy to be feared for its own sake. Rather, the focus ought to be its sudden and unpredictable onset, leaving one unprepared for the life to come and frustrating one's manifold and extensive hopes for attaining the things and pleasures of this world. The following exchange between Muhasibi and his questioner is telling:

> I asked, "How does one attain to shortening of hope (*qasr al-amal*)?" He said, "By fear of suddenness of death while one is heedless, for a slave's soul (*ruh*) is a loan and one does not know when the giver asks it back and takes back the loan. So if he feared suddenness of death, his hopes in this world are severed and he would be ready for his appointed time, acting as someone who is waiting for death to descend upon him any moment." I asked, "How does one attain the fear of suddenness of death?" He said, "With great awareness (*bi 'azīm al-ma'rifa*) of the uncertainty of one's appointed time to die, and that death would not look at him nor wait for his permission nor listen to him when it decides to take his soul from his body, just as the deaths of those who died before him." I asked, "How does one attain such awareness and such a lesson from the deaths of others?" He said, "Through continuous remembrance and reflection about the uncertainty of the appointed time of death and the descending of death and the termination of one's life and remembrance of the deaths of those to whom death came suddenly."[47]

Often enough when someone we know dies, we have a feeling, "it was not their time" and we are surprised and dazed about what almost always feels like a sudden and untimely departure. Our feelings are not based on some firm sense of a proper time for someone to die. For many of us, there is never a good time for anyone to die. In our everyday life, we often tacitly and unconsciously expect that the people we know would simply continue to live. As a matter of intellectual exercise, the Muhasibian ideal subject reminds himself and avows that death has no fixed time and place and one's unthinking assumption that it will not come anytime soon is unwarranted, not supported by empirical evidence. The subject should thus avow that the onset of death is entirely unpredictable even as they (intuitively and mistakenly) feel that the sick and the old are more likely to die or those travelling by air or sea are at greater risk of dying than those on land. They have a false sense that the young and healthy would not suddenly pass away or be afflicted suddenly by a disease and then die quickly from it. Muhasibi recommends a deliberately cultivated, uncertainty and anxiety about the time of one's death and the suddenness of its onset that would enable one to cut one's hopes short in matters of this world and cease postponing repentance and fulfilling God's rights. The subject's motivational economy must then have a place for the practice of contemplating death in order for them to feel the urgency of taking remedial action. Muhasibi says,

> No one is safe from death neither little nor big, neither young nor old. Death does not have a known reason. One can neither be secure from it in health, nor in sickness, neither in settled populations nor in the wilderness, neither on land nor at sea. If one remembers death, with a heart free from all other things and remembers that death has no fixed time, no single cause, no regard for age along with intense remembrance of what death may bring, either news of God's punishment or good news of God's mercy along with remembering those who have passed away before him, some of whom were higher/stronger

> than him and some who were below him, and also similar to him, then his awareness of death and the suddenness of death is heightened and that it may descend upon him like it descended upon those who died before him without exception. When his awareness thus intensifies, his hope is shortened and when his hope is shortened, the heart would become wary (*hadhara qalbahu*) of death. When the heart becomes wary of death, he would act with a sense that death may come. And when he acts as a person wary of death, he would hasten to prepare for it, rushing to good deeds (*istibāq ilā al-khayrāt*) before his soul meets its Owner.[48]

Contemplating death is part of a broader psychic economy in which the quality of one's life after death is a real concern for the subject. Without belief in a life after death, contemplating impending, sudden death would make no sense. The subject is not to think that they are insufficiently committed to the truth of a life after death when they disregard fulfilling God's rights or even finding out what they might be. They are instead to feel they have been postponing acting on their commitment. Contemplating death's suddenness is a method of shaking off the hold of passions upon the subject's mind and make them hasten to good deeds.

WARINESS OF SATAN: DEFICIENT, EXCESSIVE, AND EFFECTIVE

An important aspect of an ideal subject's psyche is the right kind of attitude toward the enemy, Satan. How much, if at all, should a religious subject concern themselves with Satan, its snares and whispers? And why should one pay any attention to Satan at all? Satan represents the epitome and the embodiment of all the most serious threats to ideal religious subjectivity. Satan, along with the desires of the *nafs*, stand between a subject and the fulfillment of God's rights. In a nonreligious sense, Satan is analogous, psychically, to something that stands between an agent's earnest desire for a known good and the attainment of that good. It is the cause for a set of subjective failures that a person may blame when they fail to achieve their goal. The reason I put this idea in these general theoretical terms is because I would like to facilitate an imaginary dialogue between Muhasibi's position on Satan and our own, familiar moral experiences. The question we, today, can ask (as people who may or may not be interested in Satan or religion): How much of our intellectual foci and affective energies ought to be spent contemplating the challenges that often stand between our knowledge of our cherished goals and their realization or actualization?

Muhasibi notes that some people take wariness of Satan to be nothing but a distraction. They think that it takes one's attention away from God and the hereafter.[49] A second group of people, he reports, holds that one must worry about Satan all the time. One must keep Satan front and center in one's mind so as to avoid falling into the many subtle traps he sets for those who wish to obey God.[50] Muhasibi thinks both positions are mistaken. He thinks that whereas the first option pays too little attention to the real threat that Satan poses, as per God's own guidance in the Quran, the second option obsesses about Satan a bit too much. He speaks approvingly of a third option that prioritizes the positive remembrance of God with a secondary, "back of the mind," yet active, wariness of Satan. There is a psychic standpoint proper to someone with a commendable desire to be safe from Satan's whispers and it is attained by engaging in the following discursive practice.

> The likeness of the one who dedicates his heart, or some of it, for anticipating a suggestion from Satan (*khatra min al-shaytan*) is that of a person who wants to empty a well from its dirty water, while dirty water continuously streams into it. He cleans the well but dirty water continues to pour in. He spends all his days cleaning the well but it would not get cleaned from the dirty water. On the other hand, the likeness of one who commits to preoccupation with God is the person who blocked the stream of dirty water so that with this block, he rejects the dirty water easily, purifying the well from filth with little difficulty and hardship. Such is the one who preoccupied himself with God and easily rejected the suggestions of Satan through the preoccupation of his heart with his Lord and His light and the strength of his resolve. This group follows properly the Quran and the *sunna*. . . . They are more capable of repelling the suggestions of Satan and farther away from deception and deficiency. They commit their hearts to wariness of Satan without being preoccupied with the enemy and they do not fear his power over them, but rather fear their Lord. They obey God and rely upon Him, following His command, and they do not get distracted from their preoccupation with their Lord by being preoccupied with Satan and remembering him instead of remembering God.[51]

According to Muhasibi's metaphor of the well, to spend time and effort cleaning the heart from suggestions would be a self-consuming and ultimately ineffective endeavor. As long as the source of the dirty water is left unblocked, the well cannot remain clean for long despite heroic efforts. Muhasibi favors a more proactive approach to Satan's whispers—the ideal religious subject should make it harder for Satan's suggestions to enter the heart, by actively filling his heart with the remembrance of God. The ideal attitude then is to have an *effective wariness* of Satan that is neither deficient nor excessive. The ideal religious subject engages in the remembrance of God and preoccupies himself with God as an active, intellectual strategy for blocking Satan's suggestions. Proper wariness of Satan, Muhasibi argues, is like wariness of a person who is asleep yet worried enough about oversleeping past a certain time that he wakes up at the desired time. In other words, Muhasibi thinks one ought to be wary of Satan in a "back of the mind" sort of way because one is to believe such a wariness has the desired effect of shielding one from falling into error at Satan's prompting. Remembering God is to be a means of remembering Satan effectively and *not* a forgetting of Satan.[52] Let us briefly think analogously and comparatively about Muhasibi's teachings in order to reflect about our attitude toward impediments, setbacks and challenges we face in our pursuit of ideals.

I think it is easier to see that thinking too little about challenges can catch us off guard, ignorant and ill-prepared to deal with them. This increases our chances of failure in achieving our goals. But we give less attention to the problem of over-thinking about challenges, especially when they are many and intractable. This often causes fatigue and despair, leaving us with less energy and with beleaguered hopes of attaining our desired ends. Our well-intentioned focus on problems can, if excessive, demotivate us and push us toward paralyzing cynicism or, perhaps, an escapist apocalypticism (things will likely remain bad now but become great at some point in a distant future or in the afterlife) or self-consuming worries and despair. This can happen, we can learn from Muhasibi, when we think only and directly about the challenges that we need to overcome, and forget to think enough about why the goal or end is cherished and valuable and that these worries tell us about the value the desired end has for us. We may fail to engage the world with creative and spirited hope for "the possible but the not yet" if we pay no attention to the good that "already is."

Many people today feel, and for good reasons, that we are living through dark and dying times. From politics to the environment, the problems that confront us as a globe can seem despairingly intractable and worsening by the day and the people in power often failing us. But if we continue to only focus, with ever increasing emotional intensity and zeal, on the problems and challenges and the follies of men, we may forget to celebrate the beauty and justice, which are our goals, and the meaning of our deep love for such goals. If we feel that all talk of the beauty and justice that already exists or all talk of the meaning of human desire for such qualities is a naïve, repulsive, "feel-good," cheap optimism, we can constrict the mental and emotional space for genuine hope and perhaps even joy to sprout.[53] In an effort to maintain seriousness, clarity and realism, we can become so obsessed with the problems and challenges that we forget to understand and remember (adequately anyway) those beautiful things whose decline or destruction is, quite mysteriously and inexplicably, the cause of our anxieties and worries. In time, our obsession with the problems can begin wearing us out and weighing us down. It can breed what feels like an intelligent, courageous and honest realism whereas it is an excessively ironic, self-defeating cynicism and failure to exercise effective wariness. I think we can learn from Muhasibi that sometimes the best way to deal authentically with real and imminent threats and problems, is to spend time and mental energy thinking about, and becoming more cognizant of, the goods, such as beauty and justice (to take two generic examples) and our desire for such goods. We ought to remind and nourish ourselves with thoughts of the good(s) we are so afraid to lose and affirm their desirability as worth hoping and fighting for. All the while that we focus on the goods, we never forget the challenges. Rather, we think about the goods as a deliberate strategy for keeping an excessive, overwhelming obsession with problems and impediments (known and unknown) at bay and from making us forget the meaning of our desire for beauty, which is, Muhasibi would say, is a desire and love for God, the Beautiful One. What might seem to us naïve distractions might just be the discursive practices that nourish our commitments and our resolve in the face of adversity to keep alive our hopes for the possible, and real, but not yet (fully).

AḤKĀM DISCOURSE, SUNNA AND SUBJECT FORMATION

Several scholars of Islam have argued that if we want to study practical or normative Islamic ethics, that is, discussions about what Muslims should and shouldn't do, we should look to positive Islamic law or *fiqh*.[54] If ethics is understood primarily as a catalogue of dos and don'ts and practical, action-guides, it is true that we find the most robust and detailed discussions of such ethics in Islamic law or Muslim *fiqh*. But if we think of ethics in a Foucauldian key, that is, as a study of the discursive practices people use to become, by their own means, willing subjects of specific religious/legal/moral codes, then Muslim *fiqh* is but one such set of codes, among others, that we can study for analyzing Muslim ethics. In order to understand the role of legal codes from such a Foucauldian ethical perspective, we should look at the psychic work that *fiqh* discourses are expected to do for subjects that engage in them. In Muhasibi's case, we should raise our gaze from the plethora of specific juridical rules that he discusses in his various works and consider *fiqh* discourse as a conceptual framework, with which agents organize and form their psychic standpoints, especially the standpoints that pertain to their own moral agency and natural moral intuitions.

As a conceptual framework, *fiqh* discourse functions as a classificatory scheme, comprised of five values or categories of act analysis (*aḥkām al-khamsa*).[55] An ideal subject who engages in *fiqh* discourse ought to organize their actions and reorganize their intuitions according to these categories of act analysis. These five categories of act analysis are: obligatory, encouraged, neutral, discouraged and forbidden. It is not only that *fiqh* prescribes and proscribes actions. More fundamentally, these categories of act analysis offer agents a matrix for organizing human actions and thus a particular mode of orienting themselves in, and interpreting, the world. In Muhasibi's teachings, these categories help a subject shape and order their natural or intuitive sense of propriety and help to make themselves into a religiously well-ordered subject. A key function of these categories is to empower an agent to override their natural intuitions, ethical or otherwise, and re-order their conduct in line with the order encoded in these categories. This ordering is not unique to Islam and we find it in a different form in, for instance, medieval Christianity. Briefly looking at the Christian example will help clarify and illuminate the role of these categories in Muhasibian religious formation.

In his study of medieval Christian discipline, anthropologist Talal Asad observes that the virtue of obedience was cultivated through the *structuring* of daily activities within monastic communities.[56] Describing a novice's voluntary self-confinement in a Benedictine cloister, Asad writes,

> The major concern was not simply one of observing legal duties but of knowing how to avoid falling into sin. For this, it was not enough to do what one was told by the Abbot, but to *want* to do so because obedience was a virtue, and disobedience a sin. It was a matter, as Bernard knew, of constructing the desire to become a subject.[57]

Asad argues that the structuring of everyday activities in terms of space and time was a method or technique for "constructing the desire to become a subject."[58] This is an important observation because it helps us see that rule-following, on its own, cannot be obedience without some desire, that needs to be constructed, to follow the rules. Such a desire needs to be produced and is not, in Benedictine thought, but also in Muhasibi's teachings, a natural one. The structuring of desire was not directly aimed at inducing an ethical other-regard but to transform oneself into a religious subject, properly desirous of obeying God's will.[59] For Muhasibi, the categories of act analysis are the means by which an agent resists being moved to action by their instinctual, arbitrary, self-centered moral preferences. Instead, one sees oneself as someone who is choosing, and hence desiring, obedience to God.

Muhasibi teaches that, "God has made some of His obligations more obligatory than others with respect to time."[60] There is often a need, then, to rank obligations. But how shall a person determine which obligation is more obligatory than any other? Thus, distinguishing different obligatory acts in terms of their proper time of performance requires some criteria for rank-ordering. Would the ranking be a matter of personal preference? Can the criteria be one's natural, intuitive sense of what is most urgent, appropriate or important in a given situation? Consider the following passage from Muhasibi where he responds to a question about any additional duties that fall upon a slave who might otherwise observe God's rights:

> Yes, there is an additional duty. For God has prescribed his ordinances in His book as a text, as a summary of the obligations, that require the commentary of the *sunna* of the prophet. He has made some of his obligations more obligatory than others and two obligations can coincide in time. He has imposed an

obligation with a time which will pass; if its time passes without excuse, before it is performed, the slave was disobedient to God. And He has imposed an obligation that has two times and it is more excellent for him who does it in its first time, but if he does it in its second time, he will not be guilty. And He has made obligatory that the obligations He imposes be applied in regard to that which He has forbidden to His slaves. And He does not prefer a work of supererogation by which one seeks to draw near to Him over and above the performance of obligations. You and the slaves of God must not postpone a duty with which God made it obligatory for you to begin, nor put first what He commanded to be postponed until after some other obligation, nor omit an obligation in order to seek nearness to God with a supererogatory act or by other than that.[61]

Clearly, fulfilling obligations has an order to it. And the ideal subject cannot, without courting disobedience, think they can exercise discretion and rational judgment to order these obligations without failing to remain, in their own minds, a religious subject. The mediating concept here is the *sunna*, which Muhasibi implies is necessary for ordering the obligations. The questioner then asks Muhasibi: "Explain all that to me: with which to begin when they (obligations) occur and which to postpone; which has a time that expires and which has a time that does not expire?"[62] He responds by referencing a well-known hadith of the Prophet Muhammad.

If two obligations are obligatory for you, begin with the one more obligatory for you in the Book and the *sunna*. If their times concur, such as taking care of the need of the father or the mother, then begin with the need of the mother. This is but an example concerning parents, upon which the commentary is lengthy. *It is only one example of this type of thing.* So let the servant begin with the need of his mother, because filial piety to her is put first in the *sunna* of the prophet, and the scholars agree upon her precedence over the father in regard to filial piety and obedience. In like manner, if the slave does not have a mother or a father, but has kinsmen who are in need, then let him begin with helping the nearest of kin, then the next and so on.[63]

Sunna, and the putative agreement of scholars about the latter's implication in a given context, expresses the social and ethical norms of the times. In Muslim societies, the *sunna*-derived rules were generally accepted as principles and rules to live by, principles that were expected to override any contrary personal preferences. The two passages just quoted give us a good idea about how Muhasibi wants a person to engage with what I have called the categories of act analysis. In the above example, the prominent category is *obligatory* and it is brought to bear on one's decision through what the *sunna* teaches. The category of obligatory (mediated by *sunna*) helps a slave of God correctly order what he may experience as two courses of action, both discernably ethical (attending to the needs of the father or addressing the needs of the mother) should one confront both these needs at the same time. The example is telling because we can see that both options are, prima facie, ethical—one either helps the father or helps the mother. There is no option not to help them when they are in need. But consider a scenario, not hard to imagine, where a person may intuitively feel that their father's need is more urgent than their mother's. The person may then, based on their intuitive, natural, commonsense view of things, determine that they ought to help their father before they help their mother. Imagine, for instance, that a person's father and mother need to talk to them about problems they are both having at work or they need the person to have a conversation with them because they are feeling lonely. Now imagine that the person, for any number of reasons, feels that their father is more in need of the conversation than their mother. Their own sense might be that it is better, more appropriate, for them to talk to the father first and call the mother later. In this situation, if an agent engages in the discursive practice cited above, we can clearly see they are asked to overrule their sense of what is right, good or appropriate, if they truly desire to be an obedient, religious subject. We see here that an ideal religious subject must overrule their natural or intuitive sense of the ethical. And Muhasibi is explicit that this example, that is, the example of who has a greater right to be attended to, is just one example of how moral duties may conflict and need an ordering principle. One is still acting on a value (helping another) but the value is lived in a way that negates the person's sense of the order of things in a given situation and replaces it with a *Sunnaic* stance, consistent with the order encoded by categories of act analysis. A psychic space thus opens for a properly *religious* subject to emerge, having subverted or ignored his natural sense of the good in a given situation if the latter is at odds with the *Sunnaic* order. Obedience to God is properly observed, Muhasibi's teachings suggest, by ordering one's actions according to *aḥkām* discourses, an order embodied in the *sunna* and not common sense whenever the two stand at odds in lived experience. In this particular example, Muhasibi asks the questioner to give priority to meeting the mother's need and postpone meeting the father's need even if the questioner should incline toward addressing the father's need first. Another example Muhasibi gives is as follows:

> There will appear to the slave two matters which are good (*fadlān*), the time of one could pass but not so with the other. The *nafs* will be adamant that he begin with the one just at hand and do the former at a later time. The *nafs* and the enemy will stop him from the one whose time could pass by urging him to do the one whose time does not pass; for example, attending a funeral or a sick call to a friend wherein he does not fear sudden death of the friend from the symptoms of the illness.[64]

In this example, Muhasibi suggests that the slave may be confronted with the choice of either praying the funeral prayers of a deceased person (something time-sensitive) or to visit a friend who has been sick but whose death is not imminent (something good to do but that can be done later). He thinks that the *nafs* would tell the person to visit the sick friend first (something he can do later) and forego attending the funeral (something he will not be able to do once the body is buried). In such a circumstance, the person will not be able to perform an action as an obedient slave of God without recourse to the categories of act analysis. Again, we can imagine scenarios where someone might find it more appropriate and responsible to attend to a sick, living friend than to pay respects to, for instance, a more distant deceased person, even as that person thinks the latter is a religiously meritorious thing to do. But this order of desire must be changed if one is to be an ideal religious subject because it is more likely that the *nafs* is postponing the time-sensitive action simply to avoid the self-disciplining, a restructuring of desire by means of the categories of act analysis.

In a sense, engaging with *aḥkām* discourse is a tool for disciplining moral agency in the service of religious self-making. The goal is not ethical but religious: to cultivate the ability to rearrange one's desires and actions according to God's will instead of one's own sense of what is appropriate without recourse to the categories of act analysis.[65] A person who performs his actions in the incorrect order, such a person has disobeyed God in Muhasibi's view because, "he has put first what God put last and last what God put first."[66]

> I said, "What if two matters, which are both obligatory commands or both beneficial appear and it is not clear to the person which of these is the more beneficial or the more obligatory?" He said, "He will consider which of them is lighter upon his heart, and if it is lighter by reason of passion he will do the one which is burdensome because to do it for the passion and not for his Lord will not give him security; and if it easier because he is sounder in religion or his heart has a great abundance of works—how few are such sincere hearts—he will do the easier because to serve God with cheerful obedience is more excellent than to serve Him with unwillingness and endurance. . . . And if it is not clear to him why it is light or burdensome, I prefer that he do that which is more burdensome since it is not clear to him that the lightness is from the strength of his heart and from its search for soundness and desire to increase in piety. And the burdensome action brings near to passion, the fear of that which the burdened ones have experienced in themselves and upon which they are fashioned [i.e., their natural inclination to disobey God].[67]

The ideal is cheerful obedience but Muhasibi clearly registers his doubt that many could achieve it. Here we notice, once again, how the categories of act analysis urge introspection and urge the self to find out the truth about oneself, lest it obey his desire instead of obeying God. In cases of doubt, one is to choose the more burdensome of the two obligations. In so doing, one is to feel more sincere in one's desire to obey God and avoid the confusion that would come from doing something one finds easy (did one do it for God or because it was easy and liked by the self?).

When two obligations or commands appear to be equally important to the subject, he then launches into examining himself, asking himself: which one is lighter or heavier for the heart and why? The person must then try to uncover the source of the weight of the obligation on his heart: is one obligation easier or lighter because of his passions or desire for worldly pleasure? Is the other heavier because the *nafs* does not like it? In choosing what is burdensome, the slave forms himself into a subject who is able to refuse his *nafs*'s desire (which would naturally prefer the lighter, easier action) and instead choose/desire to obey God, against the wishes of the *nafs*. The choice to perform the more burdensome obligation is to be seen by the subject as establishing the truth about their rebellious nature to themselves through reflecting on the burden one feels in choosing a given course of action. The categories of act analysis enable a particular kind of self-analysis and self-understanding—one affirms that one has a *nafs* that is reluctant to obey God and inclined toward its own short-sighted and transient pleasures. One becomes aware of the unsound condition of their *nafs* and its desires, thereby forging an embodied desire to obey God in and through the act of choosing the obligation that is psychologically more burdensome. The function of the category, obligatory, in Muhasibi's discourse is not simply an exposition of *legal* injunctions. Engaging with the categories of act analysis allow the subject to impose, when necessary, discomfort and pain—the pain that comes from choosing the burdensome obligation and leaving off the lighter obligation—on himself, revealing thereby his heart's condition to himself and inhabiting the standpoint of an ideal subject.

RATIONALITIES OF A MUHASIBIAN RELIGIOUS SUBJECT

Our discussion of the role of *aḥkām* discourse raises questions about the ideal subject's standpoint toward its God-given capacity to reason about what is appropriate or good. If we were to articulate this question in the most pithy and direct form, we could ask: Should an ideal Muhasibian religious subject use their reason or should they ignore it and instead follow God's commands? In other words, should they follow God's commands unthinkingly? The answer, unfortunately, cannot be as straightforward as these questions. The answer is both a yes and a no because there are situations in which a Muhasibian subject would voluntarily restrict the use of reason in the interest of proper religious formation and there are other situations where he would not.[68] What is important to understand is that Muhasibi teaches there is more than one kind of reason at a person's disposal.

Muhasibi distinguishes between at least two main types of reason, the rational capacity to understand the meaning of speech and therefore tell the difference between what is beneficial and what is harmful for oneself in this world. He calls this *'aql al-bayān* or what we may call *diagnostic reasoning*. This kind of reasoning helps a person understand and recognize the meanings of what is said or written and know the consequences of actions and their benefits and harms.[69] Any creature who has the ability to understand has the capacity to reason in this sense. The second kind of rationality he calls *aql 'an Allah*, which we may render *devotional reasoning*. This form of reasoning also discerns things but the objects of its discerning efforts are the harms and benefits that pertain to the hereafter, as well as to recognizing God's majesty and exaltedness. It is a form of reasoning that looks out for the subject's transcendental interests and organizes thoughts and desires to align with those interests. This is the kind of reason that alerts the subject when he is being derelict in his duties toward God.[70] The ideal subject must not only have diagnostic reasoning, which is the minimum requirement for a person to be a candidate for fulfilling God's rights in a formal, legal sense but also use devotional reasoning. Whereas those who lack the ability to use diagnostic reasoning suffer from a disability that frees them of knowing about or fulfilling obligations to God, those who have it are responsible because they have the ability to distinguish benefits from harms but ignore or reject the use of devotional reasoning.

The mark of having the standpoint of devotional reasoning is that one fears doing something that God dislikes.[71] And interestingly, there is no limit to how much one could progress in this form of reasoning and hence, Muhasibi says, one should not talk about perfection (*kamāl*) when it comes to devotional reasoning.[72] One may endlessly increase in how much one recognizes God's exaltedness. An ideal subject, one whose uses what I have called devotional reasoning, must not restrict their vision of benefits and harms to this world but extend their concerns to life after death. Muhasibi thinks it is human reasoning itself, in its devotional mode, and not a lack of rationality, that asks and enables human beings to endlessly increase their understanding of the awesomeness and exaltedness of God and hence His rights over his creatures.

But there is indeed a context in which an ideal subject voluntarily suspends and diligently avoids the use of reason altogether—any kind of reason. This is the context where one simply wants to mimic a role model—in this case, the Prophet Muhammad. A modern reader can easily understand that when one's goal is to mimic, the use of reason would be counterproductive because reason works to understand what is good and what is not. The ideal Muhasibian subject will encounter moments in his life when discerning the truth would not be his immediate goal, even though it may remain his general interest. Imagine an artist who decides to replicate someone else's work of art, a specific work of art. If the artist's goal is to draw as exact a replica of the original as possible, it would be counterproductive, perhaps even illogical and contradictory, for the artist to simultaneously try and express their unique, personal style in the process, however valuable and legitimate this personal style may otherwise be. The nature of the enterprise (mimicking a model) renders personal preference, understanding and creativity unreasonable. It is in the context of following, rather mimicking in a tangible, external form, the prophet as a role model that Muhasibi warns against the use of reason. He argues that the use of reason in such a case would ruin the "correctness" (*thawāb*) of one's bodily action. Correctness of action (or aptness of practice) is to be judged, in other words, not by appeal to reason or understanding but instead by the degree of one's following (*ittiba*) and surrendering to (*istislām*) the *sunna*, as a model of behavior to be imitated insofar as the external fulfillment of God's rights is concerned.[73] If the imitation of external prophetic behavior were to be considered the sole mark of ideal subjectivity, then surely reflection and reasoning would not be among the desirable qualities or standpoints of the ideal subject. But in Muhasibi's case, this imitation of *sunna* is one aspect, among others, of ideal religious subjectivity and those other aspects of ideal subjectivity, as discussed above, require the use of introspective, devotional reasoning.

ZUHD: UNBURDENING THE SELF

I want to say a few words about a topic that many scholars take to be a quintessentially Muhasibian theme and attitude, namely *zuhd*. Literally, *zuhd* means "to abstain, renounce, relinquish, forsake and shun." In scholarship on Islam, it is often rendered by the imprecise term, asceticism.[74] It is commonly agreed that an attitude of abstention and renunciation is characteristically ascetic. We find Muhasibi recommending abstention and renunciation as ideals in some contexts. And it is important to consider what those contexts are. We need to ask: What does a subject practically accomplish by engaging in a *zuhd* discourse in Muhasibi's teachings? To be sure, like many other religious thinkers in other traditions, Muhasibi counsels moderation when it comes to indulging one's worldly appetites and desires. What is more interesting is the way he thinks this idea should be used by the subject to bring about what we may call a functional and strategic psychic reversal: a person who is daunted by the difficulties and burdens of fulfilling God's rights would, through engaging in a discourse about *zuhd*, focus his attention on the ways in which an abstemious attitude lightens those voluntarily assumed burdens that attend one's religious life. Muhasibi's interlocutor asks him, "how does one incline toward things that God summons to?" Muhasibi responds with what an ideal subject ought to avow:

> By carrying less burden and by escaping arduous toil. When a person's *zuhd* increases, then he lessens the burdens that attach to the journey of life, he rests on the journey and his heart remains content. If a *zāhid* [i.e., the one who practices *zuhd*] looks upon the world with this [a *zuhd* perspective] so that he wants to be free from servitude to the world, he is saved from tribulations and he does not lose his dignity and self-respect. His heart is free from sorrow and grief. He is free and protected from abasement of servitude (to created beings). His burdens are lightened. He is forbearing and his life is joyous and he dies a martyr. His heart is free from the cares of this world. It is free from the suffocating constrictions of cravings. Calmness and dignity is preponderant in him. When someone thinks about these consequences of being a *zahid*, it becomes easier for them to bear the initial burdens of renunciation.[75]

What we have here is nothing short of a therapy of desire. The subject finds it difficult to resist overindulgence in pleasure initially, leading him to disregard God's rights. Here Muhasibi presents a discourse that ought to empower the subject to choose the path of fulfilling God's rights despite its difficulties and burdens, now elided with the more general "burdens of the journey of one's life." Whereas obedience itself may mostly be difficult, contemplating the liberating effects of adopting a *zuhd* perspective, a relaxed, reasoned detachment and freedom from the grip of things other-than-God, would help the subject overcome their natural, initial hesitations about renouncing worldly pleasures and the burdens they have to bear to attain those pleasures. Being subject to God is to be conceived of as freedom from self-destructive and undignified bondage to everything lesser and less abiding than Him. To be a religious subject is to feel freed from the burdens of life without losing interest in life and pleasure altogether. Muhasibian *zuhd* is a tool for self-empowerment, not a call for self-mortification or depravity-inducing renunciation of all material pleasures *tout court*. We shall see this more clearly in the next chapter where we discuss Muhasibi's views about the importance of working and earning a decent livelihood.

Crucially, desire and possession of desirable things itself are not the real problem. It is the undignified, harmful attachment that makes one lose sight of other, bigger, spiritual goods that is the problem and the solution is to regain perspective through practicing detachment. Greed can bind and blind. Avarice can subjugate and enslave. Greed and avarice shred human dignity by goading the self on to want more without end, making it cling to what tears at one's proverbial hands. They make one salivate after things not worthy of such intense desire, things that disappoint even after one attains them. It breeds perpetual discontentment and gratitude as a disposition becomes impossible. *Zuhd* then is a perspective and a choice. It is a desirable standpoint quite independent of the magnitude of the subject's material possessions. It is a way of transforming the quality or meaning of one's relationship with things. For instance, in response to a question about showing off and ostentation, Muhasibi says that it ultimately relates to a person's social standing. If a king donned the attire of a pauper and if a poor man tried to wear expensive clothes so that he would be given respect, both of them would be going against social convention and would rightly invite blame and reproach. "If a person who is not a sailor," Muhasibi says, "were to adopt their way of dressing, people would look down upon him; but a sailor would not be condemned for wearing the same."[76] This shows that Muhasibi's *zuhd* is tied to actions or behaviors that betray a desire for rank, praise or standing in the world and not, strictly speaking, renunciation of particular worldly goods per se. In the sailor's example, *zuhd* is an attitude that can save one from taking on the burden of breaking social conventions (dressing as a sailor when one is not one), merely for the sake of spearing different, *counter*cultural, for getting the attention and appraisal of other people. The purpose of *zuhd*, a discursive practice, is relief and an unburdening of the self, to the extent possible as one fulfills God's rights.

IDEAL SUBJECT: A DESIRER OF GOOD

By way of concluding our curatorial synopsis of ideal Muhasibian religious subjectivity, we can say that Muhasibi provides a vocabulary for talking about ideal subjectivity without relying on Aristotelian notions of moral excellence and the ideal of a wise and virtuous sage. One interesting phrase Muhasibi uses to refer to an ideal subject is *ṭalib al-khayr* or desirer of good. Muhasibi says that such a person ought to have five qualities: (i) *thawāb* or correctness in action that comes from imitating Muhammad, (ii) *ṣidq* or truthfulness, (iii) *shukr* or gratitude, (iv) hope, and finally (v) *khawf* or fear.[77] This list itself indicates that these are not stable moral qualities and are more appropriately understood as modes of being or standpoints that the self may adopt, through the kinds reflective and discursive avowals we have seen above. Indeed, for instance, Muhasibi does not explain gratitude as a character trait or moral disposition. Instead, he says gratitude is "to know that all the blessings are from God."[78] In other words, gratitude is a standpoint with a cognitive core—when one fails to avow that a particular thing is a blessing from God and does not relate to a blessing as arriving from God, one loses the standpoint of gratitude to God with respect to that blessing. Also, part of having a standpoint of gratitude is that should the subject suffer from a misfortune or hardship, he ought to avow that God is the one who takes hardships away. How is that gratitude, we may wonder?

The key here is to notice that a Muhasibian ideal subject does not dwell on why he was afflicted in the first place and why the blessing was withdrawn. He chooses, or ought to choose, to look upon the hardship as an opportunity to appreciate the blessing that this new situation makes available to him. Muhasibi thinks affliction is a blessing that allows the subject to relate to and know God as the one who takes away the kind of hardship he is made to face. There is a choice involved here and that is why one can talk meaningfully about ideal (or non-ideal) religious *subjectivity* as opposed conceiving of Muhasibian subjects simply as arational, habit-driven automatons. A desirer of good chooses to think about God not as the sender of affliction but as the One who takes them away. The inclination to focus on God as someone who afflicts humans, as if for no wise reason, can occur to the mind and should be rejected as Satan's suggestion, a suggestion to have a bad opinion about God. The ideal subject is formed, or else deformed, as he chooses, or fails to choose, desirable psychic standpoints amid the constant onslaught of suggestions that entice him toward ignoring God and His rights or make him complacent about fulfilling them in only outward ways. This chapter has briefly documented the nature and formation of ideal Muhasibian religious subjectivity, the psychic standpoints that a subject ought to have and the kinds of discursive practices by means of which the subject achieves those desirable standpoints, while avoiding and overcoming undesirable ones. How does such a psyche manifest in the real world? What forms and modes do the intersubjective, social encounters and interactions (real or anticipated) of an ideal religious subject take? It is to these questions that we turn in the next chapter.

NOTES

1. William James, *The Varieties of Religious Experience: A Study in Human Nature* (London: Longmans Green, 1910), 337.
2. The Islamic juristic tradition that started to stabilize soon after Muhasibi's time classified human obligations into two types, obligations owed to God (*ḥuqūq allah*) and obligations toward other human beings (*ḥuqūq al-'ibād*). Muhasibi did not seem to make this formal distinction in his teachings and the two kinds of obligations are inseparable in his works. Indeed, all obligations to other human beings must be understood, by an ideal religious subject, as obligations to God. For a concise discussion of the two types in early Islamic juristic discourse, see Baber Johansen, *Contingency in a Sacred Law: Legal and Ethical Norms in the Muslim Fiqh* (Leiden: Brill Press, 1999), 212–216.
3. Muhasibi probably has in mind the Quranic passage "Does man, then, think that he is to be left to himself to go about at will?" (Q. 75:36). The word here is *sudā'*, which in classical Arabic applied to a camel who was left to pasture on its own. See Lane, *English-Arabic Lexicon*, s.v. "sudā'." This, for Muhasibi, is the state of a person who is not on a religious path.
4. Al-Muhasibi, *al-Ri'āya li huqūq allah*, ed. Abd al-Halim Mahmud (Cairo: Dar al-Ma'ārif, 2003), 47. He says, "*awwalu mā yalzimuka fī ṣalāḥ nafsak.*" Josef Van Ess has suggested that Muhasibi, a traditionist theologian, was interested in the reform or improvement of people, in general, and not just a few spiritual elites. See Josef van Ess, *The Flowering of*

Muslim Theology, trans. Jane Marie Todd (Cambridge: Harvard University Press, 2006), 142–143.

5. He says, for instance, that worshipful obedient actions must be done with awareness (*ma'rifa*) or else they bear no fruit. In one place he says, for instance, "If a slave (*'abd*) lives his life exerting himself in devotional activities (*mujtahidan fil 'ibāda*) but is not aware of them (*lam ya'rifuhā*), and thus does not act with it and goes to God while still ignorant of it, none of his devotional activities would benefit him, unless God decides to extend His grace to him." Al-Ḥārith b. Asad al-Muḥāsibī, *Sharḥ al-ma'rifa wa badhal al-naṣīḥa* (Damascus: Dār al-Qalam, 1993), 29.

6. Muhasibi, *Ri'āya*, 83.

7. Discussion of hypocrisy in various forms, and related concepts, takes up a significant portion of Muhasibi's main work. See: Muhasibi, *Ri'āya*, 137–237. Similarly, large portions of *Ri'āya* are organized under the rubric of other vicious suggestions, as will be seen in subsequent notes.

8. Muhasibi, *Ri'āya*, 267–295.
9. Muhasibi, *Ri'āya*, 343–383.
10. Muhasibi, *Ri'āya*, 299–339.
11. Muhasibi, *Ri'āya*, 387–409.

12. Lane says *gharīza* means something natural or native, implanted by God, good or bad. Interestingly, the examples he gives are cowardice or courage. It seems then that these are things somehow already planted in one's nature that one cannot remove. One may do things to make these qualities manifest in one's behavior or else let them remain dormant. Lane, *Arabic-English Lexicon*, s.v. "*gharaza*."

13. Muhasibi's reference to strength is noteworthy and Aaron Stalnaker's discussion of virtues as processual and as capacities rather than settled dispositions is relevant here. See Aaron Stalnaker, "Virtue as Mastery in Early Confucianism," *The Journal of Religious Ethics* 38, no. 3 (2010): 404–428.

14. Muhasibi, *Kitāb al-ri'āya li ḥuqūq allāh*, ed. Margaret Smith (London: Luzac & Co., 1940), 146–147.

15. In this mode, the *nafs* may be rendered as the lower or ego self and had to be controlled as an ethical duty. See Saeko Yazaki, "Morality in Early Sufi Literature," in *The Cambridge Companion to Sufism*, ed. Lloyd Ridgeon (New York: Cambridge University Press, 2015), 78.

16. See Gavin Picken, *Spiritual Purification in Islam: The Life and Works of al-Muḥāsibī* (New York: Routledge Press, 2011), 199–204.

17. I have elsewhere discussed the self-effacing effects of Muhasibi's emphasis on suggestions as a central concern for an ideal subject. See Faraz Sheikh, "Encountering Opposed Others and Countering Suggestions [*khaṭarāt*]: Notes on Religious Tolerance from Ninth Century Arab-Muslim Thought," *Comparative Islamic Studies* 11 (2015) 2: 179–204.

18. While I think Muhasibi is not best understood in the vocabulary of virtue ethics, he is often counted among the early Sufis and scholars of early Sufi ethics have often used the language of virtue ethics to describe Sufi morality. For instance, Atif Khalil speaks about gratitude as a virtue in Muhasibi in "On Cultivating Gratitude in Sufi Virtue Ethics" *Journal of Sufi Studies* 4 (2015) 1–2: 1–26 and in "The Embodiment of Gratitude in Sufi Ethics" *Studia Islamica* 111 (2016) 2: 159–178. Consider, however, what Muhasibi says: "No one can attain the higher form of gratitude because gratitude does not have a limit or end." Muhasibi, *Bad' man anāba ila Allah wa yalīhi ādāb al-nufūs* (Cairo: Dār al-Islam 1991), 79.

19. Two prominent examples are Saba Mahmood, *Politics of Piety: The Islamic Revival and the Feminist Subject* (Princeton, NJ: Princeton University Press, 2004), and Charles Hirschkind, *The Ethical Soundscape: Cassette Sermons and Islamic Counterpublics* (New York: Columbia University Press, 2006).

20. Muhasibi, *Ri'āya*, 85.
21. Muhasibi, *Ri'āya*, 85

22. Angels in the Islamic tradition are considered beings who do not have free will and hence commit a sin. They only do what God has commanded them to do. They glorify Him without the possibility of failing to do so. Hence insofar as human beings obey God by choice and not compulsion, many Muslims have deemed human beings potentially superior to angels.

23. Muhasibi, *Ri'āya*, 33.
24. Muhasibi, *Ri'āya*, 34.
25. Muhasibi, *Ri'āya*, 63.
26. Muhasibi, *Ri'āya*, 45.
27. Muhasibi, *Ri'āya*, 267–268.
28. Muhasibi, *Ri'āya*, 269.
29. I shall say more about the vices in the following chapter. Suffice to note here that for Muhasibi, conceit due to acts of piety, which includes repentance, is a particularly pernicious problem and threatens to destroy sincerity and obedience to God as the person starts to think highly of his own piety, becoming blind to self-exaltation.
30. Muhasibi, *Ri'āya*, 278.
31. Muhasibi, *Kitāb al-riāya*, 32.
32. Muhasibi, *Kitāb al-riāya*, 33.
33. Muhasibi, *Kitāb al-riāya*, 32. Muhasibi says that in such a situation, the *nafs* and Satan urge him to claim that he repented because of his own resolve and will power.
34. Muhasibi, *Kitāb al-riāya*, 34.
35. Muhasibi, *Kitāb al-riāya*, 35.
36. Scholar of early Islamic literature and the Quran, Michael Sells remarks that Muhasibi's thought seems almost too simplistic in this respect. Michael Sells, *Early Islamic Mysticism: Sufi, Quran, Mi'rāj, Poetic and Theological Writings*, Classics of Western Spirituality (Mahwah, NJ: Paulist Press, 1995), 171–195.
37. Muhasibi, *Kitāb al-riāya*, 24–25.
38. In some early Muslim theology, obligations were understood in terms of God's reward and punishment. See Richard Frank, "Moral Obligation in Classical Islamic Theology," *Journal of Religious Ethics* 11 (1983): 204–223.
39. Muhasibi, *Kitāb al-riāya*, 41.
40. He uses expressions like *karīh fī al-ṭab'* and *karīh fī al-nafs*. This may be seen as a rhetorical move to equate, in this context, one's nature (*ṭab'*) with one's self (*nafs*). I think he does this to help the slave see his "natural" likes and dislikes as deeply flawed and mistaken.
41. Muhasibi, *Kitāb al-riāya*, 22–23.
42. Muhasibi insists that God has promised reward and threatened punishment out of his love and mercy, as an aid for human beings so that they may be able to bring themselves to obey Him. Muhasibi, *ādāb al-nufūs*, 57.
43. Talal Asad's observations on asceticism might help us understand Muhasibi's views on the psychic and formative work that the idea of divine punishment does for a subject. The pain and burden is psychic in Muhasibi's case and not bodily but it is pain nonetheless—a generative pain that, as Asad says, is part of an "economy of truth" about oneself. Indeed, Talal Asad has interpreted Christian ascetic practice as follows: "Pain was necessary because the involuntary connection of the self with sensations, feelings and desires required a constant *labor of inspection* and of testing the body lest the soul be betrayed . . . inflicting pain in an ascetic context becomes part of the discipline for confronting the body's desires with the desire for truth on the part of a suspicious will" [emphasis added]. He says of the body that it was, "a medium by which the truth about the self's essential potentiality for transgression could be brought into the light, so that it could be illuminated by a metaphysical truth, a process in which pain *and discomfort* [emphasis added] were inescapable elements. Foucault in effect makes us aware that it is not the traditional symbolism attributed to ascetic pain to which we must finally look (chastising or mortifying the body) but the place occupied by bodily pain in an economy of truth." Talal Asad, *Genealogies of Religion: Discipline and Reasons of Power in Christianity and Islam* (Baltimore and London: The Johns Hopkins University Press, 1993), 110.
44. Muhasibi, *Ri'āya*, 110.
45. Muhasibi, *Ri'āya*, 122.
46. This practice became well known in the tradition. The famous Muslim theologian and mystic Ghazali included a whole book on the subject in his magnum opus, *Iḥya*. See *Al-Ghazali on the Remembrance of Death and the Afterlife*, trans. Timothy Winters (Cambridge, UK: Islamic Texts Society, 2016). In later Sufi writings, contemplation about death was seen as a way of dying to the world so that one would become alive to God's presence. See, for instance,

Jamal Elias, *Death before Dying: The Sufi Poems of Sultan Bahu* (Berkeley, CA: University of California Press, 1998). The poet's moniker *bahu* means "with Him," that is, "with God."

47. Muhasibi, *Kitāb al-riāya*, 73–74.
48. Muhasibi, *Kitāb al-riāya*, 74–75.
49. Muhasibi, *Kitāb al-riāya*, 115.
50. Muhasibi, *Kitāb al-riāya*, 115–116.
51. Muhasibi, *Kitāb al-riāya*, 116.
52. Muhasibi, *Kitāb al-riāya*, 117. It is worth noting that Satan was never seen as a rival power to God in Muslim thought. His creation was interpreted as another means, among others, for God to attract forgetful human beings toward Himself. See, for instance, Nader Ahmadi and Fereshteh Ahmadi, *Iranian Islam: The Concept of the Individual* (London: MacMillan Press, 1998), 75–80.
53. We can contrast this view with those espoused by the philosopher and popular public intellectual Slavoj Zizek. See Zizek, *The Courage of Hopelessness: Chronicles of a Year of Acting Dangerously* (UK: Penguin Press, 2017). For a good argument in favor of an ironic eschatological optimistic disposition for Christians in the world, as opposed to an apocalyptic "we already know what should go on" triumphalism, see Charles Matthewes, *The Republic of Grace: Augustinian Thoughts for Dark Times* (Grand Rapids, MI: William B. Eerdmans Publishing Company, 2010), 218–243.
54. A good example is Kevin Reinhart, "Islamic Law as Islamic Ethics," *Journal of Religious Ethics* 11 (1983) 2: 186–203.
55. Other scholars have analyzed ethical aspects of the structure of Islamic legal discourse but their analyses have been quite different than the one offered here. Cf. Kemal Faruki, "Legal Implications for Today of *al-Aḥkām al-Khamsa* (The Five Values)" in Richard G. Hovannisian, ed., *Ethics in Islam* (Malibu, CA: Undena Publications, 1985), 65–72; Omer Awass, "Fatwa, Discursivity, and the Art of Ethical Embedding," *Journal of the American Academy of Religion*, 87 (2019) 3: 765–790.
56. Asad, *Genealogies of Religion*, 160.
57. Asad, *Genealogies of Religion*, 161.
58. Asad, *Genealogies of Religion*, 161.
59. Muhasibi teaches that insofar as following the law is concerned, it should only be a matter of proper comportment before God. I think it is only as a corollary to the ethical nature of obligations to God, in Muhasibi's view, that following the law also results in fulfillment of ethical obligations to others. Muhasibi, *ādāb al-nufūs*, 57.
60. Muhasibi, *Kitāb al-riāya*, 49.
61. Muhasibi, *Kitāb al-riāya*, 49.
62. Muhasibi, *Kitāb al-riāya*, 49.
63. Muhasibi, *Kitāb al-riāya*, 49–50.
64. Muhasibi, *Kitāb al-riāya*, 60.
65. There is a casuistic element in Muhasibi's discussion of the *aḥkām* in that one may assess an action as more or less obligatory (and similarly, as desired, discouraged and neutral) according to specific circumstances or conditions and not according to nonnegotiable rational principles. For a classic statement, see Joseph Schacht, *An Introduction to Islamic Law* (New York: Oxford University Press, 1982). However, it should also be noted that the *aḥkam* operates with constant reference to the "Book of God" and the *sunna* of the prophet. It is an interpretive exercise delimited by being tied to particular textual sources deemed normative.
66. Muhasibi, *Kitāb al-riāya*, 51.
67. Muhasibi, *Kitāb al-riāya*, 63–64.
68. For a discussion of the derivative but important role of reason in relation to revelation among the so-called rationalist theologians in the Islamic tradition, see Richard Martin, Mark Woodward and Dwi Atmaja, *Defenders of Reason in Islam: Muʿtazilism from Medieval School to Modern Symbol* (Rockport, MA: Oneworld Publications, 1997).
69. Muhasibi, *Kitāb al-ʿaql*, In *al-Masāʾil fī aʿmāl al-qulūb wa-al-jawāriḥ wa-maʿahu al-Masāʾil fī al-zuhd; wa Kitāb al-Makāsib; wa-Kitāb al-ʿAql*, ed. Khalīl Imran (Bayrūt: Dār al-Kutub al-ʿIlmīyah, 2000),172.
70. Muhasibi, *Kitāb al-ʿaql*, 175.

71. Muhasibi, *Kitāb al-'aql*, 176.
72. Muhasibi, *Kitāb al-'aql*, 176.
73. Muhasibi, *Ādāb al-nufūs*, 78.
74. For instance, see Christopher Melchert, "Transition from Asceticism to Mysticism in the Middle of the 9th Century." *Studia Islamica* 83 (1996): 51–70.
75. Muhasibi, *Kitāb al-zuhd*, 11.
76. Muhasibi, *Ri'āya*, 57–58.
77. Muhasibi, *Ādāb al-nufūs*, 79
78. Muhasibi, *Ādāb al-nufūs*, 79.

Chapter Two

Living with Vulnerabilities

Muhasibian Moral Subjectivity and Self-Care

In the broadest sense, Muhasibi narrates the ideal moral subject in the register of sincerity. Sincerity ought to be the moral subject's most cherished value and guiding principle. For Muhasibi, to live with sincerity is to be concerned exclusively with God's pleasure and displeasure. A sincere action is one that is done without desire for the praise of created beings (*makhlūq*) and without fear of their reproach. In this sense, sincerity is grounded in the subject's commitment to desiring none other than God with his actions (*la yarād bil 'amal ghayr Allah*).[1] It is, in short, the manifestation of a subject's *tawhidic commitments*. As such, sincerity is a religious ideal but one that the subject must never claim to have achieved, because to claim purity for oneself is simply conceit, a kind of self-appraisal that aims at pleasing the self and hence, a subversion of sincerity.[2] Yet, the moral subject must aim for sincerity in his day-to-day life, as a matter of practical reflection. The demand for sincerity provides the frame and impetus for exercises of introspection and acts of practical reflection, through which the subject becomes an ideal subject, someone who strives constantly to protect the integrity of his *tawhidic* commitments.

In Muhasibi's view, threats to religious subjectivity do not only arise from dereliction in the performance of rituals or outward religious duties. The health and propriety of one's inner states is more important than the aptness of outward religious performance. God, Muhasibi is categorical, has prioritized the fulfillment of inner obligations over correct performance of outward actions.[3] This being the case, a moral subject must constantly examine their *nafs*'s inner state to prevent vicious suggestions such as delusion, conceit and pride, from becoming preponderant in the heart. Should vicious states dominate the heart, they spoil the subject's otherwise lawful outward actions by compromising their sincerity.[4] It is worth remembering that the ideal moral subject is not merely a lawful, legal subject. Rather, it is an agent beset by a set of dynamic, inner, vicious suggestions and must constantly evaluate these suggestions and take timely, preventative and remedial actions in order to attain moral subjectivity. These preventative and remedial actions, as we shall see, often take the form of discursive exercises and practices that aim at protecting or restoring the sincerity of a religious subject's actions. Immoralities are not merely illegalities in the sense of breaking some positive religious law or rule. Rather, immoralities are those modes of engaging with the world that are products of a heart that has accepted vicious suggestions, such as hypocrisy, conceit, delusion, envy and pride.

Remarkably, Muhasibi teaches that the most serious threats to a subject's sincerity arise out of two situations, both of which are ubiquitous and ineliminable aspects of a person's everyday life: (i) outwardly good actions and (ii) social interactions, especially with intimate others. Muhasibi says that socially valued, outwardly good actions are a trial (*fitna*) for the agent because such actions naturally invite the agent to expect others' praise for the same.[5] Thus, taken together, the two things most disruptive of religious subjectivity confront a religious person on a daily basis: doing outwardly good actions while living among people whose opinions one may care about, and who respond to one's actions with either praise or dispraise, often in somewhat unpredictable ways. Nonaction is not an option for a Muhasibian subject as it also opens a path to hypocrisy and insincerity. For the one who abandons actions from fear of being insincere will inevitably think he has overcome the suggestion to hypocrisy and will hence think highly of the ascetic scrupulosity of his *nafs*, falling victim to its conceit.[6]

The ideal moral subject must *discursively negotiate* the threats that arise from its own good deeds and other people's knowledge of those deeds in order to preserve its sincerity. The Muhasibian subject can neither claim to have become a purified, virtuous soul, as I have discussed in the introduction chapter, nor simply recuse himself from good public action. It is in this sense that the moral subject exhibits an *ethics of againstness*, a form of life marked by a constant, discursive negotiation with the negative, contingent effects of good public actions.[7] The subject is ever-engaged in deliberate, discursive interventions to respond to inner challenges wrought by the subject's awareness of its social location and standing among a community of similarly located agents. No isolated, mystical ascent beyond (or ascetic retreat from) an active, deliberative and discursive mode of social existence is possible for a Muhasibian subject. The challenges life brings are to be confronted, as we shall see, discursively, while remaining within society and fulfilling one's social responsibilities.

It is worth noting that Muhasibi's demand for constant self-scrutiny trades on a sense of imminent moral failure and an irreducible fragility of sincerity as a religio-moral standpoint. A subject's recognition of his embattled and vulnerable religious subjectivity gives shape to his moral-cultural form of life, a life that can keep track of and respond to the vulnerabilities as they arise. Moral considerations are most pronounced and urgent when the subject apprehends themselves as acting among, and interacting with, other people whose praise and blame one takes to be an accurate index or sign of divine praise and blame. That is the only way the desire for the praise of people can actually act as a substitute for a desire for God's praise *for the same action*. One way to begin exploring Muhasibian moral subjectivity is to thus ask: How does a subject interact with, and act among, intimate others without compromising its sincerity and religious integrity? By means of which discursive practices does a subject negotiate and fulfill its duties of religious self-care, while living as a participating, responsible and responsive member of society?

NEGOTIATING SOCIALITY AND SELF-CARE

Muhasibian moral agents must negotiate social obligations on the one hand and self-care on the other. On the one hand, they must fulfill whatever obligations they have toward their families, kin, friends, neighbors and people in the marketplace. On the other, they must protect themselves from vicious suggestions that are occasioned by their interactions with these people. Muhasibi counsels against feeling secure in associating with the apparently pious, especially those the subject may think are his friends or brothers in religion (*akhi fil dīn*).[8] It is not altogether unsurprising that Muhasibi makes one's like-minded friends a bigger threat to one's religious and moral integrity, more than the company of strangers. Many of us can relate to Muhasibi when he observes that one feels uninhibited and carefree in the company of close friends and this can lead one to engage in speech and actions that one might generally find inappropriate, even reprehensible and therefor avoid when one is not in such company. Should the subject then prefer seclusion and retreat from social life? We find an implicit but clear answer in the negative in Muhasibi's discussion of the best forms of worship (*afḍal al-'ibāda*). He is asked, "What is the most excellent worship?" He responds,

> The best worship is to know God, to recognize His greatness through continuous contemplation of the change of one's state from one condition (*hal*) to another. And after one has acquired these qualities (*khisāl*), the most excellent action is kindness toward the weak and needy (*al-'aṭf 'alā al-ḍauf*). The prophet was asked, "what action is the most excellent?" and he replied, "It is

that you help a person in need or help your brother." And similarly, he said, "the one who runs around and expends effort in order to care for widows and the needy is like the person who struggles in God's path and like the person who stands in prayer all night and fasts during the day." And also, he said, "all of creation is the family of God and the most beloved to God is the one who benefits His family." To make ease in religion and helping the needy are the most excellent of actions.[9]

A total disengagement from society and cessation of interaction with others is not an option because helping others, especially one's brothers and those in need, are among the most excellent of practical, worshipful actions. Desirable qualities, such as knowledge of God's greatness, shape the psyche of an ideal religious subject but the highest practical expression of that psychic standpoint, comparable to prayer, fasting and even jihad, is the act of taking responsibility for all of God's creatures as if they were God's family. In other words, one has to interact with others. Now Muhasibi does say that if a person has repeatedly found himself sliding into sin in the company of his so-called "brothers in religion," then he should avoid their company to safeguard his piety. But this is a temporary measure, a context-specific judgment that a person would have to make in light of his experience.[10] It is not a general action-guide or the most desirable attitude for the ideal moral subject. And even here Muhasibi makes an exception for situations where one must interact with people, despite the moral risks, in fulfillment of some duty to God, such as visiting them when they are sick and things of that nature.

Crucially, one can only really help others if one knows what their needs are and this implies that the moral subject must live in a way that would allow them to be aware of the needs of people in their surroundings. Muhasibi speaks about fulfilling obligations to others and cautions against abandoning their company out of an *unfounded* fear—without any prior negative experience of falling into sin in their company—that one may become heedless in their company. According to Muhasibi, an ideal subject should sit among his brothers and interact with them, not from a desire for personal enjoyment but as a matter of fulfilling a duty to God, such as, for instance, keeping their company if his livelihood is in some way tied to being with them.[11] But something more needs to be done to neutralize the dangers of being dutiful in this way. The ideal subject can safely court the company of his friends, as a duty, by engaging in a discourse about God's protection in return for his obligation-driven motivation. The subject ought to reason along the following lines:

> When he reflects and decides to break off sitting among his friends/brothers (*al-ikhwān*) until he was obligated by some duty toward God or some indispensable sustenance, then God would know that were it not for His sake, the person would not have sat in their company and likewise would not have

visited them. God is too magnanimous to then forsake him, considering that he had abstained from sitting with them simply for the sake of pleasure and comfort. Were it not for the sake of his Lord, he would not have sat in their company nor visited them, but because he was obligated out of duty to God, God then does not leave him in perdition when he chose God above his pleasures.[12]

In the ideal subject's mind, God reciprocates with protection against sin when the subject sees his social interactions as justified in terms of the fulfillment of one or another duty he owes to God. To invoke God's protection in this way is a discursive practice that warrants that one meets one's social obligations despite the personal risks to one's moral integrity as a religious subject. One can feel safe, to some extent, despite the real risks that always lurk beneath each interaction. But why does Muhasibi think one courts the most serious moral danger in the company of one's friends and brothers in religion? The following passage is helpful:

People are of four types: A man you do not know or whom you know but you are not his friend; a man who is an innovator [in a negative sense]; a deviant or sinful man or a wanton; and a person who was unknown to you and you befriended him. As for the innovator, your heart is averse to him and likewise the wanton, even if they were to call you to truth, your heart would not incline toward them for how can you embark upon something with such obviously sinful people? And the one who is no friend to you nor do you know him, you would not converse with him nor will you entertain or adore him. Therefore, you are not going to be duped or fooled by all these people and your heart would not be so relaxed with them that you become heedless or careless and say things that your Lord dislikes. However, when you approach someone as a friend, the one who is your type, who is like you or similar to you and dear or close to you, then your heart becomes relaxed and heedless regarding them and you are heedless along with them, until you commit a transgression or sin against God while you are unaware that you are doing it. You do not remember God or you remember Him but you are unconcerned because of being overcome by pleasure in your friend's company and your conversation with him. It is but among the tricks of Satan (*iblīs*) and one of his snares.[13]

Muhasibi is clear that one's brothers or friends could be those one gathers around with an express intention to remember God and thus to be, ostensibly, in good company. Yet, on account of the heedlessness triggered by the friend's company and their presumed piety/like-mindedness, one would fall into sin. Thus, we see that neither does Muhasibi want the ideal subject to abandon the company of his friends and brothers entirely nor does he think that like-minded brothers should be approached as providing, in any straightforward fashion, some sort of safe and spiritually supportive community.

It is worth pausing to notice that this picture of a moral subject's anxieties about courting the company of his brothers in religion is particularly striking when we juxtapose it with the uniformly positive assessments of the role of religious community and good company in contemporary Muslim discourses. Religious community, we find commonly asserted among religious circles, is very important for keeping individuals safe from the corrupting and dangerous, anti-religious influences of godless, secular, modern culture. For Muhasibi, the ostensibly sinful are not a threat because the ideal religious subject is assumed to not be keen about following their ways. There is some confidence that an ideal subject would simply not find forms of life exhibited by sinful others, or total strangers, as presenting him with compelling or enticing ways of acting or thinking. It is the like-minded religious that pose the most potent threat. Muhasibi goes so far as to recommend that if one is well-known where one lives, one should leave the city and relocate to a place where one is anonymous. Social anonymity is a moral ideal. There is certainly a sense in which the Muhasibian moral subject ought to be more individualistic and self-centered than we might expect, given our biases about the modern discovery of the individual and assumptions about the collectivist/communitarian nature of premodern religio-moral life.[14] But are we to conclude that the Muhasibian moral subject ought not to value any real sense of religious community and fellowship with his co-religionists? Is there no community that the subject can cherish and in whose company it can feel joyful and comfortable without fear of falling into heedlessness and sin? These are important questions for probing further the moral texture of the lived life of Muhasibian subjects. When we turn to Muhasibi's texts with these questions, we find an answer in Muhasibi's view of the role of *hisba* (enjoining the good and forbidding the wrong)[15] as a crucial feature of proper intersubjective relations. *Ḥisba* allows for the possibility of establishing and maintaining bonds of trust, friendship and community, despite the risks for heedlessness and sinfulness that social interactions always pose.

FRAUGHT INTIMACIES: MUTUAL DIRECTION AS FRIENDSHIP

Enjoining the good and forbidding the wrong is a well-known feature of Islamic thought and practice.[16] Muhasibi allows for intimate relations with such others as would stir in one the fear of God and one who cautions one before one falls into sin and disobedience. Such counsel and moral direction is a way of supplementing one's mind with the mind of another, to mutually safeguard each other's religious well-being. Here is how Muhasibi describes trustworthy friends, persons in whose company it is proper for a moral subject to feel safe:

> Umar said, "Beware of your friend except the most trustworthy among the righteous ones, and there is no one trustworthy except he who fears God." When you become heedless, he will stir up fear of God in you. When you

come in contact with him and you start to feel secure from committing mistakes and begin to speak foolishly and say things that are objectionable to God, he will turn your mind to the remembrance of God, he will stop you and caution you (*nahāka 'an dhālik wa nabhaka*). When he calls your attention to something that you know is not appropriate or permissible for you, you become regretful and repent from it . . . Al-Sha'abi also said, "Half of your mind derives from your brother." He was right. Because if your brother alerts you regarding what you are ignorant about, it was as if your mind was in him and he returned it to you. And if your mind was completely in him, then he returned all of it you in that instant. However, throughout the times you shared, half of his mind was in you because it may occur to you when your brother becomes unmindful then you will arouse him (to repentance and obedience). Thus, you are serving God by means of two conjoined minds. You become aware of your faults with your mind and your brother's mind. Therefore, whoever does not fear God among one's friends, even if they be always praying or constantly fasting or fighting in God's path or performing the pilgrimage, they are a liability (*wabāl*) for you.[17]

We thus see that the kind of ideal intersubjective relationship Muhasibi envisions and idealizes involves mutual admonition and counseling—a complementarity of the minds—as well as an assumption that there would be an evaluative convergence between the two parties, that is, both would agree about what is good and bad for them and hence take the other's admonition as offering valid counsel or direction. The mutual trust and evaluative convergence implied in engaging in mutual direction would be a recognition of one another's corrective direction and arousals as not only valid but also desirable. In a sense, a moral subject's relationship that is both intimate and safe is a *nasīḥa*-based relationship. Mutual corrective direction constitutes intimate and intersubjective relations that are morally appropriate. Those who are not afraid to alert the subject to his potential and real heedlessness through forthright and timely admonition are his trustworthy friends, whose company he can court without fear and anxiety. One could only be at ease in another's company when the other can be trusted to safeguard one's transcendental interests. Muhasibi's account of intimate relations invites us to reflect about modern, liberal anxieties about injudicious interference into the lives of others, even intimate others.

To many modern ears, juxtaposing mutual moral direction with friendship might seem odd if not entirely misguided. Many people today tend to think that good friends are those who don't judge us and who support us even when they disagree with our choices. How can a relationship as gentle, caregiving and joyful as friendship bear the weight and harshness of hortatory moralism and mutual direction?[18] We learn from Muhasibi that trust and intimacy can be tied to the practice of mutual direction, including moral direction, which yet avoids the pitfalls we tend to associate with hierarchical relations. His account has the potential to challenge and perhaps enrich our conventional, liberal views about noninterference and a "live and let live," disengaged, laissez-faire association with others.

Interestingly, the idea that direction and friendship can cohere has been argued by modern thinkers as well. Philosophers Dean Cocking and Jeanette Kennett have analyzed the strengths and weaknesses of what they call the Aristotelian "mirror" view of friendship, where true friendship is possible between two similarly virtuous people who see themselves reflected in each other.[19] They argue that our experience shows we can be good friends with those entirely unlike us and whatever the merits of Aristotle's account, it does not quite capture our everyday experiences of friendship today. They also criticize what they call a "secrets" view of friendship, which holds that friends are those with whom we share secrets that we wouldn't with nonfriends. But they retort that we can give special access to private information about ourselves to all kinds of people without being their friends in any deep sense.[20] Against the "mirror" and "secrets" views, they propose a "drawing" view of friendship. They argue that a core feature of a relationship that we characterize as friendship in actuality is the assent that the two parties in that relation give to mutual direction and see the relation as an agreement to be formed/drawn by the other. Friends are those others that we allow to shape us in multiple, profound and direct ways and those who, in turn, allow us to shape/draw them. If one is unwilling to be drawn or directed by another, unwilling to trust their view of what is good or worthy for one to do, and unwilling to yield, at least sometimes, to their view of things, one cannot be counted as their friend in a deep sense. To use that language of the eminent modern philosopher, Charles Taylor, friends would have to be people with whom we share our "horizons of significance" so that we are ready to take seriously their evaluations of the good and right (and bad and wrong) and allow them to shape us. This idea is sometimes expressed by the term vulnerability and how the latter is critical for healthy, intimate relationships. As well, if one is uncomfortable or fearful about disclosing one's honest assessment of the other's choices or attitudes, and finds oneself reluctant to direct or advise them (without, of course, forcing them or being nasty and rude to them) from fear of interfering unjustly into their lives, then one's claim to be their friend is placed under some strain.[21]

Understandably, Cocking and Kennett are reluctant to allow *moral* direction as a component of their "drawing" view of friendship. They insist that one gets drawn by a friend or draws the friend only in nonmoral ways. Moral advice is ambiguous in friendship because one need not be intimate with someone to preach to them. But drawing is not the same as preaching. In drawing, the other agrees to and welcomes direction and there is reciprocity. I don't think the exclusion of moral direction from friendship is necessary if we make a distinction between speaking with moral advice at someone and speaking with moral advice to someone. For one thing, can moral and nonmoral aspects of our lives be neatly separated? Perhaps we can then acknowledge that direction is not inevitably and always a paternalistic intrusion and unwelcome interference into the affairs of another. Mutual direction can be the cement that defines and strengthens intimate relationships of trust and mutual goodwill. A relationship that allows for mutual direction, including moral direction, can be a relationship that has matured from being mere friendliness, mutual affirmation and fun, to being a friendship, because such mutual direction signals the existence of, and strengthens, deeper mutual trust and a deeper sense of shared horizons, a shared sense of what is worthy and valuable for human flourishing and a sign that the two people in the relation care enough about the other to bother engaging with them in deeper ways about weighty, personal choices.[22]

A theocentric, nonhierarchical ready-to-direct-and-be-directed standpoint of a Muhasibian moral subject also sheds light on contemporary ethical discussions about legitimate moral authority in intersubjective interactions. Richard Miller has recently argued that the notion of moral authority suggests that one party in a relationship takes higher moral ground: the critic takes the "high ground" in relation to the object of his criticism and thus a gap (implying some asymmetry and inequality) emerges between the critic and the one critiqued. By authority, Miller means having a certain standing within a relationship, a standing that vests an individual or group with responsibilities, entitlements, or powers to affect the lives of others. Miller draws on the work of Bruce Lincoln who defines authority as "the effect of a posited, perceived, or institutionally ascribed asymmetry between speaker and audience that permits certain speakers to command not just the attention but the confidence, respect, and trust of their audience or . . . to make audiences act *as if* this were so."[23] Thus, Miller and Lincoln suggest that, "there are credentials necessary to possess authority, and thus ways to forfeit it, or to deny it to others." They suggest that *moral* authority means having the authority to make moral criticisms of others. In the case of *naṣīḥa* as discussed above, Muhasibi clearly envisages the possibility that an intimate relationship can involve what we might call moral authority and criticism: the advisor may come to see himself (and sometimes with the consent and approval of advisees) as entitled to deference, rank (*manzil*) and authority (*riyāsa*). Yet, Muhasibi's encouragement of mutual advice doesn't allow for such entitlements and expectations and in fact deems them perversions of a healthy relationship. The ability to direct is not a sign of the director's higher status. It is a marker of a morally safe relationship for a religious subject.

Muhasibi wants to make the advisor-advisee relationship levelled and nonhierarchical despite the asymmetry that must practically obtain in any given instance of direction or admonishment. One reminds or informs the other of something that the other forgets or does not know. And one reciprocates at another occasion when the roles are reversed and one is directed by the other. Muhasibi notes that if one wants to give advice but is not ready to reciprocate, one suffers from pride and sinful self-exaltation.[24] Among the ideal comportments of the *nafs* is to accept advice from others.[25] Similarly, to refrain from giving advice to others is to promote disobedience and sin and to not want their well-being. To dislike for others what God dislikes and to like for others what God likes is a means to purifying one's heart in Muhasibi's reckoning. It is to confirm to oneself that one is committed to God and not to the praise and love of friendly others.[26]

In a sense, Muhasibi's account of the ideal moral subject asks us to consider if it is possible that an asymmetric relationship (between an advisor or censor and the advisee or a heedless person) where the roles can switch at any moment, can be simultaneously devoid of hierarchical moral authority in Miller's and Lincoln's sense.

Muhasibian subjects ought to think about their knowledge or discernment, which allows them to be in a position to counsel others, as warranting a more rigorous accountability before God. This should be reason enough for them to be even more careful not to think of themselves as better off than the one they counsel.[27] The relationship between the advisor and advisee, in Muhasibi's teachings, must thus be deliberately made, through this thought exercise, horizontal and nonhierarchical (on account of a subject's theological commitment to fulfilling God's rights inwardly). In Muhasibi's view, the advisor would have moral authority, should we call it that, only in the sense that he is in a position to utter "consequential speech" (to use Lincoln's phrase) but must remove and negate, reflectively and discursively, any claim of possessing superior merit. Muhasibi's conception of *naṣīḥa* as a religious act, is undertaken not as an expression of higher, self-ascribed virtue but as a response to God's unmerited favor: the advisor ought to see himself favored in the form of awareness of what is wrong or sinful, fear of God, love of obedience, covering up of his own faults in the eyes of the advisee (who therefore is willing to lend him an ear), and so on. These thoughts are supposed to correct for the religiously disastrous effects such as pride, conceit, contempt for the other, and so on, of the natural asymmetry that emerges in any situation where one party feels they know something good that may benefit or help someone else.[28] Instead of choosing to avoid being friends with others who may have greater discernment or feeling exalted in relation to those who may know less or who may be doing something one finds contemptible, one enters into a relationship of friendship with others that gives prominent place to the practice of reciprocal mutual counseling and honest and total mutual self-disclosure.

THE MORAL SUBJECT BETWEEN PRETENSE AND ROLE MODELLING (*IQTIDA*)

In Muhasibi's teachings, one of the most vicious suggestions and the biggest threats to sincerity is the suggestion of *riya*, that is, ostentation, showing off, pretense or hypocrisy. Muhasibi calls *riya* a minor form of *shirk* (idolatry or associating partners with God). One is acting from or with *riya* when one plays to the gallery, does something or omits doing something because one fears losing reputation or status among people and desires their love and praise. The opposite of *shirk* is *tawhid*, which is unifying the source of all good into the One, God, and see Him as the only One whose pleasure one ought to seek and whose displeasure one ought to fear. Hence, a tawhidic perspective requires fearing God alone and desiring only His praise and pleasure.[29] A sincere religious subject performs actions and omits actions from a singular concern for God's like and dislike. Muhasibi suggests that when one allows the opinions of other people to influence one's choice to commit or omit an action, one's status as a sincere religious subject is profoundly compromised. What then are the options that the subject has? Can he choose to stop doing actions that were being done so he could show off? Should he hide his actions from others and act only privately and secretly? Both options are discussed by Muhasibi.

As for giving up an outwardly good action, that one was doing for the sake of others' praise, Muhasibi is clear that this would be insincerity. Non-action from a fear of hypocrisy and insincerity is not a moral option. Muhasibi says,

> He will leave his act of fasting and prayer stopping after he has begun them, out of fear that he is not free from hypocrisy, desiring God through cessation of action. That is an error. He is required only to struggle against and reject vicious suggestions such as hypocrisy and required to not desire them. Man was not commanded to abandon action in such a case. Now he can stop acting in public in order to do those actions in secret but he is tempted by the deceitful *nafs* to abandon the action altogether or be lazy about it. If God gives him strength therein, let him do it secretly and it will be better and more excellent than doing it openly . . . but if he leaves off good actions he was doing in public view fearing lest they say, "Hypocrite!" that is an error and the giving up of a great good. His decision to leave good actions is hypocrisy on his part because he desires to retain their praise and have them consider him sincere and not a hypocrite. Furthermore, he has thought evil of them. He will sometimes stop a good work out of fear of evil opinion or anxiety concerning how he appears to them. His *nafs* has deceived him in order to give up the action. And he has thought evil of others (assuming that they would think he was doing good things in public only to be seen and be praised).[30]

The ideal moral agent cannot give up actions and must struggle against the suggestion to hypocrisy. As for acting openly versus acting secretly, there are considerations that pull in opposite directions. The argument for acting secretly is that the subject who is happy to do a good action in secret, that is, without anyone knowing about it, can feel sincere because they are content with only God's knowledge of their action.[31] But at the same time, as the passage quoted above shows, it is possible that one does an action secretly for the wrong reason: avoiding the charge of hypocrisy and desire to be judged sincere by others. In doing this, the subject is being a hypocrite in wanting their praise for being sincere and a person who is so zealously averse to hypocrisy as to abandon doing good deeds altogether.

Moreover, if a person gives up acting publicly, Muhasibi teaches that such a person would be guilty of thinking ill of others. His choice to act secretly would mean that he thinks that others would consider him a show-off if he acted publicly. He has thought ill of them by imputing onto them an accusation against himself that they have not yet made, and may not have made. In light of these considerations then, the moral agent should not give weight to the opinions of others in the choices he makes—he should act secretly for his personal religious reasons, that is, to be content with God's knowledge of his actions and he should act openly if the reason for doing so is not a desire to be considered sincere by others and not a fear of being labeled a hypocrite by others.

But there is another positive reason why the agent should act openly in general. When the agent acts openly, then he may indeed attract the praise of others but his public action is good in terms of encouraging others to follow his example or be inspired by him. The agent must interpret this praise in the right way if he is to be a moral subject: "And he is happy for them for being dutiful to God through him by praising him for his good deeds and he is happy that they may emulate or follow him because he could be an object of emulation or an exemplar for them; he probes his heart, besides all that, to make sure that his delight is not because of love of rank or prestige among them."[32] Ideal moral subjectivity is discursively attained, through reflecting about, and rethinking one's reason for acting publicly.

While acting publicly carries the risk of hypocrisy, the moral subject takes joy in being a role model for others. The idea of being a moral role model is not a fashionable one today but it is quite ubiquitous as a feature of moral subjectivity in the history of religions. Comparative religious ethicist, Cheryl Cottine uses a simple but elegant framework for describing moral exemplarity and ideal moral subjectivity in classical Confucian thought. She identifies two forms of role modeling at work in classical Confucian texts that she calls (i) *imitation* modeling and (ii) *influence* modeling. Imitation modeling is at work when we try to be like our role models, people that we think have noteworthy qualities that are worthy of our emulation. Cottine writes, "Influence modeling, in contrast, locates the source of the activity with the model herself. Here, it is the model—the person being imitated—who works to become worthy of imitation because she knows she will influence others."[33] I think Muhasibian moral agents are supposed to embrace what Cottine calls influence modeling.[34] The ideal subject is to exhibit behavior that others find worthy of emulation to encourage them to do good. One is to make one's exemplary deeds public. The question that confronts the moral subject then is this: How does one act as a role model *and* avoid falling into hypocrisy and showing-off? To play the role of a role model is, quite deliberately and intentionally, to show off so that others would admire what they see and desire to emulate it. In this context, Muhasibi's interlocutor asks him about a person who is well-known for his piety and good deeds and who rejoices at the fact that others regard him as someone worthy of emulation. How can one be happy about being a doer of good in public, and yet not be a hypocrite?[35] This dilemma ought to be of great concern for the ideal moral subject.

Muhasibi's answer lies in a subject's examination of their intention and their reinterpretation of the happiness they feel at being praised and the sadness they feel at being rebuked. The subject must engage in a discursive practice. Muhasibi asks the subject to realize that a hypocrite may or may not actually get the praise he seeks (and quite often he won't) but his intention for doing something good publicly in order to gain praise and repute among the people is sufficient to compromise his sincerity. A moral subject too likes praise and dislikes censure but must avow that he does not intend it as the aim of his action. He interprets others' praise and his resulting joy as God's act of covering up his faults (*satr Allah*) from others so that they see only what is good and praiseworthy in him.[36] Upon such a realization, his response ought to be gratitude that his real, morally tainted nature was kept hidden from others by God and they were made to see, by God's favor, what they found, through no power of his own, good. By thus interpreting his elation about other's praise through a theological lens, he should come to feel that his aim was not others' praise. He is to be happy for God's favor and protection from censure because censure, Muhasibi teaches, is naturally disliked and praise naturally liked, by human beings, religious or otherwise.

Similarly, for the moral subject, the censure of others should indicate that one has fallen in the eyes of fellow beings and has made them unhappy with oneself due to some real fault of one's own. One is to regret that one has made them criticize him (which, for them, could be a sin if they are not careful to do for God's sake alone).[37] For these reasons, it is alright for the moral subject to be unhappy about dispraise and censure as long as one does not allow one's indignation to transform into disdain or hatred for one's critics or an eagerness to be liked by them. Engaging in the correct personal interpretation of one's emotional responses to praise and blame (joy and sadness respectively) is what differentiates an ideal subject from a morally compromised hypocrite with identical (because natural) affective responses to praise and blame. The hypocrite remains sad about censure and hates his critics *because* his aim was to be well-liked by others whereas ideal moral subject sees praise and blame as ways to go back to God in gratitude and repentance by engaging in the kinds of thought exercises I have briefly discussed above.[38]

It is interesting that while Muhasibi advises the moral subject to disengage from others' opinions, he allows them to be happy about their praise and disappointed about their censure if one responds to the latter in the proper way. While he is very aware of the dangers of public action—to the extent of seeing anonymity as an ideal—Muhasibi is not advising a revolt against community feedback, unlike the *malāmatiyya*, which was a diffuse group among early, ninth-century Muslims. Their name is derived from the root word *malāma* meaning "blame" and they considered being held in good esteem, anathema. They taught that one ought to act in ways that invites scorn and blame. They discouraged the performance of publicly visible good deeds.[39] In contrast, Muhasibi allows the ideal subject to experience public blame and praise, but of course with utmost care and scrutiny so as not to fall into hypocrisy as a consequence of acting publicly. One intellectual strategy, in addition to those just noted, for achieving this delicate balance, is to engage in a discourse about God's predetermination or *qadar*.[40]

While acknowledging that human nature desires praise and hates dispraise, Muhasibi presents his listener with what I call a *qadar-centered* discursive practice or intellectual exercise that ought to help the person attain a standpoint where his natural love of others' praise and natural dislike of their dispraise does not lead to showing-off or hypocrisy. *Qadar* discourse helps a subject engage in normative social exchange (i.e., receiving and offering praise and blame) without choosing voluntary self-sabotage (like a *malāmatī*) or a retreat from social/public view into private/secret actions. Muhasibi says of the ideal subject:

> He must be well acquainted with hypocrisy and the scattering of the heart's purposes in desiring people's praise. There is no end to it because the one who works to please other people does not attain this goal because some of them are pleased by that which displeases others. If he did what some of them are pleased with, others are displeased with him for it and if he did what displeases some of them, others are pleased. This is so because some of them think evil what others think good and some of them praise him about the thing that others reproach him for. . . . His heart is fragmented and his aims and purposes become numerous and confused because he does not attain fully what he desires from them. He attains what comes to him from them with great hardship. They will not increase, with their praise, his life-term or his sustenance. Nor will their praise bring health or protect him from trials, nor will it repel the

disliked *that God has already decreed.* As for greed for what they possess in their hands, he will never get what has not been already decreed for him. If something came to him, then what came was already decreed for him. If he made his servitude pure or sincere for his Master, what came would have come anyway. But by seeking their praise, he compromised his actions and earned the anger of his Lord and lost his reward, without any increase in his sustenance and life term and without getting any benefit in religion (*dīn*) or world more than what was decreed for him. So how does a *reasonable* person not abstain from what would harm him in this world and in the hereafter without adding any benefit for him in his worldly life?[41]

Here then we have a discursive practice by which the agent argues with himself about the futility of trying to please others. The subject addresses himself and reasons his way to realizations that help him out of his predicament: What pleases some will displease others and so the goal of pleasing others is unattainable. It is tiring and futile to try and please others. It is a burden not worth carrying. Here we have an interesting incorporation of what theologians call the doctrine of divine predetermination/destiny.[42] Here we see how this doctrine is put to use in practical reflection as part of a moral argument that allows the self to engage in public moral action without feeling like a hypocrite. The agent says to oneself that they will receive the praise God has decreed for them without seeking after them. Why aim for something that one is destined to get? Why try to avoid dispraise that is already decreed? To seek after something already decreed is to express, by one's attitude, a lack of trust that they *have* indeed been decreed. It is to expend energy in vain. What is noteworthy here is that the subject invokes divine determination, paradoxically, so as to convince himself to make a better choice about the motivations for his actions. In other words, destiny *isn't* invoked to say: "your intentions or actions don't matter, God will create as God likes, you have no choice anyway." Rather, given that predetermination is real, the subject is told: "you have a choice to seek the goal that reflects you trust God and see Him as the source of all harms and benefits."

Also, there is an argument here against moral fatigue that is a part of acting in ways that the public appreciates because, presumably, it serves some public good that would otherwise not be as fully achieved. Good actions become harder to do if the outcome one seeks is the unpredictable praise of others and often difficult to satisfy, high expectations. To free oneself from the desire of others' appraise and fear of their censure frees one as a moral agent and makes one less ambiguous about the value of performing good actions publicly.

EMBARRASSMENT AS MORAL IDEAL

It should be evident by now that the issue of others' praise and blame is central to the formation and practical functioning of moral subjectivity in Muhasibi's thought. Praise and dispraise of others implicates another important emotion with complex moral implications for the ideal moral subject: the emotion of embarrassment or shame. Should one be embarrassed about anything at all? Shame is a fraught emotion in modern times. Are we not taught to be ashamed and embarrassed about things by society as a form of social control, to make us conform to its norms and ideals? Many of us may say yes to this question. At the same time, we can ask: Should we not be able to say that a potential sex-offender should feel ashamed about contemplating, let alone committing, a sexual offense? Should such persons not feel ashamed about their offense, if committed, and should society not deem their conduct shameful? Is it not the case that sometimes our natural or instinctive embarrassment or shyness helps us do something good that we might otherwise ignore or omit? Is not conscientiousness a salutary form of shame? Does not the desire to avoid embarrassment sometime stop us from doing certain unethical things (unethical by our own lights) that we may well be tempted to do? It seems that the emotion of shame or embarrassment *per se* is not the real culprit but rather the discursive contexts in which this emotion is evoked and invoked determines whether we would consider it a morally valuable guide or a tool of social oppression.

Let us turn to the Muhasibian moral subject with these thoughts in mind. For Muhasibi, embarrassment (*al-ḥayā'*) itself is a positive disposition insofar as it encourages actions that are beneficial for others in situations when, in the absence of embarrassment, the subject may not undertake those actions. In a sense, embarrassment stands in for what, in an Aristotelian vocabulary, we might call character or moral virtue. If one does not have some permanently virtuous trait necessary to do good to others, embarrassment can provide the necessary motivation. This is true for actions done for God and those done to benefit other people. Consider this telling example that Muhasibi uses to convey the choices faced by a moral subject in interpreting their embarrassment.

> Imagine a man approaches two men. He asks one of them for a loan or gift. One of them had the means to help but no sense of embarrassment so he immediately turned him down since he did not feel generous. The other was asked what he could not afford to give but the embarrassment of being stingy prevents him from turning down the request. So he did not refuse and complied with the request. Satan then finds an opportunity to tempt the person and so does his *nafs* which says to him, "Give him so he does not say 'what a stingy person he is!'" or "Give him so that he may reciprocate later" and the person gave credence to these suggestions and gave the loan . . . but another

person . . . this idea came to his mind but he said, "No! Rather, for God's sake I shall give" . . . he did not give in to the thought of pretense or reciprocal gain from the receiver of the loan. . . . He who combined embarrassment with the intention of doing the act for God and His reward, that is the best because embarrassment is a noble disposition that God does not give to everyone.[43]

Embarrassment is God's mechanism for making people do good things they otherwise, because of natural self-interest, would avoid. It is a disposition that is given to humans by God and is hence, for the ideal subject, an internal voice and not a socially imposed emotion. Once it is given, it can either be used for God's sake or it could serve the goals of pretense and dissemblance. One may respond to embarrassment by doing things to please others and not for God's sake alone.

However, Muhasibi's teachings about other concepts such as *istighnā* and *ghinā* (independence), *al-'izza* (self-exaltedness) and *tafwiḍ* (relegation) suggest that the ideal moral subject ought to be aloof and independent of the opinions of others.[44] The love of self-exaltedness can produce a desire for status and rank over other people and this leads to pride and envy, which compromises religious subjectivity. One is to thus rid oneself of the desire to be exalted by others and free oneself from it by cultivating a despair (*al-ya*'s) regarding other people.[45] All this suggests that the moral subject ought to be free from the constraints that come with worrying about others' opinions and giving their evaluations some sort of authority over one's life. But life is more complicated than a simple rule of ignoring what others think, hence it is not surprising that Muhasibi feels the need to make room for shame. Indeed, Muhasibi gives an important role to being embarrassed or ashamed and generally being responsive to and concerned about the opinions of others in specific contexts:

> The person who is closest to the path of justice is the one who is always reflecting about every state and condition of their *nafs*, whether or not the *nafs* likes this scrutiny or not. He reflects whether he is in such a state *that if it was to become known to people, would he be embarrassed and would people dislike him*? If he finds himself in such a state, then he returns to a state which, if it became known to people, he would not be embarrassed. Because the state which is the cause of embarrassment before others is the opposite of the state that is not a cause for embarrassment. When he in a state such that he would like this state to become known to people, he hastens to a state that he has no desire to make known to people [emphasis added].[46]

Here we see that the ideal subject inwardly gives authority to the opinions of others as part of the process of self-scrutiny and as a way of keeping its *nafs* in check. If one is embarrassed thinking about others' knowledge of one's condition, one does not ignore their opinion but responds to it. The important thing is that it is all an internal conversation and so the agent himself or herself gets to decide subjectively what state of their *nafs* does or doesn't embarrass them before others, in their own minds. Only when the person himself understands the dispraise of others as an indication of God's displeasure with them, would he be justified in disliking the dispraise and changing his course of action.[47] If they do not think the other's reproach represents God's reproach, the reproach ought not to be of any consequence for the subject and if he were to get upset with it, it would compromise his moral status, as it would suggest that he valued that person's opinion more than, or in addition to, God's. It would signify that he cares about others' praise and dispraise, in addition to God's, and hence he is in a state of hypocrisy or pretense and not sincerity.

The case of shame nicely illustrates the need to pay attention to discursive practices and subject formation. If we were to look to Muhasibi's discourses to simply find his theory of embarrassment, for instance, we might come away thinking his theory is rather clumsy and riddled with inconsistencies because he simultaneously advises against being embarrassed before other people and counsels in favor of giving weight to being embarrassed before them. But understood as a *pedagogical discourse* and as practices of the subject formation that track the changing contexts and psychological alterations of lived life, Muhasibi's conflicting counsels about embarrassment become more intelligible. Approaching Muhasibi through a Foucauldian lens helps us see how religious discourses help a subject form himself and how it ought to express its religious commitments in shaping its social and intersubjective encounters. In one sense then, Muhasibi would be an intellectual ally for those who think that the question of shame and embarrassment need not be decided at the level of theoretical abstraction or moral principles. In different life situations and different contexts, it can be useful to consult one's sense of embarrassment to evaluate one's inner state and to use this self-awareness as an aid for one's own religious and moral well-being.

The Muhasibian moral subject, in its own context, inhabits a complex and dynamic emotional space. Their moral life does not comprise a simple and consistent application of theoretical and moral principles. They are presented as living a life which presents to them complex situations and they respond to those situations in complex and discursive ways in order to preserve, to the best of their abilities, the sincerity and integrity of their religious standpoints. Their moral life is complex because their religiously formed psyche is threatened in complex ways and thus needs complex (often paradoxical) discursive solutions and remedies in different circumstances. Far from hollowing it out or suppressing it, a Muhasibian theological anthropology gives depth and sophistication to a subject's emotional and intellectual life.

UPBRAIDING FAULTY OTHERS:
CRITICISM AND OTHER-REGARD

If one were to single out one ethical issue that generates the most controversy and argument in the world today and that inflames people's moral sensibilities the most, it would be the issue of moral criticism, the issue of passing judgments on others, especially when those judgments are not favorable and offered by a cultural-religious other. Who in our world, if anyone at all, can claim to have a license to legitimately criticize another? And this thought leads us to ask a prickly question: Is all criticism illegitimate? Is all criticism legitimate? Is it neither? And if it is legitimate sometimes and unacceptable at others, how ought we to distinguish between the two? Is there a way to tell them apart that is not simply an assertion that one's criticism of others is, a priori, valid and others' criticism of oneself is, a priori, illegitimate? What do we gain, as individuals and as societies, when we permit and encourage criticism (or render it mere opinion or preference) and what, if anything, might we lose? These are questions that interest many in the humanities today, not just religious ethicists. The answers to these questions are indeed of consequence for the peace and well-being of our deeply polarizing world. Moreover, the rise of social media has made our world smaller and made direct, immediate and often vitriolic criticism of different others easy and largely unaccountable. Of course Muhasibi does not have answers to all these questions, but his discussion of how a moral subject ought to approach the act of criticizing, reproaching and upbraiding others, may offer us some useful resources and insights that may help us think more deeply about these issues.

We have already encountered Muhasibi's views on enjoining the good and forbidding the wrong. I argued that for Muhasibi, an intersubjective relation where criticism and direction are acceptable is one in which both parties voluntarily and happily accept the principle of mutual direction as a ground for intimacy or friendship and as a remedy for the dangers that the latter pose to ideal subjectivity. There would have to be enough trust and enough shared commitments between two persons for them to give each other the authority to allow the other to utter consequential speech. For Muhasibi, the main reason one would engage in criticism of the other would be to help the other fulfill their obligations to God and help them avoid falling into sin or disobedience. Thus, when criticism is other-regarding and concerned about the other's religious welfare, it has to occur within a relationship where there is reciprocity and a shared commitment to an ideal, the fulfillment of God's rights.

Now insofar as criticism of others outside of such *naṣīḥa*-relationships is concerned, Muhasibi takes a strong position *against* criticizing another person. It is relevant here to briefly consider arguments that ethicist Richard

Miller offers in favor of legitimate critique in his recent essay, "Moral Authority and Moral Critique in an Age of Ethnocentric Anxiety."[48] Miller's aim in this essay is to assuage what he thinks are unreasonable worries about ethnocentrism and judging when it comes to cross-cultural and social criticism. He formulates and elaborates five conditions which, if met, would make a moral critic, and hence their criticism, legitimate and judicious. Space does not allow an expansive discussion of Miller's interesting ideas. To put it briefly, according to Miller, a criticism is legitimate if, (i) it contains intelligible reasons that justify the critique, (ii) if the critic acts in good faith and with an aim to seek the truth, (iii) if the critic attends to the context and causes of the practice he may be critiquing, (iv) if he does not pre-judge and is judicious, and finally (v) if they are mindful of their location and the power asymmetries that might exist between them and those they critique.[49] Overall, Miller is interested in exploring if there are adequate and non-ethnocentric intellectual grounds for confident, cross-cultural and honest moral critique. The point I wish to highlight is that the entire logic of the enterprise of criticism in Miller's account is self-regarding, that is, it focuses on the right of the critic to express genuine criticism if he meets certain conditions. The critic stands to lose something if they are not able to offer the critique when the conditions are met and what the one critiqued may stand to gain or lose as a result of the criticism is not a focus of Miller's argument. This may seem like a minor point but it does make a significant difference. Miller's argument in favor of valid critique is self-regarding, that is, it is ultimately focused on the well-being of the critic qua free and legitimately outraged individual. The receiver of the criticism is left free to do with the criticism as they choose. The critic bears no further moral responsibility, beyond satisfying the conditions Miller elaborates, to the one criticized.

Now let us turn to Muhasibi and see how he addresses the issue of self-regarding criticism, that is, a criticism which is not part of a *naṣīḥa*-relationship and hence does not worry whether it would or would not be effective in helping the other person change in the way the critic desires. Muhasibi writes,

> When a person becomes aware of a fault of his own, he becomes aloof but when he becomes aware of some fault of another's, then he becomes an eagle-eyed critic and sharp evaluator.... For himself, he finds an excuse but he does not do so for others. He is rigorous in finding an excuse for himself but simple minded about finding one for others. Then he holds an opinion about the other that he does not like anyone to hold about himself. So when you see someone's faults and mistakes, put yourself in their shoes and think "what would you have wanted others to do with you if you were making that mistake or had that fault?" then do that same thing with him because he also wants to be treated as you would want to be treated.... If you want to be safe from envy, then this is the best way for you. For you, the least bothersome people are

those who find an excuse for your faults and if they can't find an excuse for you, then at least they do not make their criticism known to you.[50]

Muhasibi counsels the moral subject to find excuses for the person he sees worthy of upbraiding, especially in cases where one would want others to overlook the same behavior in oneself. The reasoning that the subject uses is something akin to the golden rule. One should not criticize people for things that one would not like to be criticized for oneself. The difference from the golden rule is that the thing being talked about is not something good or neutral but a fault or mistake. So that even when one sees someone doing something that one finds worthy of reproach, one ought not to criticize it because, Muhasibi assumes, the subject himself would not want to be criticized for those same actions. Muhasibi's reason for cautioning against critique is to avoid becoming bothersome for others. Here it is important to mention that for Muhasibi, the concern about not bothering others is premised on the critics assessment that there is no real hope the other will be receptive to one's critique. That receptivity, we have learned above, only happens in a *naṣīḥa* relation for a Muhasibian subject. But outside of that relation, when one is thinking about responding to people who are doing things one finds reproachable, the ideal subject should realize that his critique would simply be a form of unwelcome interference and a nuisance for those criticized. Of course, here, Muhasibi isn't talking about criticizing a manifest injustice that the person is doing to someone else. Rather, this is a circumstance where the person one wants to criticize is disobeying God and thus causing himself religious or spiritual loss.

Why should an ideal subject care about *not* bothering people with his criticism? Why should he not find solace in the fact that he is confidently and honestly expressing his indignation and critique and at least ensuring his own well-being in the process by not repressing his judicious judgments? Two things can be said here. First, Muhasibi does indeed give a cautious permission to the subject to express their criticism in a gentle way, in the hope that the other person, even as they may not be in a *naṣīḥa* relation with them, may respond and correct their ways. To presume, without trying, that the other will certainly respond negatively would be to think badly of them without warrant. But such criticism would have to be minimal and tactful and without any expectation that the other must respond positively to one's criticism. If the response is negative or neutral, one is to refrain from offering unsolicited advice. Second, Muhasibi thinks criticizing others, when it becomes clear that they are not responding kindly to one's criticism, is to cause others undue trouble and, and this is important, it is to cause them to respond with anger and hatred toward oneself thus causing them to sin. In view of this, other-regarding concern, in other words, to save them from sinning, an ideal moral subject overrides his own legitimate urge to criticize such others. The subject restraints himself with a sense of compassionate concern for the other's transcendental well-being. The subject should not want to be a cause or excuse for their sinful and hateful behavior. This is one important, and I suppose from a contemporary perspective, intriguing consideration for the Muhasibian moral subject when he voluntarily decides to forego legitimate criticism of those whose actions he rightly finds condemnable.[51] We can certainly ask whether such restraint is, in a broader sense or from a contemporary ethical perspective, a salutary one or one that would impede or entirely foreclose the possibility of constructive criticism and positive transformation. Ought the critic take into such deep regard the emotional (or other) excesses of the other's response that he forego legitimate criticism?

Furthermore, Muhasibi thinks that as a result of criticizing others for their moral lapses while thinking of his own lapses as small or few, the subject becomes deserving of God's punishment, who punishes him by taking compassion and mercy away from his heart so that he himself becomes stern and contemptuous of others and has only disdain for them. He starts to get closer in disposition, as a punishment from God, to other arrogant, self-righteous critics who feel the same way about other mortals so that he ends up becoming one among other contemptuous, self-righteous, abrasive critics who consider everyone except themselves morally corrupt and in need of correction and change. To be in this situation, Muhasibi says, should be seen by the ideal subject as being distant from God and His mercy and in a state of being punished by Him. The subject becomes deserving of God's anger and contempt when he treats his creatures, especially those he sees as faulty (and they may well be faulty in a given case), with contempt and reproach. His condition becomes like that of a person who God is letting go astray but who continues to think he does not have many faults and it is others who are truly worthy of reproach. The subject thus ends up ruining his religious subjectivity by engaging in a self-conceited and self-exonerating critique of others, without realizing that a criticism that is not going to help others is going to increase his own conceit. It is going to increase his contempt for those he would come to see as irredeemable, stubborn, ignorant, immoral and unresponsive others.[52] The ideal subject cannot let his desire for the salvation of others express outwardly in patronizing and harmful ways. In fact, Muhasibi asks the person who finds himself in such a predicament to focus on his own flaws and see them as big and see his excessive worries about others' salvation as a worrisome sign of his self-delusion and self-conceit.

INTENTIONAL EXCHANGE OF GREETINGS—SACRALIZING MUNDANE SOCIAL ENCOUNTERS

In addition to emphasizing close inner scrutiny in interactions, Muhasibi also occasionally prescribes specific, apparently minor practices as essential for proper social intercourse. For instance, he talks about the commonplace, every day act of exchanging greetings as a practice through which the moral subject can legitimately help others and help the self, without others even knowing that the subject is helping them. The "ideal" subject should ask others, "how are you" out of a concern for their well-being *and* a desire to attain reward from God. Both motivations must be present. Interestingly, in Muhasibi's view, God's reward depends on a selfless and sincere concern for the well-being of the other. If one asked after someone only for God's reward, this would make it a dishonest act: one would be pretending to care about the other but one only really wanted reward from God. And God does not reward dishonest actions. Quite literally then, to ask someone how they are sincerely and with a sincere desire to know their condition is a moral practice of high significance for an ideal Muhasibian moral subject. Through it, one properly expresses one's sincere concern for the other's well-being and also expresses a desire to receive God's reward.

The practice of greeting is also significant because the ideal subject intends and hopes that the person greeted would respond by mentioning the blessings of God (saying something akin to *Alhamdulillah* or "all praise belongs to God") and thereby earn God's pleasure and reward for himself. As a result of his greeting and question ("how are you?"), God will be mentioned and thanked by the one greeted. If the person was in a bad state, he would share his problems and afflictions and that would allow the subject who initiated the greeting to act with sympathy and compassion, deeds liked by God. What is important is that both parties to the exchange are thoughtful and deliberate about the theological-sacral framework and purpose of the seemingly routine and trivial ritual. The one asking does so from genuine, loving concern for the other (not from mere habit or as a social lubricant), a sincere desire for God's reward and a hope that the one asked mentions God's blessings and praises Him for them. The one answering acknowledges this intention and does not simply respond by asking in return "and how are you doing?" Muhasibi says that they should actually say they are good (if they are good) and then say "*thanks be to God*" or they should honestly share whatever is keeping them from feeling grateful to God so that the other person may become aware of their real state and make an informed decision about how to behave toward them.[53] For an ideal moral agent, the most ordinary and fleeting social encounters are, ideally, occasions to remember, thank and praise God. Mundanity lies in the agent forgetting the mentioning of God's blessings, not in the brief, repetitive and ubiquitous nature of the interaction itself. The articulation of thanks is never supposed to be mere verbal, formulaic, insincere repetition. It ought to express publicly, a privately felt emotion and state of being. Even so, it is always something more than a report about one's condition. The desire for God's presence, remembrance of His blessings, or else one's felt need for His blessings, ought to trickle down to the level of everyday exchange of greetings during countless, everyday encounters. There is something to be said about this Muhasibian teaching given how superficial and dishonest our everyday exchange of greetings can become. "Hey! Whats up?" and countless variations of that inquiry are rarely put forth, or responded to, with a sense that the one asking really desires to truly know or the one replying is actually telling the whole truth.

DELUSION (*GHIRRA*) HABITUATION AND GOD'S PROTECTIVE CONCEALMENT (*SATR*)

In contemporary religious studies scholarship about subjectivity, the concept of habitus has been quite prominent. Scholars tie subjectivity to habitual bodily. When we think about habitual practices, we often think about the role that societal norms play in the making of individuals because practices are socially authorized and legitimated. On the one hand, Muhasibi thinks habits are real and have real effects on subjects. He says,

> Who is purer of heart or who is worthier of being granted help and success than the one who did not do sinful deeds when he was young and grew up with obedience and service to God and is accustomed to fulfilling God's rights? Observing the rights of God is easy for him because of the length of his habit of fulfilling them. Rejecting the inclinations to their opposites requires little struggle and effort from him.[54]

On the other hand, these same habits and this ease of obedience that comes with it opens the door to dangerous and vicious dispositions such as conceit and delusion. While Muhasibi discusses many types and causes of delusion, two that suffice for our purposes are, (i) the delusion that comes from righteous and worshipful actions and (ii) delusion from the prolonged favor of God in covering up the subject's faults.[55] As we shall see, therefore, Muhasibi's account of the ideal moral subject is distinct from some contemporary anthropological accounts of the same, especially insofar as the place of habitual bodily actions in constituting moral subjectivity is concerned.

In his discussion of the delusion that comes from worshipful actions, Muhasibi notes that subjects who start to feel good about themselves on account of the ease with which they are able to carry out obedient actions and give up sins have the wrong idea of what really matters. While a *nafs* can start to find outward actions easy, the main thing is God-awareness or *taqwa*, which is an inner state of the *nafs*. All actions gain or lose value on account of whether they are done with God-awareness. In order to discern the state of one's God-awareness at any given moment, one has to query oneself, examine the *nafs* and remind it of all the ways in which it did not inwardly fulfill God's rights. And Muhasibi is categorical that this process of self-examination is hated by the *nafs*. And, Muhasibi thinks it is always delusion to think that one's ease at performing outward actions comes from an inner, stable virtue. Outward habit can blind one to one's inner state and one comes to have a delusional self-regard. In short then, one can only really develop a habit insofar as outward, bodily actions are concerned but it is not possible to attain *taqwa* as a stable, habitual disposition.[56]

As well, the moral subject can succumb to delusion if it takes the praise and regard that others give to it as an affirmation of its virtue. Rather, whatever regard one gets from others is to be seen as a protective concealment from God, who covered one's faults so that others were led to see good in the person. This gives us an indication of how far Muhasibi goes in ensuring that the moral subject does not let itself be formed by society and the subject's performance of socially authorized, bodily practices. One cannot find any comfort in being socially acceptable and well-liked. The others are not deluded in their praise; God's concealment is real and they are not misguided for praising one. One can and should thank God for this concealment but one ought not to fall prey to delusion and start to think that one is consistently acting well outwardly and recognized as virtuous by others due to any habituated virtues that one has inwardly stabilized. This would be delusion and would lead to reduced self-examination, conceit and pride. It would lead one to think much of oneself and have contempt for others who one may see outwardly disobedient to God or those who do not have a great reputation. Good repute is no indication of virtuous character but only God's favor and concealment of one's real, pitiful inner states. It is also a test for the subject, to see whether he did the praiseworthy for God's sake alone or for the sake of others' praise.

In the section of the text where Muhasibi is explaining to his listener how a slave of God (*'abd*) may attain to awareness that could be a means to attaining wariness of hypocrisy, Muhasibi is asked if all slaves of God must struggle hard to attain wariness of hypocrisy and thus attain sincerity of action. Muhasibi responds as follows:

> Yes, it is intense struggle and effort when a seeker of God (*murīd*)[57] first begins because sincerity is the beginning and end of piety. Its beginning is with extreme struggle and toilsome effort because of the strength of worldly appetites and weakness of resolve, lack of sincere worship and the length of habit (*al-'āda*) of hypocrisy. This is because the slave is weak with respect to his reason (*'aql*) in his youth, before mature adulthood, and does not desist from pretention before other slaves of God. And so, when he decides to wean

off his *nafs* from the habit of hypocrisy and tries to weaken the strength of his worldly appetites, because of the weakness of his resolve and scantiness of his habit of sincerity, his *nafs* refuses and makes it difficult for him. Thus, he has to struggle hard and exert strenuously until, once he applies himself to rejecting (the habit of) his *nafs* and attains sincerity and negates hypocrisy, the blessing of sincerity returns to his heart from God with light and insight.[58]

It is interesting to notice the concept of habit (*al-'āda*) in this passage. Due to a slave's habit of acting with pretension and hypocrisy, he has to mount a tremendous struggle against the *nafs*, which is used to its sinful ways. One's weak resolve in the past in standing up to worldly appetites means that one now needs to exert great effort to attain sincerity of action, which is nevertheless given to the heart by God. As a result of the slave's struggle and the resulting "help and favor of God" (*al-naṣr wa al-ma'ūna*), Muhasibi goes on to say, the calls of the desires of the *nafs* calm down and one's resolve is strengthened.[59] Thus we see that an insincere slave is understood by Muhasibi as the one whose heart has become overpowered by desires. The heart is the entity that attains to fear of God, struggles against the appetites and desires of the *nafs* and is finally rewarded with sincerity and strength of resolve (in the form of favors from God). Once this happens, Muhasibi says, the heart can overcome the incitement to hypocrisy quickly and "without great struggle and difficulty."[60] The heart, in other words, *can* build some capacity or capability that would make it easier to overcome the desires of the *nafs* in the future. But there is no suggestion here or elsewhere in Muhasibi's writings that one would thereby become a person of virtuous character or actually attain mystical proximity to, or union with, God.

ACQUISITION AND RELIANCE ON GOD

Muhasibi's non-ascetic ideal of moral subjectivity is clearest in his discussion of the need and value of labor and the acquisition of livelihood. In his *al-Makāsib*, a book dedicated to the theme of earning one's livelihood through work and commerce, it is clear that there were some people in Muhasibi's time who claimed that those who truly rely on God as the provider and sustainer ought not to work. For them, working to earn a livelihood indicated a lack of trust in God's providence. Muhasibi takes strong exception to this view. He argues that reliance on God is a belief that one has in one's heart that God is the only creator and provider (*al-khāliq al-rāziq*) and has sole authority over everything.[61] In a sense, this is a psychic state that defines a religious subject. Yet, as a moral subject, one is obliged to endeavor and work to meet one's needs.[62] Muhasibi cites Quranic verses as well as sayings of the prophet and the prophet's companions to argue that God intends for human beings to work as a matter of practical ethics even as He wants them to put their trust in Him. He cites, for instance, Muhammad's saying that "The best of what a man eats is what he has acquired through labor."[63] One is to earn through lawful means and one is to avoid the acquisition or consumption of unlawful things and greed. But beyond that, Muhasibi thinks that an ideal subject should not be destitute and needy before other people. As long as reliance on God is firmly established in the heart, this reliance is consistent with all requisite diligence, effort and enterprise through which human beings acquire material things and means. Muhasibi teaches that God does not obligate human beings to worship Him by giving up these natural efforts but instead asks them to worship Him by actively establishing obedience to Him and by acquiring only things that God has allowed them to acquire.[64] As long as the source of what one receives is God, whose power, order, wisdom and generosity makes it possible for there to be commerce and for human efforts to yield desired material outcomes, one's reliance on God is strengthened, not weakened, by engaging in work and benefiting from the outcomes God produces as a result.

ARROGANCE AND INTERSUBJECTIVE RECEPTIVITY

It is widely known that among the most important ethical values in the Islamic tradition is humility and one of the worst offenses that a Muslim can commit against God and others is to be proud. Pride, after all, seems to be the offense for which Satan is rebuked in the Quran's telling of the story of Adam, the first human being. When told to bow before Adam, Satan refuses, arguing that he is superior to Adam for he is made from fire, a superior material in his view, and Adam from clay. He is rebuked by God for his pride and expelled from heaven (Quran, 7:11–13). The mythos of Islam then makes pride (*kibr*) a fundamentally destructive and vicious attitude.

Muhasibi uses the term *mutakabbir* to refer to God's majesty and dignity and *kibr* as an attribute that makes a person haughty and arrogant toward other beings. He explicitly connects arrogance (*kibr*) with conceit (*'ujb*). He says,

> The slave may estimate highly or consider great what he has been given by God of religion or the world but if he does not boast with it over someone, then it is [still] conceit when he forgot the favor of God in regards to this [favor]. But if he was arrogant and haughty with it [i.e., with the favor] over another and disdains him, then scorns him haughtily, then he acted proudly (*fa qad takabbara*) because when he was conceited within himself (*'ujb*) and did not disdain another, he was conceited and not proud or arrogant. But when he was conceited within himself then looked at another, then he said in himself, "I am better than him" disdaining him and looking down upon him, then at that time the conceit is called *kibr*.[65]

For Muhasibi, the root or essence ('*asl*) of *kibr* is a subject's ignorance or lack of awareness of his value or worth; "when the slave is ignorant of his value or worth, he becomes arrogant or proud."[66] Pride involves looking at others with disdain ('*unf*) and contempt or scorn (*haqriyā*'). Because of disdain for others, *kibr* entails rejecting truth that comes from such others, while knowing it is truth.[67] An arrogant person "rejects the truth after knowing it" when it comes from those he considers inferior to himself.[68] Refusing to accept a truth that one knows to be truth is one of the most grave consequences of *kibr*.[69] Speaking of the behavior of the person who is prideful on account of his knowledge and the behavior of Muslims who exalt this knowledgeable and proud person, Muhasibi says,

> When he [the proud person] looked at them as being lowly or with condescension (*bi-al-istighṣār*) and feared for them more than he feared for his *nafs* [i.e., the fear of being damned or punished] and hoped for his *nafs* more than he hoped for them [i.e., the hope of being saved], while they looked upon him with respect or exaltation and looked at themselves as being lowly or with condescension and they feared for themselves more than they feared for him for they thought that he (the knowledgeable one) is surely saved and they are destroyed or damned. And they deem he will be saved more than they deem themselves saved. They serve God more and are more obedient in serving Him then the knowledgeable one.[70]

Muhasibi describes the proud person's behavior in terms of his feeling more concerned about the fate of others and less hopeful about their eternal fate than his own. Those who regard him highly on account of knowledge display the opposite behavior: they think highly of the proud person and think low of themselves. He considers the latter group more obedient to God and more properly subjected to Him. In explaining their behavior, I think, Muhasibi suggests a subtle strategy that a person may use for their own ethical formation. He says,

> And if it was not for the love of God and respect or exaltation of Him, they would not love him (i.e., the proud person) nor exalt him. Thus, they love him and exalt him for the love of God and hope of proximity or nearness to God through their exaltation and love and so they become deserving of God's mercy and forgiveness and that God takes them to His station [or closeness] in servitude and great struggle or religious striving (*al-ijtihād*). And he [the proud person] deserves that his actions are wasted and he is transformed to evil conditions or states (*sharr al-aḥwāl*) for he was arrogant with what God bestowed upon him of good action and he looked at other slaves [of God] with disdain or contempt.[71]

Muhasibi seems to be suggesting that reflecting on the attitude of those at the receiving end of one's pride should make one realize that in their admiration of one's religious knowledge and good actions, they display a love of obedience to God, a mark of ideal subjectivity. Once the proud person reflects about why others consider him worthy of exaltation, he would realize that they are better in obedience to God and his pride and scorn in relation to them is baseless and wrong. He will see the paradox: his knowledge and good actions help them attain ideal subjectivity while the same knowledge is pushing him further into disobedience (through thinking himself better than others who are in fact better than him). Such thoughts may enable him to not exalt himself over others (especially those who respond to his prideful scorn with exaltation and praise). It seems that to think oneself more likely to be saved than others who have fewer good actions and are lesser in knowledge subverts ideal subjectivity. But what about feeling that one is better than the unbelievers?[72]

The questioner asks, or rather tells, Muhasibi that he cannot help but think of himself as better than the people of innovation (*ahl al-bid'a*) who disbelieve in God and whom he knows to have no goodness in them.[73] Muhasibi doesn't budge. He reminds the questioner that such a person may always repent to God before his death and he, the questioner, may die while disbelieving. He says that the command or determination of God in regard to such a person is enmity or antagonism (*al-'adāwa*) and anger or indignation (*al-ghaḍab*) because of the falsehood of their action, that is, their disbelief. However, because God has hid the end of persons and his own end too is hidden, he cannot be arrogant toward that person.[74] Moreover, since the subject's own act of unifying God (presumably the ability to do so), *al-tawḥīd*, is a bestowal or favor from God, the slave should become grateful (*shākiran*) and also fearful (*mutakhawwifan*) for his *nafs* before God.[75] Muhasibi thus makes the rejection of pride, contempt and disdain toward others an important and basic feature of ideal religious subjectivity. Without such a deliberate and considered rejection of pride, one would simply fail to be properly subjected to God. While indignation and enmity are allowed inwardly toward the disbelievers and polytheists—even commanded according to Muhasibi—pride and disdain are not. An ideal subject must inhabit any tension such a paradox may produce without complaint and without easy escape into either love or indifference toward such others or prideful condescension and physical violence.

ENVY AND HEALTHY RIVALRY: RESPONSES TO ASYMMETRIES OF GOODNESS

Envy is a major moral flaw for an ideal Muhasibian subject. Envy is to not only resent that others have goods that one does not have, be it piety or material goods (wealth, number of friends and so on) but to also want others to be deprived of those goods. Envy is particularly relevant when someone else's possession of a good makes the subject feel diminutive, deprived and belittled and this likely happens in relation to people that one knows and not when the well-endowed are total strangers. According to Muhasibi, a stranger with many friends, for instance, may not threaten one's sense of self-worth in the same way that a close friend or a sibling with more friends or who is more well-liked by others than oneself. Again, we see that the subject is most threatened by people that are proximal in some relevant way—in a way that their possession of a good renders one lesser than them in one's own eyes.

There is an aspect of envy that adds another layer of complexity to Muhasibi's account and that is his positive appraisal of something that looks like envy but is actually a healthy rivalry, a desire to outdo others in good actions and achievements. The response to the possibility of envy is not a renunciation of human effort and desire to attain distinction and excellence. But again, to aim for distinction for its own sake would be mere pretense for a Muhasibian subject. One ought to aim for distinction as a way of expressing one's love for God and love for His reward.

> The conditions from which hypocrisy or pretense come: Competing with others (*al-mubāha*) in knowledge and action and boasting (*al-tafākhur*) about one's piety and material possessions. Boasting also comes from pride (*kibr*) but boasting from the perspective of hypocrisy comes from fear that one may be exceeded by others and the desire that one exceeds them. Thus, the person strives for increase or abundance in wealth and other things of the world and in knowledge and good action and accepts envy with regards to knowledge and action, not as competing with each other in healthy rivalry (*al-munāfasa*) but from fear that the one he envies would attain a station or rank and praise higher than him.[76]

There is a form of envy which is simply wanting to have the goods that one appreciates others possessing. If one is impressed with someone's knowledge, one would want it for oneself and may try to attain it. Muhasibi allows for this sort of envy, should we call it that. He does not consider it harmful or immoral. It is more akin to inspiration that one gets from encountering people whose qualities or possessions one admires and values. The ideal subject would look upon these as blessings of God with which God has blessed the person they admire. And one would ask God for those same blessings without wishing that someone else be deprived of them and without wanting to be praised by others for them. In this sense, the differences among people with respect to knowledge, wealth and other things can become opportunities for the subject to aim higher and exert effort to acquire more of whatever good he admires as a blessing. But if one did not see the good as God's blessing, one would see it as someone else's achievement and possession on account of either their merited superiority, which produces resentment, or their unmerited possession of that good, which would feel unfair and, again, cause resentment and indignation. One would succumb to making a horizontal comparison between them and oneself and find oneself smaller, exceeded by the possessor of those goods. This could engender feelings of resentment and instead of turning to God to ask for those same goods, one would focus on exceeding others or reducing others to one's own size by any means possible. One would want the other to be deprived of those goods, especially if it is difficult that one could easily acquire them. Thus, the moral subject's approach to others who possess varying levels or degrees of goods—from wealth to knowledge and piety—is an important issue. How does an ideal subject respond to the unequal distribution of abilities and goods in society? It seems they have two choices. Either they would fall into envy, which is a vicious disposition and a vitiation of religious subjectivity. Or else, they would invoke God as the source of all good, who can give the same or more to anyone who asks and petitions with their words and actions. Again, we see that religious and theological ideas, such as the idea that all the good things that people possess are to be seen as God's blessings and not their own property, should produce a form of life that is not characterized by envy and resentment directed at people endowed with material, moral or spiritual goods. They produce a form of life characterized by a rivalrous, spirited pursuit of goods without resentment toward fellow beings. Since it is God who blesses his creatures with good moral qualities and material goods, anyone can, so to speak, knock at God's door for the same and need not feel threatened or belittled by those who have been already blessed by Him. One may not get exactly what, or the same amount as, others have but one would have saved oneself from falling into envy, feeling lesser and resentful.

Moral subjects compete to attain what others have, cheerful in knowing that there is a God who possesses limitless goods, from which He has given to other creatures without discrimination (the impious and disbelieving are given the goods they seek just as the pious and believing). Goods are not possessed by people in different degrees according to random, accidental factors or due to some notion of merited desert or superior capacity or virtue. People have them, in the eyes of the moral subject formed by religious discourse, due to God's unmerited and non-preferential grace and favor. The subject ought to do their part by seeking those goods from their real owner, God, and accept the results of their efforts as God's wise and just decree and, in case conditions exist for making further efforts, to continue to seek those goods from God without despising those who have received them and without desiring that they be deprived of those goods. The admirable and blessed states of people ought to be encouraging reminders for the ideal subject that God *can* give him what he desires and the onus to seek these goods from Him, is on him. We can generalize from this that for a Muhasibian subject, theology is culturally relevant and is a mode of cultural interpretation. Consider for a moment how one may interpret salutary cultural practices or values as objectionable on account of envy, dressed as a reasonable-looking argument in favor of cultural specificity and by invoking the idea of multiple histories and temporalities. For instance, equal liberty and equal dignity for men and women might simply be a good idea but many nevertheless may oppose it if they see it as a hegemonic, superior, imperialistic, "Western" value. If the same values of equal liberty and equal dignity are elaborated as manifestations of the justice, favor and wisdom of God with which He has endowed a people, and not as the achievements of an oppressive political and cultural other (the West), they may well solicit approval and allegiance. Desire for equal liberty and equal dignity could be understood as indications of what the Divine wills for human beings to ask Him for, rather than patronizing and oppressive demands of a hegemonic cultural other. One's sense of *whose qualities* are manifest as values in the cultural realm can affect how people respond to those values, whether they embrace and seek them as goods they desire for themselves for internal reasons or else reject and despise from envy toward those seen to, or claim to, possess those values as their superior achievements. It is important to notice that once values are assigned to a culture *as the source* of those values, culture is made into, from a Muhasibian perspective, a sort of partner unto God as the praiseworthy owner of those inherently beautiful and desirable qualities. Ideal Muhasibian subjects are to think carefully about their response to the values and goods possessed by others and choose to see them as either their merited achievements or the unmerited blessings from a generous God. They ought to reject envy and instead affirm and desire all that they see good in others. They ought to see those goods equally available to all, equally-undeserving humans and cultures and strive for those goods in a healthy competition. To overcome envy, without giving up on the competitive pursuit of goods, is part of living a life informed by a commitment to seeing God alone as the owner of all that is good in the world.

In sum, Muhasibi envisions the formation of an ideal moral subject as involving discursive practices to dissuade the *nafs* from being heedless and arrogant toward others. The subject also pushes back against the power that the opinions of others unwittingly exercise on him. He needs to struggle to find his own truth as someone who serves and seeks to please no created being but only his maker, God. Muhasibi's approach shows how engaging with religious ideas serves the ideal subject's moral and psychological well-being. We see a particularly elaborate discussion of the practical and psychological implications of living with God's oneness in the teachings of Said Nursi, to whose accounts of religious and moral subjectivity we turn respectively in the next two chapters.

NOTES

1. Muhasibi, *Kitab al-zuhd*, In *al-Masā'il fī a'māl al-qulūb wa-al-jawāriḥ wa-ma'ahu al-Masā'il fī al-zuhd; wa Kitāb al-Makāsib; wa-Kitāb al-'Aql*, ed. Khalīl Imran (Bayrūt: Dār al-Kutub al-'Ilmīyah, 2000), 34.

2. Muhasibi affirms the subject's agency and, interestingly, says the agent does not need address itself about it, indicating how his discourses are meant as forms of self-address that a subject can use to transform. He says, "Your awareness that you did the action is awareness, firmly or clearly established by nature. You do not have to struggle about whether you did the action. And you do not remind yourself of this and do not address the *nafs* about it." Muhasibi, *Kitāb al-ri'āya li ḥuqūq Allāh*, ed. Margaret Smith (London: Luzac & Co., 1940), 210–211.

3. Muhasibi, *Bad' man anāba ila Allah wa yalīhi ādāb al-nufūs* (Cairo: Dār al-Islam, 1991), 59. The inner, hidden state (*bāṭin*), has to be in order and the outward action (*'amāl ẓāhir*) has to be consistent with one's *bāṭin*.

4. Muhasibi, *Ādāb*, 61.

5. Muhasibi, *Ādāb*, 84.

6. Muhasibi, *Ri'āya*, 164–165.

7. I borrow and adapt the term *againstness* from Sylvia Chan-Malik's recent work on African American Muslim women's religious subjectivity in the 20th century. She uses the term to refer to the notion of a continuous affective struggle that African American Muslim women had to wage "against accepted social and cultural norms." Sylvia Chan-Malik, *Being Muslim: A Cultural History of Women of Color in American Islam* (New York: NYU Press, 2018), 5. I think the term is apt here though in a different sense, as a continuous struggle against suggestions that threaten one's fulfillment of God's rights.

8. Muhasibi, *Kitāb al-ri'āya*, 190–191.

9. Muhasibi, *Kitāb al-zuhd*, In *al-Masā'il fī a'māl al-qulūb wa-al-jawāriḥ wa-ma'ahu al-Masā'il fī al-zuhd; wa Kitāb al-Makāsib; wa-Kitāb al-'Aql*, ed. Khalīl Imran (Bayrūt: Dār al-Kutub al-'Ilmīyah, 2000), 31.

10. Muhasibi, *Ri'āya*, 244.

11. A contrast with Nursi could be that Muhasibi regards enjoyment always as a temptation, hence, cannot see enjoyment as a gift to be thankful for or as a sign pointing to a generous and merciful God.

12. Muhasibi, *Ri'āya*, 244.

13. Muhasibi, *Ri'āya*, 245–246.

14. For an interesting discussion of individuality in the Islamic tradition from an academic perspective, see Fazlur Rahman, "The State of the Individual in Islam," *Islamic Studies* 5 (December 1966) 4: 319–330.

15. For a discussion of the contemporary relevance of the practice of mutual counseling, see Talal Asad, *Genealogies of Religion: Discipline and Reasons of Power in Christianity and Islam* (Baltimore: The Johns Hopkins Press, 1993), 200–238. The classic work on this topic is Michael Cook's commanding right and forbidding wrong.

16. For a thorough, unsurpassed and encyclopedic survey of the nature and importance of this practice in the various Islamic disciplines over history, see Michael Cook, *Commanding Right and Forbidding Wrong in Islamic Thought* (Cambridge, UK: Cambridge University Press, 2000); Cook, *Forbidding Wrong in Islam: An Introduction* (Cambridge, UK: Cambridge University Press, 2003).

17. Muhasibi, *Ri'āya*, 247.

18. For a good discussion of the potential importance of friendship for liberal democratic societies, see Jason A. Scorza, "Liberal Citizenship and Civic Friendship," *Political Theory* 32, no. 1 (2004): 85–108.

19. Dean Cocking and Jeanette Kennett, "Friendship and the Self," *Ethics* 108 (1998): 502–527. In a later essay, they specifically argue that those relationships that pose a moral danger to the parties involved are still properly described as friendship and are valuable in their own right. See idem, "Friendship and Moral Danger," *Journal of Philosophy* 97 (2000): 278–296. Muhasibi of course thinks that those friends who distract one from God are no true friends at all. Yet, this difference does not directly affect the analogy between Cocking and

96   Chapter 2

Kennett's view of friendship as constituted by an agreement at mutual direction and Muhasibi's view of mutual counseling and admonition as the distinguishing feature of trustworthy or real friendship.

20. Cocking and Kennett, "Friendship and the Self," 516.
21. Cocking and Kennett, "Friendship and the Self," 524.
22. See Charles Taylor, *The Ethics of Authenticity* (Cambridge, MA: Harvard University Press, 1992), 37–39.
23. Bruce Lincoln, *Authority: Construction and Corrosion* (Chicago: University of Chicago Press, 1994), 4.
24. Muhasibi, *Ri'āya*, 308.
25. Muhasibi, *Ādāb*, 69.
26. Muhasibi, *Ādāb*, 69.
27. Muhasibi, *Ri'āya*, 326–327. One is to respond to the suggestion to pride by deliberately avowing that one's *nafs* has no inherent value or merit and all its abilities or virtues are contingent favors of God. For an account of Mutazilite ethics and the place of merit or moral desert in moral agency, see Sophia Vasalou, *Moral Agents and Their Deserts: The Character of Mu'tazilite Ethics* (Princeton, NJ: Princeton University Press, 2008).
28. Contrast this with Talal Asad's analysis of *naṣīḥa* in contemporary Saudi Arabia as a form of public, morally corrective criticism where "virtuous individuals . . . are partly responsible for another's moral condition." Asad, *Genealogies*, 233. Asad tells us frankly that modern liberalism rejects this principle, that is, the idea that one person can be responsible for the moral condition of another. I would say that Muhasibi too would reject such a notion, not because Muhasibi is a liberal. He would reject it because *naṣīḥa* is not so much moral criticism but is a practice that makes otherwise fraught intersubjective, intimate relations, possible within the context of a concern for a subject's worries about its own religious subjectivity.
29. Muhasibi, *Ri'āya*, 131.
30. Muhasiābi, *Ri'āya*, 101.
31. Muhasibi, *Ri'āya*, 207.
32. Muhasibi, *Kitābal-ri'āya*, 171–172.
33. Cheryl Cottine, "Role Modeling in an Early Confucian Context," *Journal of Value Inquiry* 50, no. 4 (2016), 802.
34. Muhasibi, *Ri'āya*, 202–203.
35. Muhasibi, *Ādāb*, 100–101.
36. The ideal is that praise and blame become equal for him. But if they do not, he can interpret his feelings in ways that save him from compromising the sincerity of his actions.
37. One blames oneself for compelling others to reproach one. Anger toward critics would be a sign that one desired their praise with one's action and is now disappointed for not getting it.
38. Interesting that one has to make a personal judgment about which praise and blame are to be taken seriously and which are to be considered unjust and to be ignored.
39. Alexander Knysh, *Islamic Mysticism: A Short History* (Leiden: Brill Press, 2010), 95. Also see, F. de Jong, Hamid Algar, and C. H. Imber, "Malāmatiyya," in *Encyclopaedia of Islam, Second Edition*, ed. P. Bearman et al., http://dx.doi.org.proxy.library.upenn.edu/10.1163/1573-3912_islam_COM_0643. For a survey of early Malamati history see Sara Sviri, "Hakim Tirmidhi and the Malamati Movement in Early Sufism," in *Classical Persian Sufism from Its Origins to Rumi*, ed. Leonard Lewisohn (London: Khaniqahi Nimatullahi Publications, 1993), 587–592.
40. For a good discussion of this concept and debates about it in early Islam see Morad, Suleiman Ali, *Early Islam between Myth and History: Al-Hasan Al-Basri and the Formation of His Legacy in Classical Islamic Scholarship* (Leiden: Brill, 2006), 161–172.
41. Muhasibi, *Kitāb al-ri'āya*, 97–98, emphasis added.
42. See Isra Yazicioglu, "A Graceful Reconciliation: Said Nursi on Free Will and Destiny," in *The Companion to Said Nursi Studies*, ed. Ian Markham and Z. Sayilgan (Eugene, OR: Pickwick Publications, 2017), 129–145.
43. Muhasibi, *Ri'āya*, 167–168.

44. For his discussion of *ghinā*, see Muhasibi, *Ādāb*, 75 and 107–116. Also see Muhasibi, *Masā'il fī al-zuhd*, 29–30. For his discussion of *tafwiḍ*, see Muhasibi, *al-Masā'il fī a'māl*, 94–97.

45. Muhasibi, *Ādāb*, 114.
46. Muhasibi, *Ādāb*, 74.
47. Muhasibi, *Ādāb* 105.
48. Richard Miller, *Friends and Other Strangers: Studies in Religion, Ethics and Culture* (New York: Columbia Press, 2018), 75–105.
49. For a fuller discussion see Miller, *Friends and Other*, 88–97.
50. Muhasibi, *Ādāb*, 90.
51. Muhasibi, *Ādāb*, 90.
52. Muhasibi, *Ādāb*, 96.
53. Muhasibi, *Ri'āya*, 418.
54. Muhasibi, *Kitāb al-ri'āya*, 19.
55. Muhasibi, *Ri'āya*, 372.
56. Muhasibi, *Ri'āya*, 372–373.
57. In classical Sufi vocabulary that crystallizes after Muhasibi, *murīd*, which literally means "desirer," refers to the novice or beginner or an initiate on the spiritual path, who pledges loyalty and obedience to a guide or teacher, the *murshid*. In al-Muḥāsibī's usage here, it refers less formally to a person who has hitherto been heedless of God but one who now (newly) desires to make his actions pure, wants to fulfill God's rights and attain to His servile worship. Thus, here the term "seeker" [of God] is the one who seeks to or desires to fulfill God's rights.
58. Muhasibi, *Kitāb al-ri'āya*, 108.
59. Muhasibi, *Kitāb al-ri'āya*, 108.
60. Muhasibi, *Kitāb al-ri'āya*, 108–109.
61. Muhasibi, *al-Makāsib*, In *al-Masā'il fī a'māl al-qulūb wa-al-jawāriḥ wa-ma'ahu al-Masā'il fī al-zuhd; wa Kitāb al-Makāsib; wa-Kitāb al-'Aql*, ed. Khalīl Imran (Bayrūt: Dār al-Kutub al-'Ilmīyah, 2000),122.
62. Muhasibi, *al-Makāsib*, 123.
63. Muhasibi, *al-Makāsib*, 123.
64. Muhasibi, *al-Makāsib*, 123.
65. Muhasibi, *Kitāb al-ri'āya*, 232.
66. "*fa-idha jahala al-'abd qadrahu takabbara*," Muhasibi, *Kitāb al-ri'āya*, 235.
67. Muhasibi, *Kitāb al-ri'āya*, 239.
68. Muhasibi, *Kitāb al-ri'āya*, 239.
69. Muhasibi, *Kitāb al-zuhd*, 20.
70. Muhasibi, *Kitāb al-ri'āya*, 242.
71. Muhasibi, *Kitāb al-ri'āya*, 242.
72. See Faraz Sheikh, "Encountering Opposed Others and Countering Suggestions [*khaṭarāt*]: Notes on Religious Tolerance from Ninth Century Arab-Muslim Thought," *Comparative Islamic Studies* 11 (2015) 2: 179–204.
73. Muhasibi, *Kitāb al-ri'āya*, 269.
74. Muhasibi, *Kitāb al-ri'āya*, 269.
75. Muhasibi, *Kitāb al-ri'āya*, 269.
76. Muhasibi, *Kitāb al-ri'āya*, 305–323.

Chapter Three

Belief Perspectives and the Nursian Religious Subject

This chapter explores how Nursi conceives of an ideal religious subject. What kinds of standpoints and perspectives ought people to cultivate, *qua religious subjects*? What sorts of discursive practices are implicated in the cultivation of religiously ideal modes of being in the world? I think the best way to start exploring Nursi's answers to these questions is to attend to his understanding of *belief* or what I call *practices of belief*. It can be a challenge for us to proceed in this way because in order to understand the term *belief* or *faith*[1] in a Nursian sense, we would need to set aside, as much as possible, understandings of belief we might have in the context of debates about Protestant notions of private belief and the ways these notions undergird fraught distinctions between the private (religion) and public (secular) realms, and between properly American and un-American others.[2] Moreover, given the widespread distinction between belief and practice, "practices of belief" may come across as an oxymoron, but as I shall argue, belief is indeed a practice, an interpretive practice, in Nursi's teachings.

Belief for Nursi may indeed be private and personal. But it would be unhelpful to think about it as a fixed, complete, disembodied, anti-ritual, immediate and commonsensical grasp of reality or an inscrutable, suprarational allegiance to some fixed set of abstract creedal or doctrinal propositions. In Nursi's teachings, it is none of these. Rather, belief, for Nursi, is a *contemplative perspective*, with all the fluidity, fragility, incompleteness, counter-intuitiveness and transformative power that are often features of any reflectively inhabited, human perspective. Moreover, Nursi's understanding of the practice of belief is tied to constant, Quranically-guided reflections upon empirical and experiential reality, within oneself and out there in the world. The ideal subject is not to affirm a truth claim without concern for evidence for its truth. Instead, Nursi thinks belief perspectives are to be supported by clues and evidences gathered through Quranically-guided interpretations of the universe, a universe whose "doors" are otherwise "closed" to human beings.[3]

What is most interesting for our purposes is that in Nursi's view, belief is an informed choice to see or read a thing or event in a particular way at a given moment, often motivated by the psychologically devastating effects of the failure to believe. Belief is a way of reading the universe that makes the person engaged in it as a believer insofar as, and only as long as, they continue to read the universe in that way. Nursi's dynamic view of belief, and hence his view of what being a believer means, makes his teachings ideal for analyzing the relations between discursive practices and religious and moral formation.[4]

The motivation to read the universe from a belief perspective comes, Nursi thinks, from an acute sense of dissatisfaction and tragedy that a thinking human being experiences throughout his life whenever he reflects upon his existence, and especially its passing and transient nature.[5] An ideal Nursian subject does not claim to fully and finally know the meaning of the ambivalent, mysterious and tragic aspects of life, once and for all, but he also does not passively, and might I add indolently, accept meaninglessness to be the final word about existence. Rather, for Nursi, the unease and restlessness caused by the lack of meaning (meaninglessness would be a bit too drastic a term) of existence, stands in such dire need of redress that a reasonable human subject should find it unconscionable that his maker would give him this profound need and then leave it utterly unaddressed.[6] The ideal subject thus engages with the Quran as God's address to His creatures, taking it to be the speech of God whose main purpose, and raison d'état, is to reveal meanings that human beings need to flourish as spiritual, meaning-seeking, misery-stricken beings and that they find themselves unable to produce without outside help.

As we launch into a detailed analysis of Nursian religious subjectivity, it is useful to keep Nursi's historical context in mind. In the face of what he saw as atheistic, materialist and naturalist philosophies making inroads into Muslim lands and minds at the start of the twentieth century, Nursi felt that a taken-for-granted attitude toward religion and God would not suffice for sustaining people's commitment to Islam and an Islamic way of life. In this context, Nursi came to speak critically of a static, and perhaps even archaic, way of believing, what he referred to, somewhat critically, as imitative belief or *al-īman al-taqlidī* (Tk. *taklidi iman*). In its place, he presented a new ideal, a dynamic, Quranically-informed reflective belief or *al-īman al-tahqiqī* (Tk. *tahkiki iman*). Such belief would not simply add abstract, justificatory layers upon traditional religious dogmas. Rather, it would comprise a new mode of being, a mode comprising reflectively and individually chosen perspectives, energized and supported by subjectively experienced *meanings* that are revealed to the subject through a Quranically-informed reading of reality and personal experience.

Instead of treating the Quran as a settled, textual archive of Islam's early history or an archive of Muhammad's revelatory experiences or a holy book of divine commandments to be accepted and revered without questioning, Nursi approaches it as a direct, living, metaphorically rich, potential personal guide for a person's existential needs and questions. Nursi thinks people should want their maker, and not any other source, to address their deepest existential questions in a manner accessible to each at their personal level of understanding.[7] It was his optimism, perhaps a bit ambitious, that any person of average intelligence with little to no formal education, could become a direct addressee and student of the Quran and find meaningful intellectual and emotional guidance in its teachings for *their* personal needs.[8] He saw no better way to help his fellow human beings resist what he understood to be the self-injuring effects of imbibing, often without realizing, materialist and naturalist perspectives on life. He thought that appeals to spiritual authority were insufficient to empower a modern, thinking person against the onslaught of meaninglessness and anti-religion naturalism. Thus, he steered clear of recommending allegiance to himself or any other spiritual master, such as a Sufi teacher (*shaykh*), to guide one to intimate knowledge of God. Instead, he attempted to provide tools for his audience to enter into a deep and deeply personal and dynamic *studentship of the Quran*.[9]

In what follows, I analyze Nursian discursive practices through which an ideal, believing subject is formed. Given that Nursi's entire corpus is replete with, often repetitious, discourses about cultivating belief perspectives, I restrict myself to a curatorial discussion of four main elements of what I have called practices of belief: believing in God's unity (*tawhid*), believing in God's messengers (*rusul*), believing in a life after death (*al-akhira*) and believing in divine predetermination (*qadar*). In each case, we shall see, the ideal subject is to guide himself by an engagement with the Quran to inhabit a perspective that reveals a liberating and elevating divine meaning being expressed in nature, in his own self and in his relationship with the universe at large. Before we move onto unpack these practices of religious formation, I want to highlight the centrality of the Quran and certain Quranic concepts for Nursi's overall pedagogical project. Of particular importance is the distinction Nursi draws between "nominative meaning" (Tk. *mana-i ismi*) and "indicative meaning" (Tk. *mana-i harfi*) and his linking of the indicative meaning to the "beautiful names of God" (*al-asmā al-ḥusna*).

INDICATIVE MEANINGS AND THE BEAUTIFUL NAMES OF GOD

According to Nursi, the Quran makes the world speak in a particular way—it presents everything as a sign or *ayet* (Ar. *āya*) that indicates God through His beautiful names. But the human subjects who would be able to witness and interpret things as signs are not there already—religious subjectivity is an achievement and a difficult, discursive and dialectical one at that. From a Nursian perspective, a human being can interpret reality in two ways at any given moment. One could either focus on what something means in-itself, its "nominative meaning," or one could focus on what that thing indicates about other-than-itself, its "indicative meaning."[10] Practices of belief are, at their core, interpretive exercises that transform a subject's gaze from seeing nominative meanings toward the indicative meanings.[11] The indicative meanings refer to observed or felt qualities in the world, such as compassion, wisdom and mercy, which the ideal subject interprets as manifestations of the beautiful names of God, such as the Compassionate, Wise and Merciful, in the created realm. The turning of the human gaze to the beautiful names of God is to be accomplished through Quranically-guided reading of everything in the universe (including things, emotions, relations) as signs of God, that is, indicating one or more names of God. For instance, to look upon the sun as a hot, gaseous sphere is to look upon it for the sake of its nominative meaning. But to look upon it (and its relations with other things, for instance, plant and animal life) and see wisdom, magnificence and mercy in those relations is to focus on the sun's indicative meaning and to see them as signs of God's wisdom, magnificence and mercy. The ideal subject ought to find oneself constituted as a witness to the names and, crucially, also as someone who can consciously manifest all the names in the world.[12] Indeed, it is through inhabiting a believing perspective, Nursi argues, that a human being is elevated to the "highest of the high" and it is by abandoning a belief perspective that he falls "to the lowest of the low" (Q. 95:4–6).[13] How is that so? What transforms or changes, subjectively and psychologically, when human beings look upon the universe with a belief perspective and what does the psyche of a person who sees the world believingly, look like? In the rest of this chapter, we shall explore these questions.

TAWHID AND SUBJECT FORMATION

Tawhid, unifying the divine or Godhead, is often spoken about as an Islamic doctrine, a quintessential Islamic summon. Muslims are supposed to believe in the unity or oneness of God. It is presented, by Muslims and non-Muslim scholars of the Quran alike, as the fundamental emphasis of the Quran. This way of talking about *tawhid* reflects a certain conception of belief—as a *theoretical* idea and not an interpretive practice. In contrast, Nursi's speak of believing in God's oneness as a set of reflective exercises or practices that produce certain subjective standpoints. The objects of such reflection are varied and in this section we shall focus on just a few as illustrative examples. One key method by which the subject comes to inhabit a belief perspective is reflecting on natural causes and it is here that we begin.

Questioning Natural Causes

In Nursi's writings, one of the central features of believing in the oneness of God is to inhabit a critical standpoint toward what we commonly refer to as natural causes. By natural causes, Nursi means things like sunlight, the soil, oxygen, the digestive system, rain, human beings and so on—anything that we might explicitly, but more often implicitly, take to be a *creative* power, an agent possessing innate and effective powers to create (bring into being) and sustain one or more effects. To put it bluntly, an ideal Nursian subject must come to deny effective, creative powers to natural causes—he must come to deny that natural causes have the power, inherent or given, to create their effects or to sustain those effects.[14] I say "come to deny" because there is a process of reflection and a movement of thought involved here, not a knee-jerk, abstract and unthinking, fideistic rejection of the principle of causality or human agency *tout court*.[15] It should be as a matter of personal observation and reflection that the ideal subject should come to deny natural causes as creators of particular effects. This denial is the opening of doors and window unto the divine. To take one example from hundreds Nursi mentions throughout his works, consider how a Nursian subject ought to think about rain and the subsequent growth of vegetation:

> Rain comes from the sky in order to produce food for you and your animals. *Since water does not possess the ability to have mercy for you and your animals* and thus produce food accordingly, *it means that* the rain does not come, it is sent. And the earth cleaves up and yields forth food for you. But *lacking feelings and intelligence*, it is far beyond the ability of the earth to think of your sustenance and feel compassion for you, *so it does not produce the food* on its own.[16]

The denial of power and consciousness to natural causes, here rain and also the earth, is presented as part of a reflective process that starts not with God's power as the only cause but with an attention to what the observable qualities of the effects mean or indicate. The subject contemplates the compassion and wisdom exhibited by the effects but that he sees lacking in the seeming natural causes. Once he avows that the rain and earth lack the qualities needed to produce the beneficial and intelligent effects he observes, he then focuses on the gap or distance between the richness of the effects and the impotence or poverty of the seeming causes. Nursi says, "the distance between causes and effects is such that it may be seen *only with the light of the Qur'an*, through the telescope of belief" and "it is within this long distance between seeming cause and its effect that the Divine Names (*al-asmā al-ḥusna*, lit. 'Most Beautiful Names,' or 'attributes of perfection') each rise like stars. The place of their rising, is this distance."[17] This "long distance" is a reflectively achieved perspective on the relation between the effects and the seeming causes. The subject then starts to hear the names of God such as *the Life-Giver, the Nurturer, the Sustainer, the Wise*, being recited by the natural processes, that is, the cause(s)-effect(s) relations. The ideal subject is a believing subject insofar as he hears and witnesses these signs of God in the gaps between effects and their apparent causes. Such affirmations are not accomplished once and for all but rather are perspectives one must choose to come to repeatedly, each time one reflects about any cause-effect relation in the world. As we shall see later in the chapter when we look at Nursi's interpretation of the story of Prophet Jonah in the Quran, to think that causes have the power to create their effects is, for Nursi, the quintessential "non-tawhidic" (*shirkī*) and self-destructive perspective that a person can take.

It is important to note that a Nursian subject thinks about the beautiful names of God *through*, and not at the expense of, cause-effect relations in nature. The relation is not denied entirely but a gap is opened, conceptually and reflectively, between cause and effect and this gap reveals the meanings that elevate the subject. To believe in the oneness of God reflectively and not imitatively is to take such a reflective stance toward all natural cause-effect relations, as one encounters them in one's day-to-day life. Attention to the connectedness of things follows upon such a view of natural causes. The harmonious working of so many seeming causes too now becomes a matter of importance for the subject. The subject ought to now think about the principle of cooperation and make it a matter of reflection. Nursi counsels,

> Look at the principle of cooperation at work in the universe: With command of the Sustainer, the sun cooks the necessities required for the life of living beings. Similarly, the moon serves as a calendar (for computing the passing of time), and light, air, water and nutrition hasten to the aid of living beings. Moreover, plants hasten to the aid of animals, and animals hasten to the aid of human beings. Likewise, organs in a body support each other and nutritive particles hasten to the aid of the cells in the body. In other words, *unconscious* and *lifeless* beings help and support each other with wisdom and generosity and they heed each others' needs, thereby *manifesting a principle of generosity, compassion and mercy*. This reality shows that they are the servants, employees, and creations of the Unique and Single (*al-wāḥid al-aḥad*) Necessarily Existent, Self-Sufficient One on whom everything depends (*al-fard al-ṣamad*), the All-Powerful, All- Knowing, All-Merciful, and All-Generous.[18]

To believe in the oneness of God then is to take the causes as lifeless in themselves and yet wise and generous in terms of the actions and outcomes that flow through them into the world. Such a stance toward natural causes is a step toward observing these causes as servants and employees of a single, self-sufficient One, on whom they must therefore depend. The one who fails to deprive, as a matter of intellectual or discursive practice, natural causes of their powers cannot attain a believing perspective insofar as *believing as a lived practice* is concerned. Notice that this failing to believe does not have any legal or doctrinal baggage attached here but only an experiential one: the subject who does not think about causes and effects in this way would not experience the apparent causes as employees of a single powerful and knowing One, serving his needs as per His wise, knowing, and compassionate will.[19] The notion of God as merciful or wise would have little to no resonance in the person's psyche. As well, the subjects who see that natural objects and events point to other than themselves would see how the perishing of objects does not mean that the meanings they display also perish. Let us look at how a *tawhidic perspective* renders transience and death meaningful for a Nursian subject.

Transience and Dying

For a Nursian subject, believing in the oneness of God consists in taking a contemplative and imaginative standpoint toward the passing away of things—their death, their temporal and hence transient existence. To believe in God's oneness is to see a certain meaning in death and transience, one's own and that of other things. Death, for an ideal Nursian subject ought not be, "nonexistence, execution, vanishing, or extinction."[20] Instead, a believing standpoint would be one from which the subject sees death as "release from duty, a transfer from one place to another, a change of body; a retirement from the duty of this world . . . death is an orderly and wise act carried out by a Wise Maker."[21] How does one attain such a standpoint toward death? How can it be experienced as the orderly action of a Wise maker, and not as indicative of a limit on the life-giver's power or ability to give life any longer? How does the subject manage to avoid responding to death as if it were an execution and extinction, a vanishing into nonexistence, a misfortune, a failure or a divine punishment? It is important to quote Nursi at length. In the passage below, the ideal subject is being asked to focus on the passing of spring with the coming of winter:

> Seeing the passing "funeral" of the spring, human beings turn their gaze to the past and notice a wider perspective. That is, human beings are reminded of all the past spring seasons, each of which filled up the face of the earth with life. Human beings also foresee the coming of future spring seasons, each of which is a wonder of divine power bringing forth abundant life on the face of the

earth. The death of the earth in winter, therefore, brings to mind a vast and bright vision of the past and future. . . . In place of one short-lived and transitory miracle, thousands of miracles of divine power are brought to mind. . . . The fact that new springs came after the ones that vanished shows that seeming causes are naught, they have no effect. The death of living beings along with their seeming causes shows that they can only be created by a Powerful Glorious One who, with His wisdom, connects life with seeming causes. . . . *Think carefully.* How can anyone other than the One whose wisdom and power encompasses the past and future have a part in creating life on earth? How can blind chance and nature be responsible in any way?[22]

What are some of the key discursive practices that we can identify here? First, the arrival of winter and the death of this current spring should draw one's attention to other past springs. One looks away from the death of one particular spring and attains a broader perspective, a perspective that encompasses all the past springs during which the earth had been alive and all the future springs when life will, the subject imagines, emerge again. The subject condenses the springs of the past and the future into the present moment of death, overwhelming *this* moment of death with life (i.e., "springs") of the past and the future made present through an intellectual exercise, a conscious exercise of attention, recollection and also imagination (the imagining of future springs that do not yet exist). Past springs, already gone, ought to assure the person that the many deaths of past springs were the deaths of the cause-effect pairs and not just the death of the effect (spring). This thought makes the person feel that seeming causes too were made by someone, a wise agent, who must have connected them with the effects for if the causes of spring were real causes and if these real causes had died, no more springs should have been possible. But springs continued to come into existence. Future springs are contemplated as not only possible but as coming out of nowhere, that is, not from seeming causes that perished with their effects but together with the seeming causes and only to pass away again.[23]

To see this passing away as pointing to a One who must give existence to both cause and effect, connect them within an order, and take them out of existence while itself never going out of existence is the practice of believing in the oneness of God. In other words, experiencing the periodic emergence of death and life as an act of resurrection, a wisdom-displaying recreation of things and their fruit-bearing connections—such as the relations between the air/atmosphere and the soil so as to create new life in the form of colorful flowers, fruits, and so forth—is an important perspective for an ideal Nursian subject. Reality, for an ideal subject, is not merely creational but "resurrectional."

Nursi also brings this perspective to the subject's own transience. Speaking to his own *nafs* (and thus asking the subject to address himself as such), Nursi notes:

> Your lifespan passes quicker than lightening, and your life flows faster than a river. Now, since transience is the nature of worldly life, physical existence and animal life, it is wiser for you to stop restricting yourself with animality and corporeality, and enter the higher level of the heart and spirit. You will find a life much broader than the vast world you used to imagine. You will find a realm of light. The key to this world of light is in the sacred phrase, "there is no god except God."[24]

This is a significant difference here between Nursi and Muhasibi. For Muhasibi, death and transience were invoked to evoke urgency in fulfilling God's rights. Death is really to be seen as the end of life as one knows it. To be sure, Nursi too supports the notion that God's commands should be obeyed but his view of the ideal response to transience is markedly different from Muhasibi's. Nursi sees death and transience as aspects of the world that ought to be reflected on so as to see the eternal qualities of God, such as beauty, life, power, revealed by the death and transience of the things in the world. For Nursi, death is not so much a bearer of news about the end as about the possibility, and reality, of endless new ends and beginnings.

It is significant that Nursi highlights that the ideal religious subject doesn't just engage in this reflection once, but repeatedly through life—as he himself illustrates it through sharing from his own life journey, an example of which we shall see later. For now, we turn to a crucially important way in which believing in the oneness of God shapes the psyche of an ideal Nursian subject—the subject's attitude toward his own capacities and qualities.

Tawhid and Human Capacities

Nursi likens the human being to an antique work of art, valuable not on account of the material it is made up of but on account of the divine-indicative art it displays. He describes a believing person as someone who gains, on account of adopting a belief perspective, a capacity to consciously read himself as a microcosm of the whole universe in terms of being a bearer of divine meanings. He says,

> Man is an antique work of art of almighty God. He is a most subtle and graceful miracle of his power whom he created to manifest all His names and their inscriptions, in the form of a miniature specimen of the universe. If the light of belief enters his being, all the meaningful inscriptions on him may be read. As one who believes, he reads them consciously, and through that (connection), he causes others to read them. That is to say, the (divine) art in man becomes apparent through meanings like, "I am the creature and artefact of the All-Glorious Maker. I manifest His Mercy and Munificence."[25]

The ideal subject is one who establishes a *connection* with God through belief. This connection gives the subject access to valuable meanings, such as the idea that he manifests his maker's qualities of mercy and munificence (whenever he is merciful and munificent), just as a mirror may be said to gain value, not on account of its glass but on account of the beautiful image reflected in it (when it is reflected in it). The ideal subject finds his value or worth by connecting, reflectively, his limited and fleeting qualities to the abiding and absolute qualities of God. It is important to note that the subject does not gain the value associated with those qualities himself. Rather, from a subject's point of view, in and through the act of believing, of consciously establishing a *connection* with the owner of the valuable qualities, he can feel valuable on account of that *connection*. The value, for him, is in the connection/believing and does not come to reside in himself as bearer of divine qualities. Thus, if the belief-connection is severed, whether due to heedlessness or through conscious choice, those same qualities still exist in the human being but cannot be read as "inscriptions of divine art" anymore and lose their indicative value (insofar as they are then seen as qualities of the subject himself). Without a belief perspective, these qualities would only become aspects of the human being's animal, physical existence whose end is "only to pass a brief and partial life as the most impotent, needy, and grieving of animals."[26] The subject's mercy and munificence, without a conscious connection to a maker who is actively inscribing those qualities in man, are perishing along with his body and even become a liability for they make man suffer more than other creatures. A human being who sees compassion as his own quality would suffer when he sees the suffering of others. But from a perspective of belief, human being's own qualities would begin to speak, as if like messengers, about the One who is sending them to him and all other creatures and One who must therefore possess them as real, abiding qualities. The suffering of the subject, on account of seeing others suffer, would now bear news about a maker who does not like suffering and a call to act in the name of such a merciful one and do one's best to relieve others' suffering. In short, the act of believing in God's oneness, for Nursi, is a kind of intellectual practice that involves the attaining of a mirror-like stance toward the capacities and qualities one finds in/with oneself.

Nursi discusses the human self, especially what he call as "the I" in great depth and with great subtlety and a full discussion of his ideas is not possible here. But it would not be fair to the reader if I passed on without some comment about Nursi's view of the human "I," especially as it pertains to believing in the oneness of God. Here, then, is a truncated and sketchy version of his rich and complicated account.

Nursi teaches that philosophers like Plato, Aristotle, Ibn-i-Sina and al-Farabi "said that the ultimate aim of humanity is to liken themselves to the Necessary Being," that is to say, to actually resemble Him. In so doing, they "closed the doors to impotence and weakness, poverty and need, deficiency and imperfection, which are intrinsic to human beings, and thus obstructed the road to worship."[27] In Nursi's view then, the ideal way of being in the world is not to try and resemble God and become perfect like Him. Instead, Nursi proposes a three-fold conception of the "I" as mirror-like.

The first aspect might be called *apophatic mirroring*, that is, the "I" mirrors God *through* a recognition of its own lacks, needs, weaknesses and poverty.[28] That is to say, the "I," for instance as a biological being, makes known the Nourisher in the mirror of its hunger and its in the mirror of its need for food. It makes known the Wise in the mirror of its ignorance and need for wisdom. His need for help and strength reflects or makes known the Helper and the Powerful One that it looks to and seeks in all its actions that require strength. This self-negational mirroring is very important to notice because it closes the possibility that the "I" can ever become or ought to try and become God-like. Nursi talks about this form of mirroring God by referencing the famous intimate supplication of the famous seventh-century Muslim, Uways al-Qarani, by saying: "Every creature, universal and particular, is, like Uways al-Qarani, a mirror, in a form that has the meaning of supplication. All proclaim the Divine power and perfection through their impotence and poverty and deficiency."[29]

A second aspect of mirroring might simply be called *positive mirroring*. Nursi describes this aspect in the following words: "through particulars like his partial knowledge, power, sense of sight and hearing, ownership and sovereignty, which are sorts of samples given to him, man acts as mirror. . . . For example, he says: 'Just as I make this house and know how to make it, and I see it and own it and administer it, so also the mighty palace of the universe has a Maker who knows it, sees it, makes it and administers it.'"[30] Such analogies are only to be taken as acts of analogical and imaginative thinking and not actual descriptions of reality. The "I" is to think, ultimately, that it is not the owner or builder of the house at all. After having understood what the "I" indicates, the subject is to realize that the house is part of God's creation as well and the "I" does not actually own it. In this aspect again, the subject looks to its capacities and qualities as partial and limited samples of what, he must come to realize, the absolute qualities and names of God.

A third aspect of the Nursian "I" as mirror might be called *responsive mirroring*. That is to say, through his being-in-the-world, for instance, as a human being who exists and is alive, a person reflects the names Life-Giver and Nurturer. As well, to give an example that more clearly relates to ethics, in responding (involuntarily) to injustice and poverty with emotions such as sadness, indignation and melancholia, for instance, the subject reflects, as a mirror, the names, Just and Judge and Compassionate. The ideal subject sees that his emotions are a response generated by the impresses of divine names in his being. Everyday responses of the person as an "I" reflect what Nursi calls the "impresses" or "stamps" of the divine names.[31] With this discussion in mind, we turn to how an ideal subject, who believes in the oneness of God by taking himself to be a mirror-like "I," engages with his own thinking or reflective capacity, namely his intelligence.

Selling Oneself to God

For an ideal Nursian subject, believing in the oneness of God alters his standpoint toward his potentials or capacities as a human being, importantly, his intelligence or ability to perceive and understand meanings. A Nursian subject ought to be inspired by the Qur'anic verse, *God has purchased the lives and possessions of the believers in return for Paradise* (Q. 9:111) for effecting an altered standpoint toward his own intelligence. An ideal subject ought to sell his intelligence back to the One who owns it.[32] What is involved in this proverbial selling of one's "possessions" and what are the emotional and psychological consequences, if any, of making the sale? Nursi argues,

> The intelligence is, for example, like a tool. If you do not sell it to God Almighty, but rather employ it for the sake of the soul, it will become an ill-omened, noxious and debilitating tool; it will descend to the rank of an inauspicious and destructive tool. It is for this reason that a sinful man will frequently resort to drunkenness or frivolous pleasure in order to escape the vexations and injuries of his intelligence. But if you sell your intelligence to its True Owner and employ it on His behalf, then the intelligence will become like the key to a talisman, unlocking the infinite treasures of Compassion and the vaults of wisdom that creation contains.[33]

The fundamental shift here is from using intelligence for "the sake of the soul," in a nominative register, to employing it on its owner's behalf. Intelligence is seen, in the mirror of the "I" as a divine messenger or key with which the ideal subject ought to understand the manifestations of divine wisdom and compassion in creation. The change in subjective state is from being vexed and injured by the assaults of an intelligence that sees no wisdom and compassion in things, the vexations that come from a need for meaning, to a state where one experiences or apprehends the previously hidden compassion and wisdom manifest in creation. A Nursian subject recognizes his vexations and sufferings as the failure of intelligence, employed in nominative meanings, to see the indicative meanings in creation. What previously appeared only cruel and chaotic ought to, for one believing in God, show the face of compassion and wisdom that the cruelty looks to and indicates. For instance, an intelligence that was tortured by feelings of compassion and helplessness for those oppressed by a tyrant can see the tortures revealed by a *sold-intelligence* as mirroring the justice and compassion of God. Intelligence used on behalf of God ought to show the subject that his maker, God, dislikes tyranny and is therefore Just and Compassionate. Had God not been just, the subject, being a mirror, would not have been able to intelligibly grieve for the oppressed. The subject then, in response to its intelligence's witness to God's justice and compassion, hopes from this compassionate God that He will do justice to all, if not in this world then in some other realm.[34]

Another clear example of how this selling of intelligence works in practice is in Nursi's discussion of *bismillah* or "in the name of God." Nursi tells a parable of two travelers and maps the two travelers in the parable to two different ways in which a human might interact with the world in the journey of life:

> Now, my arrogant soul (*nafs*), you are that traveler. And this world is the desert in the story. Your weakness ('*ajz*) and poverty (*faqr*) are boundless. Your enemies and needs are endless. So take the name of the Pre-Eternal Ruler and Post-Eternal Sustainer of this desert and be saved from begging before the whole universe and trembling before all kinds of events. Indeed, this phrase, *bismillah* is such a blessed treasury: it connects your infinite vulnerability, weakness ('*ajz*) and poverty (*faqr*) to the source of infinite power and mercy. It makes your weakness and poverty an excellent intercessor in the Court of the All-Powerful, Compassionate One (*al-qadīr al-raḥīm*). Indeed, the person who acts *bismillah*, in the name of God, is like a government official who acts in the name of the government. Unlike an individual with no authority who is acting in his own name, such a person fears nobody. He performs every matter and withstands all challenges in the name of the law and the government.[35]

We can think about the suggestion to sell one's intelligence to God and acting in the name of God as two sides of the same coin. A Nursian subject is asked to recognize, as a matter of intellectual exercise, his poverty, in the sense of a lack of self-sufficiency, and juxtapose it with his innumerable needs and vulnerabilities. These needs and vulnerabilities pose challenges that injure and harm the human on account of his inability to meet those needs. For instance, a human being may need innocent people to remain free from tyranny and harm and may find himself unable to ensure such safety for his loved ones and perhaps for all the oppressed of the world. His intelligence will vex and torture him—it would cause him to see the chasm between his immense needs and his equally immense inability or lack of power to produce the desired outcome. In light of his realization of such a gap, the Nursian subject does not surrender passively or ironically to the gap. He ought to use his intelligence, sense of justice and all efforts to reinstate justice to end tyranny, in God's name. In other words, *bismillah* is not simply a phrase to be verbalized nor a license to be a god on earth. It is a mode of being in the world where one engages in a life-long process of consciously surrendering the apparent qualities of the "I" to their owner and then act in the name of the One who is the owner of that good or beautiful quality.

For an agent structured/formed by a *tawhid* perspective, affirmation follows negation. In negating that one is the real owner of one's qualities, one affirms that there is One who owns those qualities. A believer gives up claims to self-possession of all praiseworthy and beautiful qualities. Besides, he gives up attributing them to ignorant causes and blind chance. While Muhasibi simply reminded his audience of the obligation to do so, Nursi tries to convince the reader to do so by talking about the joy and relief that the soul experiences in choosing such a perspective. For instance, in his discussion of a prayer that Nursi notes is recited after the morning and evening ritual prayers, he comments:

> This phrase (*wahdahu*) "He is the only one" contains healing, joyful good news. Our hearts and spirits are involved with so many things. We feel connected with countless people and beings, and we care deeply about the world around us. With such intense involvement, our hearts and spirits are overwhelmed with the mess and confusion of the world. It is then that "He is the only one" ("*wahdahu*") comes to the rescue and becomes a refuge and a protector against all the confusion and misery. The phrase *wahdahu* announces to us: "God is one. Do not tire yourself begging from others. Do not debase yourself before anything or feel indebted to them. Do not tremble before them, or debase yourself by trying to please them. There is only one sovereign of the universe. The keys to all things are with the One. He has control over everything. Everything is resolved through His command. If you find Him, you will find all your wishes, and you will be saved from endless indebtedness and fears.[36]

While Nursi here also mentions the idea of being free from indebtedness to others and not trying to please others just as Muhasibi did, I want to draw attention to what the phrase ought to announce to the Nursian subject insofar as he finds himself trembling before things/causes. The phrase is supposed to *do* something for the person concerned about countless beings: transform his worry into joy and relief by handing the reins of their existence and well-being to an all-powerful and all-merciful One and releasing them from his own hands. This move, an intellectual choice, ought to rescue the subject emotionally and restore a sense of dignity to him, a dignity that is injured by a deep sense of failure and inadequacy in determining and controlling outcomes. Thus, to engage with the phrase "He is the only One" is to affect a change in one's standpoint toward one's capacity for empathy and altruism with the result that one hears *in* this phrase, and thus *in* the "I"s apparent capacity to care for others, good news about a One who has complete control over everything, a control He does not share with secondary causes, and about One who cares for the well-being of one's loved ones. Such a person hands over or surrenders the power to do benefit and harm to the One he sees as having sole control over things and who, for him, is now the sole source of wisdom and compassion with which (or in whose name) the subject now cares about others. We shall see more fully how mutual concern, grounded in a belief perspective, ought to be externalized in interpersonal relations, in the next chapter.

Supplication as Agency

Thus far, we have seen how the agency of an ideal Nursian subject lies is making a choice regarding their standpoint toward themselves and acting in God's name rather than in their own name. Interestingly, for a Nursian subject, such a shift in one's standpoint redefines and enhances agency and does not eliminate it. What we normally regard as a passive form of agency, that is, supplication, becomes the core, active agency for the ideal subject. Nursi describes such an agency while he is discussing the different types of supplications human beings and other beings offer to God. Discussing supplications specific to human beings, he says:

> The fourth type of supplication, the one that is most well-known, is our [human] prayer and it consists of two types. One is offered through our actions and our states of being, and the other through our hearts and tongues. For instance, *having recourse to seeming causes is a prayer through action (du'a fi 'lī)*. The gathering of seeming causes is not for creating the result. Rather, it is to *request the result* from the Almighty Creator through assuming an acceptable position and praying through the *language of our situation (lisān al-ḥāl)*. When a farmer ploughs a field, it is an act of prayer: the act of ploughing is an act of knocking on the door of divine mercy. This type of prayer through action is most often accepted because it is directed at the name and title of the Absolutely Generous One. The second type of prayer is through the heart and tongue. It is to ask for certain wishes that we are unable to obtain. The most important aspect, the most beautiful purpose and the sweetest result of this prayer is the following: *the person who is praying realizes that there is someone who hears his deepest wishes in his heart, who is able to do anything, who is able to fulfill all his wishes*. He feels that there is someone who has compassion for his weakness and his poverty.[37]

There are several important points to notice here. The first and perhaps the most important for our purposes is the way a Nursian subject ought to assign meaning to their active, physical agency: they see it as a "gathering of seeming causes." For the subject, believing in God as the only real cause or power, ought not mean that one does not see oneself acting at all. The transformation instead is the meaning that one assigns to the ability to act and the performance of actions. To use his example, the farmer still ploughs the field but now, insofar as he wishes to practice belief in God, ought to see his agential efforts as gathering already-existing causes and requesting results from God, a knocking on the door of His mercy. To then see one's crop growing would be seen not as a natural, unwilled and taken-for-granted outcome of one's effort and a result of blind, natural causes but a willed and direct response, an answer to one's prayer-as-action. In this way, an ideal Nursian subject transforms the meaning of his agency and sees himself as inhabiting a supplicatory standpoint, inhabiting a state of worshipfulness to the extent that an agent sees his actions as requests, and the results of his actions as responses by the One who must be someone (in the subject's view now) who hears and knows his needs (since He creates some kind of result). To the extent that believing in God is tied to the denial of the power of the seeming causes, this prayer-through-action is an ongoing semantic possibility—one either assigns this meaning to one's agency at a given moment and takes a particular stance toward it and its results or one fails to (or refuses to) do so.

A second important point here is that the prayer of heart and tongue is not just important for the sake of things or results one might be asking for but significant insofar as it produces a *realization* in the subject that there is one who hears his petitions, knows his needs and responds to them. What is implicit here is that a Nursian subject will understand his needs in a particular way, a way captured by a saying of God that Nursi cites: "If I had not wanted to give, I would not have given wanting."[38] A Nursian subject thus finds the response to his supplication in the act of, and the urge for, supplicating to God and in the act of asking Him to fulfill a need. The ideal subject sees, in the very act of asking, God as already responding by moving him to ask.[39] Thereby, the subject's agency implies and reveals divine agency and reveals what the divine wills for the subject.

Finally, the ideal subject is to see himself acting on behalf of and as a representative of all the beings in the universe. Believing in God ought to mean that one's agency is expanded beyond one's individual self and that one inhabits a sort of collective agency, where the collective is not—as we might expect—merely the Muslim community but rather the entire cosmos. It is in the act of seeing one's action as a prayer that one's agency is so expanded. One is to, ideally, represent—as God's caliph—the universe and the total dependence of all existing things on God, in one's supplicatory stance toward God. Since one comes to prayer out of a recognition of the existential poverty of all beings and the powerlessness of all causes, one's stance toward one's agency as a conscious being is that it includes the entire universe in its recognition of neediness and the recognition of the giver of those wants and needs to all beings.[40] This emphasis on "cosmic context" however, does not mean that the believing subject does not need human exemplars as models for the right way of being a religious subject. Believing in the prophets serves this important need.

PROPHETHOOD AND SUBJECT FORMATION

In this section, I reflect on some key subjective standpoints concomitant with an ideal Nursian subject's belief in prophethood. Again, we shall see that believing in prophets or messengers of God is tantamount to reading or seeing particular meanings in existing things. An ideal Nursian subject is defined by the sacred meanings he recognizes in things, the things of this world and his inner world. And prophets and prophetic stories in the Quran play an important role in making particular meanings available and intimately relatable for the subject. To illustrate, I shall discuss three examples: a person's stance toward the beauty he sees in the universe, his standpoint toward personal pain and suffering and finally (perhaps surprisingly for the reader), the meaning he ought to give to advancements in science and technology.

Prophets as the Possibility of Cherishing Beauty

An ideal Nursian subject who believes in the prophets, and specifically the prophethood of Muhammad, ought to take a particular stance, an appreciative and joyous standpoint, toward the art and beauty he observes in the world. In Nursi's understanding, the prophet is primarily a conveyor of meanings and solver of "the riddle of the mystery of the world's creation." And in doing so, the prophet enables the subject to cherish beauty and celebrate its source.[41] More specifically, in Nursi's teaching, believing in the prophet, among other things, represents a resolution to the tragedies and miseries that humans experience not despite but rather *on account of* their ability to discern and appreciate beauty. In commenting on the verse that reads, *If you do love God, follow me; God will love you* (Q. 3:31) Nursi says,

> Since in the universe there is observed beauty of art, and this is certain, it necessitates with a certainty as definite as actually witnessing it, the prophethood of Muhammad. For the beauty of art and finely ornamented forms of these beautiful creatures show that in their fashioner is a significant will to make beautiful and powerful desire to adorn. And this will and desire show that there is in the Maker an elevated love and sacred inclination toward the perfections of the art He displays in His creatures. And this love and inclination require to be most turned toward and concentrated on man, the most enlightened and perfect individual among beings. And man is the conscious fruit of the tree of creation. And the fruit is the most comprehensive and furthest part, the part with the most general view and universal consciousness. And the one with the most comprehensive view and universal consciousness may be a most elevated and brilliant individual, who will meet with and be addressed by that beauteous Maker.[42]

It is noteworthy that Nursi speaks about this verse in the language of "art" and "beauty," a "will to beautify and adorn," and adornment addressed to human consciousness. Unlike many other interpreters, he does not here talk about the importance of following the legal and ethical injunctions in Muhammad's *sunna* or the *shariah*.[43] Believing in prophethood is to take oneself to be a consciousness to which the art and beauty of the world is addressed. Nursi says that the Maker of art and beauty would want to appoint a human being who appreciates the beauty at the highest level, His prophet. The prophet, in other words, is to be seen as a person appointed as an "appreciator-in-chief" of all the divine art and beauty in the world. And believers in prophethood are those who try to emulate, at their own levels, this appreciation of art and beauty.

But what about all the ugliness in the world? The prophet, and those who follow him, cannot simply inhabit a feel-good positivity without understanding the meaning of all that lacks beauty and is therefore ugly. Indeed, the possibility of joy or appreciation the prophet feels, and teaches, comes from inhabiting a perspective that covers both the beautiful and the apparently ugly. Nursi argues that, ultimately, real ugliness is only possible when one loses a tawhidic, "there is no god but God" perspective.[44] Without such a perspective, the world would indeed become "a place of general mourning" and beings would be like strangers and orphans "weeping at the blows of death and separation." Through the "light and guidance" that the prophet offers, the ideal subject shifts his perspective:

> Now look! Through the light he [the prophet] spreads, that place of universal mourning has been transformed into a place where God's names and praises are recited in joy and ecstasy. The foreign, hostile beings have become friends and brothers. While the dumb, inanimate creatures have each taken on the form of familiar officials and docile servants. And the weeping, complaining orphans are seen to be either reciting God's names and praises or offering thanks at being released from their duties.[45]

Prophecy of Muhammad is necessary for a Nursian subject because only through the lens it offers do all other beings show themselves to be messengers and servants of God. A prophet who turns every single being and every single instance of beauty into a messenger conveying God's beauteous names, in this sense, could be seen as a seal of prophecy because nothing more radical can be accomplished in terms of making the divine fully accessible to human consciousness. Notice how the transformation affected by the prophet and by following the prophet is described in terms of the change in meaning—a different interpretive standpoint toward a world, a standpoint that grounds its approach to the ugliness and injustices in the world in a prior affirmation that there is art and beauty in the world and that such beauty would stand contradicted if it were not understood as referring to the Beautiful One, whose beauty does not perish.

The subject is to understand that to believe in the prophet is to believe in eternal happiness because the prophet is the one who supplicates to God for eternal happiness on behalf of all humanity and all other creatures.[46] Prophetic perspectives make the unfamiliar, familiar and makes otherwise painful death of beings, an acceptable completion of their assigned duties.

Belief in the prophets not only supports and enhances the *no-god-but-God* perspective on things but also signals the possibility of living out this perspective of beautiful names of God amid encounters with challenges and existential questions in personal life. Nursi's use of the example of Prophet Jonah is an important one in this regard, to which we now turn.

Prophet Jonah, Human Affliction and Prophetic Supplications

The story of Jonah is exemplary for the ideal subject in terms of diagnosing the internal reasons for the existential suffering and misery of human beings, in general, as well as in specific cases, and in terms of seeing the solution to existential angst in prophetic prayers as described in the Quran. The gist of the matter lies in something we have already encountered above, namely, the realization that causes are only seeming causes and do not have any real power—their power is entirely derivative of the One who is the real and only source of all the power manifest in the world and thus all things are directly and fully under His command and control. Commenting on the prayer of Prophet Jonah in the Quran that reads, "*There is no god except You! You are limitless in Your glory! Verily, I have done wrong,*" Nursi says,

> He [Jonah] was thrown into the sea and was swallowed by a big fish. He found himself in the belly of the fish, in the midst of a stormy sea, in the deep darkness of the night. He realized that no cause could deliver him, and he cried out, "*There is no god except You! You are limitless in Your glory! Verily, I have done wrong.*" This prayer led to his immediate deliverance. What was about this prayer that was so *transformative*? His prayer contains the realization that all the "seeming causes" are completely powerless. Since the night, the sea, the fish and the weather seemed to be all united against him, he needed someone who has power over all of these seeming causes. In other words, only the one who has power over all these elements could save Jonah. . . . When Jonah realized with the certainty of seeing (*'ayn al-yaqīn*) that there is no recourse other than the Causer of All Causes (*musabbib al-asbāb*), then the oneness of God became manifest to him.[47]

Interestingly, Nursi sees the turning point in the story as Jonah's recognition of *his responsibility* in the injustice and anxiety he encountered in his interactions with his people. Jonah's despair at the stubbornness of his audience isn't simply a response to ugliness out there in the world. Rather, Jonah, inadvertently, contributed to this ugliness through his perception, by momentarily losing his belief perspective and by assigning power to causes.

How is a Nursian subject expected to follow Jonah's example? Interestingly, Nursi does not explicitly refer to some personal crisis. Instead, casting his net wide, he interprets Jonah's impasse as representing *the* fundamental crises that all human beings face, a horizon of perception that not only shows things to pass away but shows them to be passing into nonexistence. A horizon that makes them feel subject to blind and merciless forces of history, nature and time.

> Now, we are in a situation exceedingly more awful than that in which Jonah (peace be on him) first found himself: Our night is our future. *When we think about the future with forgetfulness (ghafla) of a Sustainer* our future appears to be much bleaker and more terrifying than Jonah's dark night. Our sea is the constantly changing world in which we live. This world is full of death and separation. Indeed, each "wave" of our sea bears thousands of corpses. Hence, our sea is a thousand times more frightening than Jonah's sea. Our whale is the caprice of our ego (*nafs*), which tries to engulf and destroy our eternal life. This fish is a thousand times more threatening than Prophet Jonah's. While his fish threatened to destroy his limited earthly life, our fish seeks to destroy our eternal, everlasting life. If this is our real situation, then let us take the example of Jonah (peace be on him). Let us turn away from all of seeming causes and take direct refuge with the Causer of Causes, our Sustainer. Let us say, *There is no god but You. Glory be unto You! Indeed I have done wrong.*

As we discussed above, the agency Nursi assigns to the subject is active only in a supplicatory sense and not in a creational sense. A Nursian subject ought to transform the way he sees the passing away of things by drawing on the perceptive acuity of Jonah in realizing his utter misery and helplessness and the transforming power of a tawhidic perspective. The meaning of the prayer, for Nursi, is that it expresses Jonah's framing and reframing of reality and, more importantly, that it makes possible for people, as believers in and followers of Quranic prophets (including Jonah), to overcome the afflictions that hit them on account of the death and transience of all that they cherish (the past), fear of the unknown (the future) and a short-sighted, pleasure-seeking worldliness. Like Jonah, the ideal subject can find an eternal Sustainer if he ceases to think blind, transient causes are sustaining him in the here and now. Nursi offers a similar approach as he unpacks the story of Prophet Job in the Quran.[48] In sum, prophetic narratives are not so much stories from which moral lessons are to be drawn, as is commonly taught in conventional exegeses of the Quran. For Nursi and the Nursian subject, they are narratives whose ebbs and flows and relationalities one is to enact in one's own life in order to be an ideal subject, a true follower (at an affective and psychological levels) of prophetic perspectives on reality. One interesting example of how ideal subjects ought to enact a prophetic agency in the world concerns scientific discoveries.

Scientific Progress and Discovery

Nursi suggests that belief in the prophets as mentioned in the Quran is to believe in the miracles associated with them, which is a traditional Islamic notion. Nursi thinks that not only the ordinary parts of a prophet's living and framing of life but also their miracles should inform the religious subject's standpoint in the world. This view was already implicitly at work in his understanding of Jonah's story: his predicament in the belly of a whale and miraculous deliverance from it represents the deliverance of human being from their spiritual and existential impasse.[49] What is interesting is that Nursi also claims that to believe in the miraculous actions of prophets should predispose one to take a particular stance toward "humankind's material progress."[50] For instance, in his commentary on Jesus's miracles of healing the blind and the lepers and bringing the dead back to life in the Quran, "*I shall heal the blind and the leper and I shall quicken the dead, by God's leave*" (Q. 3:49), Nursi says,

> Just as the Quran urges man to follow Jesus' (upon whom be peace) high morals, so too it allusively encourages him toward the elevated art and dominical medicine of which he was the master. Thus, this verse indicates this: "Remedies may be found for even the most serious illnesses. In which case, O man and O calamity-afflicted children of Adam! *Don't despair!* Whatever the ill, its cure is possible. Search for it and you will find it. It is even possible to give a temporary tinge of life to death." And in terms of *meaning*, God is saying through the figurative tongue of this verse: "O man! I gave two gifts to one of my servants who abandoned the world for me. One was the remedy for spiritual ills, and the other the cure for physical sicknesses. Thus, dead hearts were raised to life through the light of guidance. And sick people who were as though dead found health through his breath and cure. You too may find the cure for every ill in the pharmacy of my wisdom. *Work and find it! If you seek, you will certainly find!* Thus this verse traces the limit which is far ahead of man's present progress in regard to medicine. And it hints at it and urges him toward it.[51]

In other words, believing in the prophets and following them, both major teachings of the Quran, is to feel encouraged "to attain to things similar to them and to imitate them."[52] Nursi discusses several prophetic miracles mentioned in the Quran—Solomon's subjugation of air (Q. 34:12) and understanding of the speech of birds (Q. 38:19), and Abraham remaining unharmed by fire (Q. 21:69) and what each of these ought to signify for one who believes in the prophets. And so, faced with sicknesses that do not yet have a cure, a believing subject takes a *religiously-grounded*, optimistic and empowering stance toward finding their cures—and toward the exploration of nature and human endeavor more generally. Needless to say, Nursi does not think that prophets are great scientists or herbalists, even as they serve to encourage exploration and discovery.[53] The meaning that a subject who engages with discourse about prophetic miracles should give to scientific endeavor is that it is becomes a supplicatory exercise, a kind of worship where one is seeking the result (in this example, cures for illnesses) from the "pharmacy" of God's wisdom. It seems that an ideal Nursian subject who believes in the prophets ought to feel encouraged, even perhaps implicitly mandated—if they have the capacity for such undertaking—to engage in scientific and technological endeavors but also give a particular meaning to such endeavors: as divinely recommended and enabled means for accessing, benefiting from and thus acknowledging the wisdom of God.[54] We can also tie belief in prophecy then to a posture of hopefulness and trust. If there is a problem, there must be a solution. To believe in prophetic miracles is to deem the seemingly impossible, possible. It is to choose hope even in the dark face of suffering and despair—if fire became cool for Abraham (one of the miracles mentioned in the Quran in relation to Abraham), the religious subject who believes in the prophets can and should hope that the fires, real or metaphorical, that burn him can cease to do so and that the keys to this transformation lie, like in the case of Jonah, in his own hand (i.e., his interpretation of reality). The prophets are interpretive guides in the journey of life, which an ideal subject should live within an eternal horizon so that nothing, in their view, goes to nonexistence. It is to the question of believing in everlasting existence, believing in the hereafter, that we turn next.

BELIEVING IN THE HEREAFTER AND SUBJECT FORMATION

Much of Nursi's discussion of the hereafter is framed as proofs of the possibility and necessity of resurrection. This discussion is rich and intriguing on its own right but will not be my focus here. Rather, I would like to attend to the kinds of psychic standpoints that characterize a person who believes in the hereafter, according to Nursi. Let us start with an idea that may perhaps resonate with us, living, as we are, in a world filled with injustices.

Unrequited Injustices

> *Behold, then, [O man,] these signs of God's grace—how He gives life to the earth after it had been lifeless! Verily, this Selfsame [God] is indeed the One that can bring the dead back to life: for He has the power to will anything!* (Quran, 30:30)

It is easily understandable that the existence of unrequited or uncompensated injustice would pose a problem for anyone who wishes to assert or feel that the creator of the world is absolutely just and that human beings ought to be grateful and worshipful toward this creator. A believing standpoint, according to Nursi, is indeed such a one—one from which a subject sees all things as glorifying God and from which a subject finds existence meaningful in all its aspects. Yet, surely there are injustices of various kinds in the world. Even if one could say that inanimate and animate beings that suffer from change and death are being "discharged from their duties" and being taken to a realm of perfect and permanent beauty, one could still be deeply indignant about the kinds of oppressions and injustices that human beings (and non-human beings) regularly suffer at the hands of other humans beings. Nursi is quite aware of this problem and he presents believing in the hereafter as one important intellectual practice for attaining a particular standpoint toward all the injustices that remain unaddressed from the point of view of a religious subject. Instead of taking such injustices to be an argument or evidence against the existence of a just or compassionate God, Nursi wants the ideal subject to interpret his feelings of indignation as pointing him toward an affirmation of the existence of eternal beauty and eternal reward and punishment. Nursi uses a parable with two people, one wise and the other foolish, travelling through a kingdom and making observations, and the wise one points out:

> Look at the organization and administration of this kingdom! See how everyone, including the poorest and the weakest, is provided with perfect and ornate sustenance. The best care is taken of the sick. . . . The ruler of this kingdom must possess, then great generosity and all-embracing compassion . . . but not a thousandth part of what that generosity and awesomeness require, is to be seen in this realm. The oppressor retains his power, and the oppressed, his humiliation, as they both depart from this realm. Their affairs are left, then, to the same Supreme Tribunal, of which we speak.[55]

While the "perfect and ornate sustenance" demonstrates that the ruler of this kingdom (the world in the parable) has great generosity, it is "not a thousandth part" of what the subject ought to expect it to be. The subject should face a conundrum: there is enough generosity that one expects there to be no oppression and enough that one cannot explain it away as thinly-veiled ugliness or a mere illusion yet not enough generosity and justice to satisfy the expectations that this evident generosity creates in the human being. Thus, the parable presents a person who moves from rejoicing and appreciating the sustenance provided for each being to a sense of deep dissatisfaction produced by evident lack of desired perfection and beauty in the world. This example is a good illustration of how religious discourse aims at the formation and transformation of subjectivities and is not simply an abstract system of thought. Here, instead of taking a "philosophical" stance toward the conundrum and resolving it either in favor of nihilism (there is no real generosity here) or zealous but morally difficult pietism (there is no oppression here), the subject is asked to confront the dilemma, feel it and then attempt to resolve it on a personal, psychological level by interpreting it as a sign, a sign pointing to the existence of a realm where perfect generosity should manifest and all the unrequited injustices duly compensated (the oppressor punished and the oppressed rewarded). In other words, the recognition of the traces of beautiful names of God in the world does not mean that one settles for the world only. For an ideal subject, contentment and hope, and yearning for more perfection are embedded within each other, which can only manifest in one's mode of responding to the reality before one's eyes, and not through an abstract system that offers some abstract, doctrinal solution and, deceptively, suggests a non-ambivalent closure. The ideal subject puts the ambivalence to work, he reflects about it to strengthen his affirmation of a just realm of existence after the present, ambivalent one. After all, the subject would not be able to notice a lack unless it was grounded in a prior sense of fullness with reference to which he identifies something as a lack! The affirmation of the lacking and transience is made meaningful by realizing the eternity and perfection whose existence the subject is inwardly, at the level of his soul, aware and which the ideal subject must become mentally and affectively aware. Without believing in an eternal realm of perfection and eternity, the subject would be left to conclude that the creator is neither just nor merciful but tries (and fails) to convince His creatures that He is.

Consolations for the Young and the Infirm

In one of his less popular works, *Dependent Rational Animals*, Alasdair McIntyre makes the important point that much of modern Western thought takes the young, healthy, adult male as its protagonist. Children, the sick, and elderly are usually forgotten.[56] Fortunately, Nursi's religious discourse is not only for healthy young adults. He observes that "an important section of mankind are the sick, the oppressed, the disaster-stricken like us, the poor and the life-prisoners," while children and the ageing together comprise half of humanity.[57] For the sake of brevity, I shall focus on Nursi's discussion of the latter two groups.

According to Nursi, belief in the hereafter is of critical importance for children and the elderly. Believing in the hereafter ought to engender hope in children and allow them to give meaning to their otherwise baffling and demoralizing losses. Nursi says,

> Children can endure the death, that appears to them so awesome and tragic, only by means of the idea of Paradise. Only by this means can they find some spiritual strength in their weak and delicate bodies, and find some hope, permitting them to live joyfully, despite their vulnerable spiritual disposition that swiftly gives way to tears. Thinking of Paradise, the child will say, "My little brother or friend has died, and become a bird in Paradise. He is playing there, and leading a life finer than ours." Otherwise . . . the death of children and

adults all around them, would overwhelm their powers of resistance and inner strength.[58]

For children then, believing in the hereafter amounts to the cultivation of their imagination so that they may envision that those who die do not perish but instead depart for a better, finer life elsewhere. It offers them resilience in the face of death and separation they see in the world.

Similarly, the elderly can find consolation in the idea of life beyond death. The aged too, Nursi thinks, suffer "distraughtness of spirit and disturbance of heart" on account of the approaching extinction of their worldly life. "Only through the hope of eternal life can they confront the painful and awesome despair that arises from the anticipation of death and separation."[59] The thought of death as total annihilation and an extinction of loved ones or oneself is especially pressing and troubling for both groups (children and the elderly) and a discourse about paradise and life after death ought to give them strength and hope. The potential of this idea of a life after death, to transform—strengthen the young and console the aged—is an argument in favor of not only its use but lends support to the idea that such a realm should exist.[60] For a Nursian subject, as we shall see below, a religious idea is necessary, important and true insofar as a person's engagement with it reconciles him (emotionally and intellectually) with an undeniably ambivalent reality. This reconciliation is hermeneutical and discursive and not a singular act or station of mystical or metaphysical self-transcendence.

The Dignity of Beings

What happens to things and people after they die in this world? A standard Muslim answer, and the Quranic answer, is that they return to their origin and source, God.[61] To put the matter in this way would be to speak doctrinally and without concern about how a person might engage with and experience the force and veracity of such a claim. For a Nursian subject, the ability of this piece of Quranic guidance to affect their life and life choices depends on the extent to which they can perceive the world with a perspective that is not imitational ("I will believe this because the Quran asks me to believe in this") but a kind of witnessing. Imitational belief, for Nursi, is a simple non-denial. It is not yet a perspective that one actually, intellectual and affectively, inhabits as positively determinative of one's life choices. The ideal subject needs to *receive*, and *not simply repeat*, Quranic claims about the unseen. A Nursian subject engages in discursive practices around the idea of life after death for their own religious formation as believer, and not as a polemic against non-Muslims or unbelievers. Two aspects of this discursive practice are especially worthy of note.

First, Nursi wants an ideal subject to awaken to the moral implications of denying existence beyond life and death in this world, not only for people but for all beings. He wants the subject to awaken to the idea that when he denies the *continuity of existence* beyond this transient world, he is, ethically speaking, accusing that those creatures, and their observed existence, are unreal and essentially illusory and bound toward nonexistence. The subject ought to think to himself:

> If there were no permanent abodes, lofty mansions and everlasting stations . . . then it would be necessary to reject the true essences of wisdom, justice, beneficence and compassion. . . . For it is plain that this impermanent world and its contents cannot be a complete manifestation of their true essences. If there is no other place, *somewhere else*, where they can be manifested fully it then becomes necessary, with a lunacy like that of a man who denies the existence of the sun even though he sees its light filling the day, to deny the wisdom that we see in everything in front of our eyes; to deny the beneficence that we can observe in our soul and other things . . . to deny the compassion we see everywhere in operation.[62]

If the subject were to deny the existence of a "somewhere else" as a place where qualities that he observes and loves here, such as wisdom, beauty and justice, could manifest permanently and perfectly, the Nursian subject would be denying what he sees with his eyes, instances of wisdom and justice, however partial, in this world. It is an affective argument that the subject has with himself and that calls into question the subject's own integrity and even sanity, should he agree to deny that the qualities he observes in the world and on account of which he loves beings that display those qualities, have no real essence. The subject is asked to trust his perception of qualities such as justice and beauty, as perceptions of entities with a reality, an essence and a truly existing core "somewhere else." To believe in the hereafter is thus inseparably tied to seeing the sensible world (material or otherwise) as truthful, as a created reality and not simply a mental or linguistic illusion. The reality of the observed qualities is affirmed subjectively when one affirms the existence of a realm of existence beyond the present world, where the essence of these qualities must continue to exist after they cease to exist here. Believing in the hereafter is such an exercise of the affirmation of the existence of true essences of qualities and thus the value and qualities of the beings (from seeds to the stars) that exhibit those qualities.

Second, believing in the hereafter is about restoring dignity to beings as small as seeds and flowers and fruits, a dignity they would lose if human beings were to see them purely instrumentally, as means, for instance, through which human beings find the existence of eternity. The beings show other-than-themselves as the source of their existence when they perish and are unable to sustain themselves but to say nothing more of the transient beings is, for Nursi, to take an unacceptably utilitarian and instrumental approach toward them. One corrects for one's instrumental, religious "use" of their transience (to benefit oneself, i.e., to attain a belief perspective) by affirming that these things do not actually go into nonexistence but leave "permanent forms" and "everlasting meanings" in another realm, the hereafter, when they perish in the present realm. A subject can only give dignity back to beings which, so to speak, served him by perishing and connecting him to God *through* their transience (i.e., by displaying in dying that they were not the source of their own existence), by recognizing their endurance in another realm. Here is how Nursi puts it,

> As for the fruit serving us as sustenance, this is merely one out of many thousand wise purposes; it fulfills its purpose, expresses its meaning, and dies, being buried in our stomach. Since these transient beings yield eternal fruits in another place, leave their permanent forms of themselves and express their everlasting meanings; since they engage in ceaseless glorification of the Maker; and since a *human being becomes a human being by perceiving these aspects of things that are oriented to the hereafter*,[63] hence finding his way to eternity by means of the transient—since all this is true, there must be some other purpose for all these beings that are cast around between life and death, that are first gathered and then dispersed.[64]

Nursi continues and asks the subject to believe in the hereafter should he wish to save himself from thinking of other beings as merely "cast around between life and death" for the benefit of human beings. A Nursian subject thus moves to thinking about the hereafter in terms of the meaning and meaningfulness of the spiritual and moral qualities he witnesses in the world and from a desire to endow beings with permanent, non-instrumental value. To believe in the hereafter is to find wisdom, compassion and other such qualities meaningful, that is, real on account of their permanent meanings that are only possible in an eternal hereafter since the present world is a transient one. Moreover, the physical beings that die do not die in all senses—they exist eternally through the real, *eternal* meanings they express, meanings that human beings have the responsibility to affirm as real and eternally existing in a realm beyond this world. As far as the religious subject is concerned, the beings of this world are either condemned to nothingness, or given eternal reality and expression, according to his choice to either affirm or deny the existence of an everlasting life after death.

BELIEF IN DIVINE DETERMINING (*QADAR*)

Nursi teaches that the one who perfectly believes in God, the hereafter, angels, messengers and the revealed books (considered the fundamentals of belief in Islam) can then inhabit a state of being that is called Divine Determining or *qadar*. For people of many religious faiths, both the past and the present, Divine Determining is a critical yet challenging idea because it raises questions about the interaction of an eternal and absolute divine will with a limited and contingent human will, the possibility of human freedom and thus the question of human responsibility as well as the issue of theodicy.[65] Like the thinkers and theologians from other traditions, Muslim theologians continue to discuss these issues in breathtaking detail.[66] What is interesting for me here is the way that a *qadar*-centered discourse functions as a discursive practice for the goal of proper subject formation.

Nursi explicitly asserts that the reason *qadar* has a place in what he calls "matters of belief" at all, is to enable the subject to *feel responsible* for his actions while simultaneously disavowing all self-exalting claims to virtue or goodness. It is important to quote him at length on this point:

> Divine determining and the power of choice are aspects of belief pertaining to state (*ḥāl*) and conscience which show the final limits of Islam and belief; they are not theoretical matters and do not pertain to knowledge. That is to say, a believer attributes everything to Almighty God, even his actions and self, till finally the power of choice confronts him and he is not saved from obligation and responsibility. It (i.e., the power of choice) tells him: "You are responsible and under obligation." Then, so that he does not become proud due to the good things and perfections which issue from him,[67] Divine Determining confronts him saying: "Know your limits! the one who does them is not you. Yes, as to Divine determining and the power of choice . . . the former has entered among the matters of belief to save the soul from pride, and the latter to save it from shirking responsibility.[68]

One affirms one's agency, as a matter of responsibility, against the overreach of belief in God's unity, which may say that God does everything, good and bad. One avows *qadar* not as a matter of knowledge of God's predetermination or some religious creed but as an ethical, normative stance against the twin threats of pride and self-exoneration. *Qadar*, for Nursi, is not a theoretical matter. It is purely about inhabiting a perspective, a religious and religiously responsible state of being in a complex world, a world where human beings can act but where the grounds and results of their actions are not within their power to fully grasp and determine respectively. The ambivalence of Quranic teachings about divine and human agency both tracks, and inscribes as inevitable, the ambivalence of living religiously and responsibly as a free and responsible, *religious* human being.

An ideal religious subject ought to feel responsible for his bad actions and feel no sense of achievement on account of his good deeds. That sounds unfair! One could say: "Hey! If I get the blame for doing the bad things, it means you are saying that I am the one who did them. And if I am responsible for my bad actions then I must be responsible for my good actions as well. And if so, I am right to say that I merit praise or reward for doing the good actions!" A Nursian subject could respond to this complaint in two ways. First, Nursi notes that people hav already been made, by God, to incline toward goodness, which is based on the Quranic concept of the *fitra*, that is, the notion that human nature is essentially wired for goodness (e.g., Q. 30:30). To give an example, if I was walking down the street and saw a person lying on the ground and bleeding, I'd instantly feel some need to help or at least the desire that the man is helped by someone. Thus, "in terms of one's natural instincts and conscience, it is much harder to intend to kill someone than to intend to save his life. Hence, when a human being makes a bad choice and goes against his *fitra*, he takes complete responsibility for it. Whereas, when he follows his *fitra*, he gets credit only insofar as he did not block the goodness he is already wired to do."[69]

Second, Nursi argues (and thus a Nursian subject could argue) that bad actions are essentially acts of destruction and negation. "While harder on the conscience, destroying needs much less energy or actual effort than building something. As Nursi explains elsewhere, there are *many* conditions for something to exist while the absence of only *one* of these conditions will result in its absence or destruction."[70] For instance, if I am part of a crew but neglect my duty and the ship sinks, I am to take all the blame even though I am just one member of a much larger crew. In contrast, if I do my duty well in the ship, and the ship sails nicely, I don't take all the praise for it, because other people in the crew also did their part.[71]

Earlier, I noted that supplication is the core of human agency for Nursi's ideal subject. Summarizing the transformative, subjective implications of believing in Divine determining, Nursi uses the metaphor of a human body as representing human will, with two proverbial hands: one hand does good actions and the other bad actions. The hand that does bad, Nursi says, should be seen as long and effective in its reach—it is easy to destroy and mess many things up at once. The other hand, the one that does good is to be seen as very short in its reach and weak. Given that this is the situation, the person should adopt the attitude of "seeking forgiveness" to counterbalance the extensive reach of the bad hand even as some good issues through his weak and short hand. The short hand doing good should practice supplication, asking the beneficial results to be created through divine will and power. The goodness that is created through its "supplication" should be received as a response and a gift, with due gratitude.[72]

DIALECTICS OF BELIEF AND MULTIPLE INDIVIDUALITIES

I have signalled this before and now it is time to address this important matter head on: in Nursi's teachings, all acts of reading the indicative meanings, all perceptions and affirmations of the names of God and all the support and comfort a subject finds in his belief perspectives—these are all fluid and fleeting states of being and never, experientially or epistemically, complete and final resting places. Thought is terminal but its movement from a beginning point to some terminal point repeats, again and again, and seldom along identical endpoints and pathways. The best evidence that this is the case comes from Nursi's method of self-narration. Here is Nursi, in old age and having spent a lifetime teaching about and trying to model belief in God and life after death, remembering his response to news of the death of Abdurrahman, his beloved nephew and student:

> Then one or two months later while thinking of once again, passing a happy worldly life together with Abdurrahman, alas, I suddenly received news of his death. I was so shaken by the news that *five years later I am still under the effect of it*. It afflicted me with a grief, sorrow, and sense of separation far exceeding the tortuous captivity, aloneness, exile, old age, and illness I was then suffering. Half of my private world had died with the death of my mother, and now with Abdurrahman's death, the other half died. My ties with the world were now completely cut. For if he had lived, he could have been both a powerful help in my duties which looked to the Hereafter, and a worthy successor to fill my place completely after me, and a most self-sacrificing friend and consolation. He would have been my cleverest student and companion. . . . Yes, in regard to humanity, such losses are extremely distressing and painful for people like me. It's true that outwardly I was trying to endure it, but a fierce storm was raging in my spirit. If *from time to time*, solace proceeding from the Qur'an's light had not consoled me, it would not have been possible for me to endure it. At that time, I used to wander alone in the mountains and valleys of Barla. Sitting in lonely places amid my sorrows, pictures of the happy life I had spent in former times with my loyal students like Abdurrahman passed through my imagination like the cinema; being swiftly affected due to old age and exile, they broke my resistance. Then suddenly the sacred meaning of the verse, "Everything shall perish save His countenance; His is the command, and to Him shall you return [Qur'an, 28:88] was unfolded to me. It caused me to declare: "O Enduring One [*Ya Baqī*], it is You Who is Enduring! O Enduring One, only You are Enduring!" and truly consoled me.[73]

I quote this passage at length because it shows Nursi's description of his thought process. Even after spending years teaching about life after death and the joys of belief in the hereafter, Nursi frankly shares with his readers that his practical relationship with those beliefs was a dynamic one. By narrating his sorrowful state along with what delivered him from that state, Nursi illustrates that belief does not transform a person into an unfeeling, unaffected, emotionally "strong," "why should I be sad? I believe in the hereafter!" kind of a person. Rather, one weeps and cries in pain and sorrow, in the loss of relations through which one had hoped to bring good into the world and only *time to time* does the Quranic guidance intervene and lends solace and, sometimes, rushes into the subject's mind, driving him to turn to the Enduring One, God. Should we think that Nursi's belief in life after death was simply weak so that even after spending years teaching about it and proclaiming it, he was mournful and sad about his late nephew? I don't think so. I think Nursi is presenting a model of being a believer that moves along authentically and viscerally, with life as human beings actually experience it, in its paradoxical fullness.

A second clue about the dynamic and fluid nature of belief comes from Nursi's conception of the individual. Nursi describes an individual as comprising of multiple individualities and thus in constant need of renewing their belief. Evidently building on the mainstream Islamic notion (Ashari/Maturidi) of continuous creation, according to which the universe is being created and recreated at every instant, Nursi suggests: "Since man himself and the world in which he lives are being continuously renewed, he needs constantly to renew his belief. For in reality each individual human being consists of many individuals. He may be considered as a different individual to the number of years of his life, or rather to the number of days or even the hours of his life."[74] His view of constantly renewed individuality grounds his view about the need to constantly renew belief and explains why he thinks religious formation is an endless, dynamic process. Moreover, this multiplicity of one's individuality, that is, being a new person every hour of one's life, is not only diachronic but also synchronic.

Again, talking about himself, as he often does as a pedagogical strategy, he says he has "at least three personalities." First, in relation to his role as a teacher of the Quran, second as a worshipper turned to God seeking refuge in Him, and third as a person who inclines toward hypocrisy, vanity and other deeply ingrained, habitual, moral ills.[75] Thus, Nursi thinks that individuals may have different personalities or aspects to their personhood and thus perspectives specific to those aspects of their personhood. To attain a belief perspective in one aspect may not mean that one has also attained it in all aspects of one's personality. In fact, perspectives of the various personalities within each person may diverge significantly while in an ideal subject—for instance, the prophets of God—all these personalities converge.[76] Be that as it may, the Nursian religious subject must act in the world to express his belief perspectives—what his moral agency and moral subjectivity ought to look like shall be our concern in the following chapter.

NOTES

1. In this chapter, I use "belief" and "faith" interchangeably, simply because neither of them is an adequate translation of the term *īmān* that Nursi uses. For my purposes here, the term itself matters less than the meanings and practical implications that it has, as we shall see, in Nursi's discourses.

2. Scholar of American religion, Tracy Fessenden has argued how New England Protestant claims about their access to the living word of God, inwardness and rational belief (as opposed to what was disparaged as the undeveloped religious lives of "brutish" and spiritually inferior Indians) were developed in Protestant terms. The language of inner belief was used to dispossess and dehumanize the natives. As we embark on an analysis of Nursi's teachings, let us be clear that his ideas about private, inner belief, and a person's interaction with the living word of God, in the Quran and in creation, bear little relation to the use of such concepts in the early Protestant discourses that Fessenden superbly documents. See Tracy Fessenden, *Culture and Redemption: Religion, the Secular and American Literature* (Princeton, NJ: Princeton University Press, 2007), 15–33.

3. "For while being apparently open, the doors of the universe are in fact closed." Nursi, *The Words: From the Risale-i Nur Collection*, trans. Sukran Vahide (Istanbul: Sozler Publications, 2004), 558. For a discussion of why Nursi considers the Quran an indispensable guide for human reason in understanding reality, see Yamina Mermer and Isra Yazicioglu, "Said Nursi's Qur'anic Hermeneutics," in *The Companion to Said Nursi Studies*, edited by Ian Markham and Z. Sayilgan (Eugene, OR: Pickwick Publications, 2017), 55–56.

4. For another discussion of belief, and related concepts of gratitude and security and contentment, in the Quran, see Toshihiko Izutsu, *Ethico-Religious Concepts in the Quran* (McGill: Queens University Press, 2002). For a contemporary discussion of the way *iman* has often been mistranslated as "faith" and "belief" by scholars of Islam, see Robert Kevin Jaques, "Belief," In *Key Themes for the Study of Islam*, ed. Jamal Elias (Oxford: Oneworld Publications, 2010), 53–71.

5. Indeed, for Nursi, transience and death are major reasons for human being to seek the light of the Quran. Thus, for instance, in a parable, the guided person confronts the atheist person saying: "If you have the means to kill death, and [make] decline and transience to disappear from the world, and remove poverty and [weakness] from human being, and close the door of the grave, then tell us and let us hear it! Otherwise, be silent! The Qur'an reads the universe in the vast mosque of creation. Let us listen to it. Let us be illuminated with that light." Nursi, *Words*, 44 (modified translation; replaced words are indicated in square brackets here, and in other quotes, from Vahide's translation).

6. While search for meaning and the existential choice for or against meaningfulness of the world is not necessarily new in the Islamic tradition, Nursi's emphasis on it is noteworthy. Charles Taylor would probably classify Nursi as a "modern thinker" as he suggests that the crisis of meaning is a quintessentially modern crisis. For a discussion see Charles Taylor, *Sources of the Self: The Making of the Modern Identity* (Cambridge, MA: Harvard University Press, 1989), 16–19.

7. For a helpful discussion of Nursi's Quranic hermeneutics, see Mermer et al., "Said Nursi's Qur'anic Hermeneutics," 51–66.

8. "The Quran spreads its light to the thousands of levels of those it addresses, the understanding and intelligence of whom are all different.... It has not lost its freshness . . . it teaches every ordinary person in a most easy, skillful and comprehensible manner." Nursi, *Words*, 409. Here we see Nursi's attempt to tie the Quran's timeless relevance and freshness to the idea that it speaks to all ages and to all humans at their own level. See also Nursi's claim that "all classes of men, from the most lowly and stupid to the cleverest take their full share of the Quran's instruction." Nursi, *Words*, 473.

9. Nursi does not reject Sufism as a path but ultimately thinks his way is different and that *tariqa* style of spiritual journey that is centered around a spiritual master is not the best at this time. Nursi also seems to have felt that it is time to make the subtle mysteries that Sufis talked about apparent and known to reflective and questioning minds. Cf. Alan Godlas, who suggests that Nursi's use of Sufi terminology is sufficient to place him among the Sufis. Alan Godlas, "A Religiological Analysis of Nursi's View of Sufism Expressed in the 'Nine Allusions' (Telvihât-ı Tis'a) of the Risale-i Nur," *Islam and Christian Muslim Relations* 19 (2008) 1: 39–52.

10. Here, I am using Yamina Mermer and Redha Ameur's rendering of Nursi's *mana-i ismi* and *mana-i harfi*. See their "Beyond the Modern: Sa'id al-Nursi's View of Science," *Islam and Science* 2 (Winter 2004), 137. Colin Turner renders these terms as "self-referential" and "other

indicative" respectively. *The Qur'an Revealed: A Critical Analysis of Said Nursi's Epistles of Light* (Berlin: Gerlach Press, 2013), 96.

11. Turner, *Quran Revealed*, 298.

12. As Nursi puts it, "All the letters of a book describe themselves to the extent of a letter and point to their own existence in one way, while they describe their writer with ten words and show him in many ways. For example: 'The one who wrote me has fine hand-writing. His pen is red, and so on.' In just the same way, all the letters of the mighty book of the universe point to themselves to the extent of their own [tiny] size and [form], but describe the Names of the Pre-Eternal Inscriber like an ode, and testify to the One they signify and point to His Names to the number of their attributes." *Words*, 307 (modified translation).

13. Nursi, *Words*, 319–320.

14. Causality is a vast subject in Islamic thought and has been discussed as a theological issue for over a thousand years by Muslims. For a detailed interpretive discussion see Yamina B. Mermer, "Induction, Science and Causation: Some Critical Reflections," *Islamic Studies* 35 (1996) 3: 243–282. See also, Isra Yazicioglu, *Understanding the Qur'anic Miracle Stories in the Modern Age* (University Park, PA: Penn State University Press, 2013), 15–68 and 123–148. Here, I do not engage the causality discussion per se, as I interpret it not as abstract doctrine but as part of lived practices of belief for a Nursian subject.

15. Richard Frank, "The Structure of Created Causality according to al-Ash'arī," *Studia Islamica* 25 (1966): 13–76.

16. Nursi, *Words*, 436 (italics added).

17. Nursi, *Words*, 435 (italics added). As Muhammad Asad notes, "*al-asma' al-husna*" (lit., "the most perfect [or 'most goodly'] names"), which occurs in the Qur'an four times—i.e., [in 7:180] as well as in 17:110, 20:8 and 59:24—it is to be borne in mind that the term *ism* [singular of *asma*] is, primarily, a word applied to denote the substance or the intrinsic attributes of an object under consideration, while the term *al-husna* is the plural form of *al-ahsan* ("that which is best" or "most goodly"). Thus, the combination *al-asma' al-husna* may be appropriately rendered as "the attributes of perfection," a term reserved in the Qur'an "for God alone." Asad, *The Message of the Qur'an* (Gibraltar, Spain: Dar al-Andalus, 1984), 231.

18. This is a quote from "10th Window" of "33rd Word" as translated in the forthcoming work *Living the Quran with Joy and Purpose: Selections on Tawhid from Said Nursi's Epistle of Light*, forthcoming, trans. with intro. and notes by Yamina Bouguenaya and Isra Yazicioglu (Piscataway, NJ: Gorgias Press, 2020). Also see Nursi, *Words*, 691.

19. Nursi, *Words*, 691.

20. 33rd Word, "24th Window" in *Selections on Tawhid from Said Nursi*; see also Nursi, *Words*, 708.

21. 33rd Word, "24th Window" in *Selections on Tawhid from Said Nursi*; see also Nursi, *Words*, 709.

22. 33rd Word, "24th Window" in *Selections on Tawhid from Said Nursi*, see also Nursi, *Words*, 709.

23. Nursi's reasoning seems to be that if the seeming causes were real causes of existence, they themselves could not have lost existence. For instance, we may think that parents give life to their offspring. But when a parent dies, we might say that her passing indicates she was not the real cause of the child's life. After their death, we could say that parents were only *seeming* causes. If they were real causes of human life, they could have caused themselves to continue existing and thereby cause their effects (themselves) to continue existing. It seems to me that some such logic is at work here in Nursi's teaching and he wants his reader to think in this way to attain a particular standpoint toward death.

24. Nursi, "Fourth Indication" of "14th Note of "17th Flash," in *Selections on Tawhid from Said Nursi*.

25. Nursi, *Words*, 320 (modified translation).

26. Nursi, *Words*, 320.

27. Nursi, *Words*, 563. Nursi does not think all philosophy, as an intellectual endeavor, is somehow illegitimate. His objections are very specific and targeted toward a way of reasoning that is unenlightened by revelation and materialist/naturalist. For a discussion of reason as

pivotal to Islamic theology from the earliest times, see John Walbridge, *God and Logic in Islam: The Caliphate of Reason* (Cambridge: Cambridge University Press, 2011).

28. Nursi, *Words*, 719.

29. Nursi, *Letters*, 286–287. He also notes, "It is as though all beings are making supplication with Uways al-Qarani through their tongues of disposition, and are saying: *'O God! You are our Sustainer, for we are mere slaves; we are powerless to sustain and raise ourselves. That is to say, the One Who sustains us is You! And it is You Who is the Creator, for we are creatures, we are being made! And it is You Who is the Provider, for we are in need of provision, we have no power! That is to say, the One Who creates us and bestows on us our provisions is You! And it is You Who is the Owner, because we are totally owned property; someone other than us has power of disposal over us. That is to say, it is You Who is our Owner! And You, You are Mighty! You possess grandeur and sublimity! As for us we look to our baseness and see that there are manifestations of a mightiness on us. That is to say, we are mirrors to Your mightiness! And it is You Who is the Possessor of Absolute Riches, because we are utterly wanting, and riches are bestowed on us that our indigent hands could not obtain. That is to say, it is You Who is rich, the One Who gives is You! And You, You are the Ever-Living, Ever-Enduring One, because we, we are dying, and in our dying and in our being resurrected we see the manifestation of a perpetual giver of life! And You, You are Ever-Enduring, because we see Your continuation and perpetualness in our demise and transience! And the One Who responds to us and answers us, the Granter of Gifts is You. For all of us beings, we are ever crying out and requesting, entreating, imploring by tongue and by state. And our desires are brought about, our aims are achieved. In other words, the One Who answers us is You! . . .'* And so on. Every creature, universal and particular, is, like Uways al-Qarani, a mirror, in a form that has the meaning of supplication. All proclaim the Divine power and perfection through their impotence and poverty and deficiency" (Ibid., italics in original text).

30. Nursi, *Words*, 719.

31. Nursi, *Words*, 719.

32. The notion of selling connotes the exchange is reciprocal and that the subject should expect something in return. In Nursi's teaching, that something is not simple, in some simplistic and unrelated way, God's reward or Paradise in an afterlife but, indicative meaning, here and now.

33. Nursi, *Words*, 39.

34. Nursi, *Words*, 61–62.

35. Nursi, *Words*, 15–16.

36. Nursi, "Twentieth Letter, First Station," in *Selections on Tawhid from Said Nursi*. See also Nursi, *Letters*, 264–266.

37. Nursi, "23rd Word, First Station, Fifth Point" in *Selections on Tawhid from Said Nursi*. See also Nursi, *Words*, 326–327. Nursi also discusses supplication in his "24th Letter, First Addendum," in *Letters*, 353–54.

38. Nursi, *Letters*, 357. For an interesting application of Nursi's understanding of supplication to human psychology, see Mustafa Tekke and P. J. Watson, "Supplication and the Muslim Personality: Psychological Nature and Functions of Prayer as Interpreted by Said Nursi," *Mental Health, Religion and Culture* 20, no. 2 (2017) 143–53.

39. Or to put it in the words of the famous Muslim sage and Sufi master Mawlana Jalal al-din al-Rumi, "From Thee (come) both the prayer and the answer." Rumi, *Mathnawi*. Book II: 692, trans. by R. A. Nicholson (Gibb Memorial Trust, 2016), accessed via http://www.masnavi.net/1/25/eng/2/692/.

40. Hence, Nursi suggests, in the core Quranic prayer *Thee alone do we worship* (Q. 1:5), "we" includes all the creatures, which the ideal believing subject ought to intend in their prayer. Nursi, *The Rays: From the Risale-i Nur Collection*, trans. Sukran Vahide (Istanbul: Sozler Nesriyat, 2002), 584–585.

41. Nursi, *Words*, 241.

42. Nursi, *Words*, 241–242.

43. Of course, as he notes repeatedly, Nursi does consider following the Prophetic example (*sunna*) important. His definition of what constitutes the prophetic example, however, is much

broader than a basis for deriving positive Islamic Law. See Nursi's treatise on the *Sunna*, *Words*, 243–252.

44. Nursi, *Words*, 243.
45. Nursi, *Words*, 244–245.
46. Nursi, *Words*, 248.
47. Nursi, "First Flash," in *Selections on Tawhid from Said Nursi*, see also, *The Flashes: From the Risale-i Nur Collection*, trans. Sukran Vahide (Istanbul: Sözler Neşriyat, 1995), 18.
48. See Mermer, Yamina B., "Bediuzzaman Said Nursi's Scriptural Approach to the Problem of Evil" *Journal of Scriptural Reasoning* 4, no. 1 (2004); and Isra Yazicioglu, "Affliction, Patience and Prayer: Reading Job (p) in the Qur'an," in *The Journal of Scriptural Reasoning* 4, no. 1 (2004). Both articles available online at http://etext.lib.virginia.edu/journals/ssr/issues/volume4/number1/ssr04-01-e01.htm.
49. Ibn 'Arabi and Rumi, who are considered among major spiritual giants of the Islamic tradition, also see prophets as representing human being's spiritual journey, including their miracles. See, for instance, Jane Clark, "Universal Meanings in Ibn 'Arabi's *Fuṣuṣ al-ḥikam*: Some Comments on the Chapter of Moses," *Journal of the Muhyiddin Ibn 'Arabi Society* 38 (2005): 105–129 and Isra Yazicioglu, "Engaging with Abraham and His Knife: Interpretation of Abraham's Sacrifice in the Muslim Tradition," in *Interpreting Abraham: Journeys to Moriah*, ed. Bradley Beach and Matthew Powell (Minneapolis: Fortress Press, 2014), 73–78.
50. Nursi, *Words*, 261. For a detailed discussion of implications of Quranic miracle stories for Nursi, see Yazicioglu, *Qur'anic Miracle Stories*, 149–163.
51. Nursi, *Words*, 263.
52. Nursi, *Words*, 263.
53. Yazicioglu, *Qur'anic Miracle Stories*, 155.
54. While this is a noteworthy point by Nursi, he expresses it in only several pages out of thousands of pages that he wrote as part of his *magnum opus*. So, it would be unfair to present his work as focused on making connections between Islam and contemporary science as Muzaffar Iqbal seems to do in his survey, "Scientific Commentary on the Quran," in *The Study Quran: A New Translation and Commentary*, in *Study Quran*, ed. S. Hossein Nasr et al. (New York: Harper One, 2015), 1684–1685.
55. Nursi, *Words*, 61.
56. Alasdair McIntyre, *Dependent Rational Animals: Why Human Beings Need the Virtues* (La Salle, IL: Open Court Press, 2001), 1–11; 81–82.
57. Nursi, *Rays*, 244–247.
58. Nursi, *Rays*, 244.
59. Nursi, *Rays*, 244.
60. Nursi also discusses evidences for life after death in many places, a most extended discussion is in "Tenth Word," Nursi, *Words*, 59–72 and its addendums 73–133.
61. *[Whoever] attest the most beautiful, We shall ease his way unto ease* . . . (Quran, 92:6–7). This translation is from Nasr et.al, *Study Quran*, 1523.
62. Nursi, *Words*, 97–98.
63. Nursi is explicit here that the ideal subject attains ideal subjectivity on account of his perspective—which aspects of the things in nature he perceives (or fails or refuses to perceive). In any case, ideal subjectivity is tied to a perception of the eternal aspects and meanings of transient things.
64. Nursi, *Words*, 98–99 (modified translation).
65. For a discussion of the theme in important Muslim thinkers, see, Maria De Cillis, *Freewill and Predestination in Islamic Thought: Theoretical Compromises in the Works of Avicenna, Al-Ghazālī and Ibn 'Arabī* (New York: Routledge Press, 2014).
66. For a good summary with a focus on Nursi's theology, see Isra Yazicioglu, "A Graceful Reconciliation: Said Nursi on Free Will and Destiny," in *The Companion to Said Nursi Studies*, eds. Ian Markham and Z. Sayilgan (Eugene, OR: Pickwick Publications, 2017), 129–145.
67. I think it is noteworthy that by saying "due to the good things and perfections *which issue from him*," Nursi is in effect avoiding talking about good things and perfections as moral virtues or character traits. These small turns of phrases, in a Nursian subject's life, ought to

134 *Chapter 3*

slowly and gradually augur significant changes in their perspective on everything, including themselves.

68. Nursi, *Words*, 477.
69. Yazicioglu, *Said Nursi on Freewill*, 136. Nursi notes "Yes, as the Qur'an states, man is totally responsible for his evils, for it is he who wants the evils," *Words*, 478.
70. Yazicioglu, *Said Nursi on Freewill*, 136. Nursi's use of "condition" is intentional here. For, apparent causes are not genuine creators, they are simply conditions which the Creator takes into account in His unaided creative action.
71. Yazicioglu, *Said Nursi on Freewill*, 136.
72. Nursi, *Words*, 339.
73. Nursi, *Flashes*, 312 (italics added).
74. Nursi, *Letters*, 383–384.
75. Nursi, *Letters*, 378.
76. Nursi, *Letters*, 378.

Chapter Four

Nursian Believer as Moral Subject

At the end of his philosophical work entitled *Ethics, Demonstrated in Geometrical Order*, the Danish Jewish thinker Baruch Spinoza says something that, I think, Nursi would want an ideal moral subject to also affirm: "Blessedness is not the reward of virtue but virtue itself; nor do we enjoy it because we restrain our lusts; on the contrary, because we enjoy it, we are able to restrain them." We have seen in the previous chapter how a Nursian subject, seeing himself as a mirror to the beautiful names of God, takes joy in a fragile blessedness that he sees in the existence of his connection to the divine, the result of choosing a belief perspective, and not as an entitative or substantive blessedness that inheres in him and that could make him more blessed than some other, not-so-blessed and inferior others. The question I want to focus on now is: How do Nursian belief perspectives ought to express themselves in everyday lived life? Nursi's elaboration of blessedness, unlike Spinoza, is not centered around the lusts that one is able to restrain therewith but the kinds of blessed intersubjective relations a properly formed religious subject may establish with other beings in the world and the kind of moral agent he ought to become in the process.

According to Nursi, standpoints of belief enable the best of human potentials to come forth. In what follows, I describe and analyze examples of how an ideal Nursian moral subject ought to think about, and respond to, things and events in his life such that his responses and interactions with other beings, human and otherwise, would be consistent with the subject's belief perspectives discussed in the previous chapter. First we shall see how a particular perspective on temporality, transience and life after death ought to inform a subject's relationship with intimate others. Then we move to an analysis of a Nursian subject's ethics in asymmetric relations of exchange, an ethics that is grounded in a standpoint that negates natural causality, in the sense discussed in the previous chapter. We shall see how a Nursian moral subject responds to and inhabits social hierarchies that emerge in various kinds of social relations and interactions. We shall then take a quick look at the moral concerns that a Nursian subject would nurture toward consumption and the environment and the kinds of theological reasoning that would inform his response to the same. Next, we move to an analysis of the ways in which a Nursian moral subject would negotiate the conflicting demands of seeking personal truth and the strength that is to be found in bonds of brotherhood and cohesive community ties. The following section analyzes how a Nursian subject would draw on religious perspectives and discourses to respond to injustices and oppressions that he may suffer at the hands of others. We shall then, all too briefly, reflect about the gendered nature of Nursian moral subjectivity and evaluate how we might understand or interpret those aspects of Nursi's thought. Finally, we cursorily analyze Nursi's counsel that the ideal subject ought to not engage in politics and political action and instead prefer a life of service to God.

TEMPORALITY, RELATIONSHIPS, AND MORAL AGENCY

According to Nursi, belief in a life after death expands the perception of temporal frame within which the moral subject understands and experiences his life and relationships. If the subject doesn't see his life in the context of eternal, unending life, if this life on earth is the only time frame for the subject, then his human potentials do not have enough room to fully flourish. For Nursi, "the virtues he acquires like zeal, love, brotherhood, and humanity are to the extent of the fleeting present, which is squeezed between the past and the future, which are both non-existent, and dead, and [dark]."[1] In such a tight time frame, one cannot fully express one's human potentials. Nursi notes, "For example, he loves and serves his father, brother, wife, nation, and country, whom he formerly did not know and after parting from them, will never see again. He would very rarely be able to achieve complete loyalty and sincerity, and his virtues and perfections would diminish proportionately."[2] To exercise these values would be difficult and inferior without an eternal dimension because the relationships themselves will lack the durability and longevity necessary for a fuller and deeper manifestation of values such as compassion and loyalty:

> Belief in the hereafter . . . expands the present moment so that it encompasses the past and the future . . . thinking of his father being the realm of bliss . . . and the fraternity of his brothers continuing to eternity, and knowing that his wife will be a beautiful companion in Paradise, he will love and respect them, be kindly and assist them. He will not exploit the important duties which are for relationships in that broad/eternal sphere of life and existence . . . his good

qualities and attainments will advance to the degree he is successful in being earnestly loyal and truly sincere and his humanity will increase/flourish . . . he becomes the most eminent and happy guest in the universe . . . the best loved and most acceptable servant of the universe's Owner.[3]

Compassion and loyalty to others and foregoing exploitation and hatred are here linked to a moral subject's standpoint toward the virtues of compassion and loyalty within the framework of believing in an eternal life. The hereafter is the continuation, and hence the longevity, of the social bonds and values one experiences and manifests in the world in one's intersubjective encounters.[4] Notice there is still no perfect sincerity and loyalty with belief in life after death but there is greater durability and increase in loyalty commensurate with the subject's sincere effort, an increase that seems to be worth the effort. The subject goes from having a short-term, instrumental and exploitative relation with one's spouse or partner to finding himself, ideally, able to respond with deep and abiding loyalty and love. The subject should live a life and love others such that he would want to live and love others for all eternity. That is the challenge Nursi presents to the ideal moral subject.[5]

But the perception of the moment as part of an eternal life does not simply enhance the natural instincts. It also complicates and shapes them. Consider what Nursi narrates in his treatise for the sick:

> Although I am not worthy of it, for the past eight or nine years, a number of young people have come to me in connection with illness, seeking my prayers. I have noticed that each of those ill youths had begun to think of the hereafter to a greater degree than other young people. The sick ones lacked the heedlessness of healthy youth. They were saving themselves from animal desires and heedlessness. So I would consider them and then suggest to them that their illness were a divine bounty within the limits of their endurance. I would say: "I am not opposed to this illness of yours, my brother. I don't feel compassion and pity for you because of your illness, so that I should pray for you. Try to be patient until illness awakens you completely.[6]

In other words, it seems as if invoking life after death may sometimes make one less concerned about the other's physical well-being! To be fair, Nursi's immediate stated goal in this particular treatise is to help people see the practical value of belief in God and the hereafter for their own lives. And he wants people to notice how apparently undesirable things can awaken them to their need for God. Thus taken in its original context, one could be charitable and say that his point here is not to counsel or advocate against compassion for the sick. But I think one can raise a legitimate question about the unintended ethical implications of thinking about the well-being of others primarily in terms of their transcendental well-being. Those consequences jump out at the reader in Nursi's blunt and cold admission, "I don't feel compassion and pity for you because of your illness." Now we may grant that pity, even if compassionate, is not a particularly admirable attitude toward others who may be suffering. Here we must frankly confront the fact that most religious thinkers, like Nursi, would prioritize otherworldly well-being over worldly well-being and might be willing to tolerate worldly suffering as long as it is within bearable limits and turns people toward God for refuge and help. The refrain about "limits of endurance" needs to be underlined so that one does not inadvertently endorse or exalt complacence about relieving unbearable and relievable suffering.

HIERARCHY, INDEBTEDNESS AND AN ETHICS OF CONJUNCTION

We have already seen that denial of real causal power to apparent causes is a key feature of Nursian religious subjectivity. In Nursi's teachings, this denial has real-world moral implications and ought to find practical expression in intersubjective encounters, especially those where there is exchange and there exists the possibility that one party in the exchange would feel indebted to the other. In intersubjective encounters and exchanges, a Nursian moral subject practices what I call an *ethics of conjunction* and shuns what we may call an *ethics of causality*. An ethics of conjunction, I think, protects human dignity from moral injury that may result due to the acceptance of favors from human benefactors. Nursi talks about this feature of moral subjectivity when he narrates an autobiographical incident:

> Some of the gifted disciples of the *Risale-i Nur*, such as Husrev and Refet, had felt overly indebted to me as their teacher. In that regard, they confused conjunction with causation. They thought: "If our teacher had not come here and taught us, we would not have learned these great lessons of the Qur'an. Therefore, he is the cause of our benefiting from these precious lessons." Yet in reality what has happened is a mere conjunction of two blessings from God: God has kindly blessed them with precious Qur'anic lessons and He has kindly blessed me with the gift of articulating the precious teachings of the Qur'an. Therefore, my friends, know that God's compassion is the real cause ['*illa*] of both blessings. I also made a similar mistake of confusing conjunction with causation in my relationship to you, my dear brothers and sisters. I have felt extremely indebted to you for your support of this service of faith, in your transcribing of the *Risale-i Nur*. I was saying to myself: "If they were not with me, how could I, a weak . . . person, serve the Qur'an?" Then, I realized that God first blessed you with the sacred gift of supporting this service to the Qur'an and then blessed me with the gift of a successful service. These two blessings are conjoined but they are not each other's cause. That is why, instead of thanking you, I congratulate you for receiving this blessing. And so you too instead of feeling obliged to me, congratulate me, pray for me.[7]

Nursi's account of his relationship with his supporters, the scribes who helped with writing the *Risale*, and their gratitude to him as their beloved teacher, provides a good illustration of Nursi's ethics of conjunction. In social exchange, material or nonmaterial, where any kind of gift-giving is involved or anything valuable flows from one party to another, hierarchy and indebtedness can naturally arise. The benefactor may or may not feel proud but perhaps, more to the point here, the beneficiary tends to feel indebted to the benefactor, obliged to exercise deference, respect and gratitude toward him. This sense of indebtedness, we can surmise, can then produce various kinds of ethically problematic attitudes: students who feel obliged to their teacher in this way, for instance, may not criticize the teacher even if it is warranted. An ethics of causation can inscribe an asymmetric and unethical system of patron-client relations—goods in return for loyalty. Examples can be multiplied but it is clear that for Nursi, there is a theological imperative for a moral subject to engage in a social exchange of benefits through an ethics of conjunction and thus to respond to goods received by *celebrating the good* that comes via others without feeling indebted to them. It is important to note that Nursi's counsel against gratitude to others does not mean that the moral subject should be ungrateful or disrespectful to human benefactors. The choice is not between gratitude and contemptuous disregard. Rather, the choice is between seeing others as the source of the good or else congratulating the other for being a beneficiary of God's blessings and for then passing along to others the blessings that are conjoined to them.

But sometimes when one is sharing with others, even if one understands that what one is sharing is God's blessing, one may feel burdened. At one point, for instance, Nursi's interlocutor expresses to him that he is burdened by the duty to provide for not only his own wife and children but also his old, needy and infirm parents.[8] In his response, Nursi also includes aunts and uncles among those one should care for, if they are in need of support. Nursi reminds the questioner that the elderly parents once took care of the questioner when he was helpless and needy. He then asks the interlocutor to engage in an intellectual exercise, in light of Quranic verses.[9] As an ideal subject, the person should think differently about what he initially feels is a strained livelihood. Nursi says,

> O you who struggles to secure his livelihood! The means of plenty and mercy in your house, and the repeller of disaster, is that elderly or blind relative of yours, whom you belittle. Beware, do not say: "My income is little, I have difficulty in making ends meet," for if it was not for the plenty resulting from their presence, your circumstances would have been even more straitened. . . . Yes, the All-Glorious and Munificent Creator, Who, as the universe testifies, is infinitely Merciful, Compassionate, Bountiful, and Generous, provides infants with the finest of sustenance when His sends them into this world, causing it to flow into their mouths from the springs of their mother's breasts. So

too, He provides, in the form of plenty, the sustenance of the elderly, who are like children though even more in need and deserving of kindness and compassion. He does not charge the avaricious and miserly with their livelihood.[10]

An ideal subject would aim for two sorts of perspectival transformations with these words. First, he is to see that he has whatever little he has (and he does feel it is little), not because he deserved to have it but because of the needy others, parents in this case, who God put in his charge. Their presence is to be seen as the cause, rather the condition, because of which God has given him whatever means he finds himself able to acquire. One is to see one's means as having the purpose of meeting the needs of such others as are under one's charge. But then the ideal subject needs to take a second step. He is asked to expand his sense of the amount of compassion that is possible in intersubjective relations through analogical reflection about the compassion manifest in the natural order. The subject ought to reflect on the mercy and compassion manifest in a mother's suckling of an infant. This reflection should lessen his burdens about caring for dependents because it should increase his capacity, to use Nursian language, manifest God's compassion in the world. One should feel like a proverbial mother, suckling its young with milk that she did not create but the sharing of which with her hungry infant brings her, Nursi could only have supposed, greater joy and fulfilment than withholding it. The larger point here is that the Nursian subject ought to see the compassion of God in all relationships of dependence in the world. But one may ask, why the conjunction, if it is all from God? Why is one's elderly parents' or uncle's provision from God linked with one's livelihood? How does one understand one's privilege (or lack thereof) compared to others?

For Nursi, the differences in the levels of livelihood that might arise or remain, within a framework of justice and compassion, should be considered intentional. Nursi invokes the wisdom in fasting to elaborate on the differences in means that people have. Nursi says,

> Human beings have been created differently with regard to their livelihoods. As a consequence of the difference, God Almighty invites the rich to assist the poor, so that through the hunger experienced in fasting, the rich can truly understand the pains and hunger which the poor suffer. If there was no fasting, there would be many self-indulgent rich unable to perceive just how grievous is hunger and poverty and how needy of compassion are those who suffer them. Compassion for one's fellow men is an essential of true thankfulness. Whoever a person is, there will always be someone poorer than himself in some respect. He is enjoined to be compassionate toward that person. If he was not himself compelled to suffer hunger, he would be unable give the person—by means of compassion—the help and assistance which he is obliged to offer.[11]

The ideal subject ought to see the conjunction between his greater means and the dependence of others on him as a means for him to feel and exercise gratitude toward the bestower, God. In the face of another who needs what one has, one can actually feel and affirm the value of what one has and thus become grateful to God for it. In a sense, Nursi is saying that my ability to feel the value of something I have is tied to someone else's need for it. Also, the ideal subject can then exercise compassion because to withhold what he is thankful to have, that is, what he recognizes as necessary for fulfilling the need of another, would be the opposite of a compassionate standpoint. It is through the need of the other being conjoined to one's greater means that one can feel and express gratitude and compassion, two key components of ideal moral subjectivity.

FRUGALITY: NURSIAN ENVIRONMENTAL AND WORK ETHICS

One of the most pressing problems confronting us today, as a globe, is rapid environmental degradation and climate change, both of which are closely connected with contemporary patterns of consumption, the global rise of a consumer culture and alarming levels of wastefulness. Single use plastic products and packaging allow us to consume more, more easily but are obviously wasteful despite salutary recycling efforts and increased use of earth-friendly and compostable materials. It can't be gainsaid that with an increased appetite for commodities come overconsumption and wastefulness. Many of us have gotten used to buying what we don't really need and discarding, without many qualms, what may still be usable or repairable. Much has been written on the nexus between religion, consumption and the environment and scholars of Islam have made important contributions to the broader field of religion and ecology.[12] Nursi's reflections about frugality, as a religiously grounded moral attitude, offers interesting perspectives that can enrich ongoing conversations about the intersections between religion, especially Islam, and the environment.

Nursi dedicates a short treatise on frugality in his work titled *The Flashes*.[13] He presents the treatise as a series of practical injunctions, seven in total, that he thinks flow from the Quranic verse, "*Eat and drink, but waste not by excess.*" (Q. 7:31) While Nursi's overall teachings take the sacredness of nature to be pivotal in the formation of religious subjectivity, his treatment of "frugality" (Tk. *iktisat*) has a somewhat different focus. I think the three main arguments he provides in favor of frugality, and against wastefulness, are elaborated in terms of *wisdom, appreciation* and *human dignity*. In other words, a Nursian moral subject is to be wise, experience and appreciate God's generosity and gain dignity through establishing a proper relationship with food, and by extension other consumables. He ought to see wastefulness, from a psychological point of view, as unwise, ungratefulness and undignified. Let us briefly look at these three arguments in turn.

Frugality and Wisdom

Nursi uses a simile and a parable to argue that frugality in relation to food, which he links with contentment, is a wise course of action, "in conformity with divine wisdom" and nourishes the human body. Its opposite is wastefulness, which causes indigestion and illness. Nursi likens the human body with a "wonderful palace" of which the human being, qua spiritual being, is a ruler and where food and drink arrive as if they were gifts arriving at the palace.[14] In this parable, Nursi characterizes the human sense of taste as a doorkeeper deserving of some gratuity, as a token of appreciation for letting in the gifts for the ruler and keeping harmful things out. But if the proverbial doorkeeper is given too large a tip, Nursi says, it would corrupt the doorkeeper and he would start to function, not as a doorkeeper, but as a ruler, who will allow only what it finds most pleasurable, causing disorder and chaos in the palace. Nursi thus wants an ideal subject to feel it would be unwise to go out of one's way to satisfy or gratify one's sense of taste, the proverbial doorkeeper and let its appetite build unrestrained. To eat bread and cheese is frugal and wise, Nursi says, betraying his subjective cultural location in Anatolia, where these items were cheap and easily available. To seek after the more delicious and expensive baklava (a traditional Turkish sweet pastry), which Nursi says is of equal or inferior nutritional value, is a disproportionate and unwise appeasement of one's sense of taste. Wisdom lies in frugality and treating "the sense of taste as a doorkeeper and giving it its remuneration accordingly."[15] To seek after an "unnecessary variety of foods" produces only an artificial appetite that causes indigestion and illness. Indulgence can be addictive. Enchantment with variety can produce an "artificial appetite." Here, we can generalize Nursi's point about food to consumable items or commodities more generally. As scholar of religion Vincent Miller notes in his book, *Consuming Religion*, research into consumer behavior shows that appetites can be artificially manipulated, misdirected and intensified.[16] Miller does not dwell on food, in particular, but his analysis of the ways in which genuine human desires and appetites can get derailed in consumer culture is a relevant consideration. If one embarks on an endless quest to gratify one's sense of taste, instead of giving it importance commensurate with its role within a larger frame of human well-being, one would end up neglecting the larger purposes of food consumption, among which are, nourishment and human well-being. To put it in Nursian metaphorical terms, the palace and its ruler (the human body and the human being), both suffer at the expense of a spoiled doorkeeper.[17] To be frugal is to be balanced and proportionate in one's consumption of food and, by extension, other consumables.

Interestingly, Nursi doesn't say that the only purpose of food is bodily nourishment, as we shall now see.

Frugality and Generosity

Nursi argues that frugality is not so much about depriving oneself of what may be considered exquisite types of food (although it is partly about that), as about the subject's attitude toward the food and toward the pleasure he derives from it. If consuming something produces greater appreciation of divine bounty and generosity, then the proverbial doorkeeper, the sense of taste, becomes "a supervisor and inspector of divine mercy."[18] Seen in this light, it is not a violation of frugality to prefer delicious foods, and more generally, whatever is more palatable and exquisite, if affordable through licit means, and one's preference for more tasteful foods "does not lead to degradation and begging."[19] It seems then that wastefulness, for a Nursian subject, is a failure to appreciate the immaterial meanings carried by the material things one consumes. Thus, for Nursi, "the sense of taste does not look to the physical stomach, rather, since it looks to the heart, spirit and mind, it has a position superior to the stomach." If one's engagement with food is "purely to carry out the duty of thanks and recognize and perceive the varieties of divine bounty," then delicious foods may be preferred in order to employ the sense of taste for giving thanks to God.[20]

For an ideal moral subject, therefore, the boundaries between frugality and wastefulness are not defined strictly in terms of the price or type of food but are also marked by one's mode of engagement with the food (and we can generalize to other consumables). The more pleasurable option can be, rather should be, preferred without fear of being wasteful if one understands and perceives the physical pleasures as bearing the meaning of divine bounties and one thinks about one's sense of taste as a tool for measuring and appreciating God's bounties. Wastefulness is to waste the opportunity to witness divine generosity and mercy. Gratitude brings a sense of contentment that puts a natural break on the otherwise insatiable drive for more, in search of an elusive, yet-to-come satisfaction.

Frugality and Work

Given Nursi's focus on gratitude and appreciation, we may start to think that Nursi's teachings would produce a deflationary effect on human industry and the will and motivation to work. It may be quite the opposite. Nursi connects frugality with contentment and wastefulness with greed. The frugal person manages what he has in a way that suffices his needs whereas the wasteful person, well, wastes what he has and then looks greedily and lustfully at what others have. The sufficiency of the frugal person is dignified whereas the apparently admirable large-heartedness of a non-frugal person is undignified because it would, in time, lead to the latter's impoverishment and then a degrading dependency on others and covetousness for their possessions.[21] Contrary to what a modern reader might expect, Nursi thinks that frugality encourages effort and work while wastefulness promotes laziness and destroys enthusiasm for work. How so?

The key for Nursi is the psychologically motivating consequences of experiencing the joys of contentment and the demotivating effects of remaining discontent with the fruits of one's work and effort. We might think that the frugal person would not want to work too much since he would be content with little. Nursi, and hence a Nursian moral subject, thinks differently. For a Nursian subject, frugality produces contentment with the fruits of one's efforts. Work and effort, in the mind of a frugal person, bear delightful fruit! This ought to encourage and motivate the subject to make the kind of effort that yields *satisfying* results. The wasteful and ungrateful person, on the other hand, would not be content with the fruits of his effort: his wastefulness is the consequence of his continuing lack of contentment and his attempt, through immoderate spending, to reach a state of contentment. Realizing that his best efforts do not produce contentment, the person will quickly burn himself out. He would be discouraged to put effort into work that does not produce a satisfying outcome at the affective and psychological levels. Nursi thinks that a discontented person cannot endlessly motivate himself to do work that produces dissatisfying outcomes. To feel that the results are not commensurate with one's efforts is to find oneself in an unfair and undignified relation with the world. For a discontented person, his efforts are not adequately reciprocated and his needs are not met and yet he must continue, as if against his will, to labor. The ideal Nursian subject then ties frugality with dignity and engages with things in a frugal way so as to preserve his dignity as well as his sense of industry and enthusiasm for work.[22] To work in order to receive a response from God, in the form of the fruits of one's labor, and to then take pleasure in those fruits and respond with gratitude is a good way to channel one's inner drive for willing, constructive and meaningful work (physical or otherwise) in the world.

The goal for Nursi is not, of course, to produce motivated labor. Rather, it is to establish a different kind of relation with one's intuitive drive to do something good in the world and to attain the goods of this world. Interestingly, Nursi thinks that the drive to work must be related, in the mind of an ideal subject, to the person's belief perspectives. Discussing the importance of daily prayer, Nursi uses the parable of a gardener who has to labor all day long in his garden, Nursi argues how the performance of the five daily prayers ought to shape the subject's attitude toward the work itself:

> If you spend your rest periods on the prayers, which allow your spirit to relax and heart to take a breather, you will discover *two mines* which are an important source, both for a productive worldly livelihood, and your livelihood and provisions of the hereafter. First Mine: Through a sound intention, you will receive *a share of the praises and glorifications offered by all the plants and trees, whether flowering or fruit-bearing, that you grow in the garden.* Second Mine: Whatever is eaten of the garden's produce, whether by animals or man, cattle or flies, buyers or thieves, it will become like *almsgiving* from you. But on condition you work in the name of the True Provider and within the bounds of what He permits, and see yourself as a distribution official giving His property to His creatures. So see what a great loss is made by one who abandons the prescribed prayers. What significant wealth he loses, and he is deprived of those two results and mines which would otherwise *cause him to work eagerly and ensure his morale is strong;* he becomes bankrupt. Even, as he grows old, he will grow weary of gardening and lose interest in it, saying, "What is it to me? I am anyway leaving this world, why should I put up with this much difficulty?" He will sink into idleness. But the first man says: "I shall work harder at both worship and licit activities in order to send even more abundant light to my grave and procure more provisions for my life in the hereafter."[23]

The ideal subject should see the results of his labor, actual fruits and plants in the case of a gardener, as glorifying God and see himself glorifying God through them. In other words, insofar as one sees a flower manifesting and glorifying the beauty of its maker, one sees one's own labor in helping the flower grow, as a part of the flower's glorification of God's beauty. In this sense, that labor should become a form of worship. This should keep the person from seeing his labor and its fruits only in terms of what they may bring to him in this world but also see them as provisions for a life after death. The weariness of laborious work can be mitigated and transformed by reflecting on the fruits of one's labor and seeing them as a type of worship and also a type of almsgiving. It is clear then that if one's work is producing ugly and unjust results, such as dehumanization or oppression of other humans or clear and discernible harm to other creatures, one would not be able to see them as glorifications of a just and compassionate God and so one should not be motivated to engage in such work. There is a subtle argument here for engaging in work whose fruits can reasonably be seen by a sincere person as praises and glorifications of a just, wise and compassionate God.

Also, the content person has patience and is willing "to act with slow deliberation" that is needed to attain one's goals in this world, as per God's decree.[24] The greedy person rushes, lacking the patience it takes to properly follow the steps that God has decreed. A person who wants a good loaf of bread needs to put it in the oven and wait. The slowness of the process is purposeful—so that the human agent can see God's wisdom and decree unfolding. The one who is hasty and greedy lacks concern for witnessing this unfolding of wisdom. Imagine how we might extend Nursi's logic to social relations and the slowness that may be a nuisance for us. When a friend is cross with you, and takes her sweet time to become convinced that you did not intend to hurt her with your comment, instead of giving up on her and accusing her for being difficult, one could instead see in the slow repair of the relation, a clearer manifestation of divine wisdom and compassion. Wisdom and compassion gets time to manifest in the slow coming to fruition of one's reconciliatory efforts. Without any interest in seeing the wisdom in the slow unfolding of processes in the natural and social worlds, there is a good chance one would lose patience with things sooner than one ought to and not appreciate the pace at which things actually, by God's decree from a Nursian perspective, work in both the natural and social worlds.

BROTHERHOOD, INDIVIDUALITY, AND DISCORD

One of the most important ethical debates of our times is one about the complex relationship between an authentic and independent individuality on the one hand and communal ties on the other.[25] How, in what ways and under what epistemic and social conditions can humans flourish, continue to be important concerns in the humanities and social sciences. It is outside the scope of this chapter to review these lengthy and important debates. Instead, here I want to simply and directly raise the question: What is the ideal standpoint of a Nursian moral subject toward the putative tension between individual autonomy and the demands that come with a person's strong ties to a community? Nursi's response, in my view, is ambivalent and this ambivalence is salutary because I think it tracks better the ambiguities and complexities of human life than a simple, dichotomous antagonism or easy reconciliation between the twin demands of individual authenticity and conformity to the norms of a community. In a nutshell, a Nursian subject neither privileges individual autonomy and self-sufficiency over relationships and shared religio-moral visions, nor idealizes community cohesiveness and agreement at the expense of authentic and confident self-expression.[26] He engages in a process of negotiation, a discursive negotiation, over legitimate moral and intellectual demands arising from both within and without. Nursi's teachings about these questions can be described as three related, but not easily reconcilable, propositions.

The first proposition may be expressed as follows: brotherhood, agreement and cohesion are important for, and strong among, the misguided due to their misguidance and not because of strength, magnanimity or any other virtue. This is primarily a negative claim, that is, a claim about what the cohesion of the misguided is not. Nursi makes several arguments in support of this proposition that aim to highlight that the misguided feel the need for solidarity because they do not have "the true source of support" (God) for their individual (atheistic and heedless) stances.[27] "The people of neglect—those misguided ones sunk in worldly concerns—are weak and abased because they do not rely on truth and reality. On account of their abasement, they need to augment their strength, and because of this need they wholeheartedly embrace the aid and cooperation of others," opines Nursi.[28]

Proposition 2 can be expressed as follows: brotherhood, agreement and cohesion are weak among the believers partly due to their strong beliefs. This claim captures Nursi's consolatory advice to a believer who is bothered and disappointed by a lack of unity and cohesion among the faithful. Nursi's argument is this:

> Dispute and disagreement among the people of guidance are not the results of weakness and the powerful union of the people of misguidance is not the result of strength. Rather, the lack of the union or cohesion among the people of guidance comes from the power that results from the support provided by perfect belief. . . . Since the strong do not feel a need for union, their unions are weak. Lions do not need union like foxes and therefore live as individuals, whereas wild goats form a herd to protect themselves against wolves. The community and collective personality of the weak is strong and the community and collective personality of the strong is weak.[29]

The moral subject is to interpret the lack of cohesion among believers as a sign of individual strength. The subject may even interpret the lack of cohesion in their community of belonging as a sign of firm belief. A weak collective personality is a function of strong individual personalities that make up the collective. But Nursi does not leave matters here. He goes on to make the argument that in reality, brotherhood is indeed a desirable good and discord is problematic and harmful. We can then formulate a third proposition to capture this aspect of his view.

Proposition 3 may be stated as follow: believers should avoid and overcome discord among themselves and realize the strength to be found in cohesion and brotherhood. For Nursi, the brotherhood, agreement and cohesion of believers is very important for the triumph of belief in God against atheism. Nursi makes a number of mainly functional arguments in favor of this third proposition. For instance, referring to Quranic verses such as *"and do not quarrel with one another, or you may lose heart and your spirit may desert you"* (Q. 8:46). Nursi says, "One must realize how harmful to Islam dispute is, and how it helps the people of misguidance to triumph over the people of truth, and then, wholeheartedly and self-sacrificingly, join the caravan of the people of truth with a sense of his own weakness and impotence."[30] The strong believer is being asked to sacrifice his firmness and assume a sense of weakness and impotence qua individual.

Highlighting that what ought to matter to a moral subject is God's pleasure and the sincerity with which he worships God, Nursi says,

> O people of truth! O people of the law! People of reality and the people of the path, all worshiping God! Confronted by the awesome disease of discord, overlook each other's faults, *close your eyes to each other's shortcomings!* Behave according to the rule of courtesy established by the criterion that is the Quran in the verse, "When they pass by error, they pass by it with honorable avoidance." (Q. 25:72)[31]

Nursi asks the moral subject to forego jealousy and petty conflicts that arise from seeking after acclaim, appraisal of one's opinion and acceptance among people and instead, for the sake of sincerity, establish union and cohesion with his brothers in religion, a union even stronger that that of the worldly.

Attention to context makes his position easier to understand: a dominant and unified Europe taking charge of a beleaguered and fractured Ottoman empire, and more importantly, the intellectual current of atheism "treacherously trying to subvert, poison and destroy [the] minds."[32] The somewhat worrying aspect of the passage just quoted is that Nursi thinks Islam would be harmed if the ideal subject did not overlook the faults and shortcomings of his fellow Muslims. The Quranic verse that Nursi cites, which refers to "passing by error with honorable avoidance" could be interpreted to mean that one is not to fall into others' errors rather than suggesting that one is to turn a blind eye to their shortcomings. Two things might be said about this worry. First, Nursi's advice about ignoring shortcomings to avoid dispute seems addressed to those who may let petty creedal differences grow into deep acrimony and sectarianism, which he sees as harmful for a united stance against atheism, the common enemy. For instance, referring to a sectarian divide between Sunnis and Alawis, he says,

> And so, O Sunnis, who are the people of truth, and Alawis, whose way is love of the Prophet's family! Quickly put an end to this meaningless, disloyal, unjust, and harmful dispute between you. Otherwise the atheistic current which is now so influential will make one of you a tool against the other, and use the one to crush the other. And after defeating the one it will destroy the tool. Since you are believers in divine unity, it is essential to leave aside unimportant matters which necessitate division while there are a hundred fundamental sacred bonds between you which command brotherhood and unity.[33]

Secondly, we see that Nursi actually provides a list of practical guidelines—nine in total—about how a subject should negotiate the demands of strong individuality and the benefits of community cohesion. To cite two key ones, Nursi asks ideal subjects, "to act positively, that is, out of love for one's own outlook, avoiding enmity for other outlooks, not criticizing them, interfering in their beliefs and sciences, or in any way concerning oneself with them."[34]

As well, he asks them to adopt a just rule of conduct, which, in his view is the stance that "My outlook is true, or the best," and not that "My outlook *alone* is true," or that "My outlook *alone* is right or good," thus implying the total falsity of all outlooks other than one's own.[35] In other words, so long as the subject is not an exclusivist about his truth claims, he can love his commitments, act on them and express them confidently. It is not the love of, or convictions about, the truth of one's standpoint that breeds hatred and division. It is to imagine one's truths to be the only truths and one's commitments to be the only ones worth having, which leads to rivalry and egotistical discord and to a failure to recognize religio-moral commitments that may in fact be shared among groups.

BEING A VICTIM OF OPPRESSION

It seems to me that many people today feel they are victims of one or another kind of oppression. In a way, it is a good thing. Advances in knowledge, social awareness and communication have made people more aware of the various, subtle varieties of injustices they, or others, are subjected to. Feminist movements and movements for racial and environmental justice are good examples. People realize that injustices can be systemic, subtle, entrenched and multidimensional and intersectional and require coordinated, prolonged and multilayered responses. Awareness about the interrelations between various sources of oppression has spawned new movements where the various at-risk and oppressed groups are trying to make alliances across racial, economic, ethnic and other traditionally dividing lines. We do well when we turn our gazes to all sources of tyranny and respond by organizing collective resistances and raising our collective voices. For a Nursian subject, the work of fighting to repair can, but should not, turn into a celebration of rancour and enmity. The collective responses, Nursi teaches us, need to be supported by an internal and reflective self-centering that happens through, paradoxically, a self-distancing and a simultaneous self-accounting, both discursively achieved. The ideal subject has to think about the injustice (and the pain of seeing injustice done to others) at the personal level as well. As we shall see below, a subject's reflective response to tyranny is a sort of self-distancing insofar as it involves being emotionally cold and mathematical. But it is also a self-familiarizing insofar as it involves acknowledging, perhaps against the protests of the ego-self, one's own and the oppressor's failings as individual human beings.

We know that Nursi was persecuted by the authorities for much of his adult life. He was sent to prison and sent into exile for extended periods of time. Nevertheless, he argues that one cannot categorically and wholly condemn the other for the evil one suffers at the other's hand. Nursi gives three reasons for his striking stance:

> Firstly, Divine Determining has a certain share of responsibility. It is necessary to deduct that share from the total and respond to it with contentment and satisfaction. Secondly, the share of the soul and Satan should also be deducted, and one should pity the man for having been overcome by his soul and await his repentance instead of becoming his enemy. Thirdly, look at the defect in your own soul that you do not see or do not wish to see; deduct a share for that too. As for the small share which then remains, if you respond with forgiveness, pardon, and magnanimity, in such a way as to conquer your enemy swiftly and safely, then you will have escaped all sin and harm. . . . If then you love yourself, do not permit this harmful hostility and desire for revenge to enter your heart. If it has entered your heart, do not listen to what it says. Hear what truth-seeing Hafiz of Shiraz says: "The world is not a commodity worth arguing over." It is worthless since it is transient and passing. If this is true of the world, then it is clear how worthless and insignificant are the petty affairs of the world! Hafiz also said: "The tranquillity of both worlds lies in the understanding of these two words: generosity toward friends, forbearance toward enemies."[36]

Nursi asks the ideal subject to apportion responsibility for the injustices being done to him by another in four equal-sized chunks. He gives one fourth to God, that is, one-quarter of what is happening is the decree of God and that aspect of decree is an entirely vertical/religious matter between the subject and God. We have already discussed, in the previous chapter, how Nursi wants a person, qua religious subject, to engage with God's predetermination. If something is happening to the subject that is outside of their control, there must be a reason behind it and one should attend to the aspect of the matter that points to the beautiful names of God. For instance, one's aversion to a tyrant's tyranny points to the One who is just and does not like tyranny. Of the three-fourths left, one-fourth is given to the oppressor's ego and to Satan, as an act of calming and distancing oneself inwardly from the indignations produced by the injustice—rather, the oppressor can now be pitied as a person who has been deceived by his ego and Satan into choosing wrongly. One does not see them as unintelligibly and irredeemably evil, incapable of regret and repentance. Another one-fourth goes toward self, not to blame oneself for bringing the injustice upon oneself but as a way of repenting for injustices of similar nature that one *may* have done (or might still be doing) to others, advertently or inadvertently. After one is done with this much cognitive activity about the injustice, one is already less passionate and single-minded about destroying the single agent one previously thought wholly responsible for one's miseries. Interestingly then, one fourth of the blame does go to the actual oppressor but Nursi quickly turns to the virtues of forgiveness, tranquillity of the soul, generosity and forbearance when thinking about the fault of the oppressor. One is indeed indignant but with an option to forgive and one is simultaneously more self-aware and, importantly, not angry with God for allowing the injustice. The other, the unjust other, is after all, a human being, responsible for his actions but also pitiably yet redeemably gullible.

NURSI'S GENDERED MORAL SUBJECTS

Nursi does not make distinctions between men and women when it comes to their abilities and responsibilities as believing subjects.[37] The distinctions he does take up are those that are mentioned in the Quran. In line with his larger goal of demonstrating Quran's truth and wisdom against challenges to the latter posed by materialistic and atheistic philosophy, he cannot ignore the Quran and wants ideal moral subjects to find Quranic injunctions ethical and just. For instance, he argues that the Quranic injunction regarding unequal inheritance shares for sons and daughters (a daughter gets half of what a son gets) are more just than "modern civil law."[38] The fact that Nursi feels the need to explain how the injunction is just already betrays an anxiety about its fairness, or at least an awareness that modern ethical thought would consider this injunction, prima facie, unfair. Nursi's defense is twofold and verges on being inconsistent. Referring to Quran's injunction as perfect justice and mercy, Nursi says,

> It is just because, in most cases and according to Islamic law, the husband provides for his wife and children, whereas the wife has no legal obligation to provide for her husband or herself or for the kids. Thus she is compensated for inheriting half of what a man inherits. It is a perfect mercy because a girl is delicate, vulnerable, and thus held in great affection by her father who, thanks to the Qur'anic injunction, does not see her as someone who will cause him a loss by carrying half of his wealth to others. In addition, her brothers feel compassion for and protect her without envy, for they do not see her as a rival when dividing the family's possessions. Thus, the affection and compassion she enjoys throughout her family compensates for her apparent loss in inheritance. It is a great injustice to give her more than her due share out of unrealistic compassion—unrealistic because no one is more compassionate than God.[39]

Since the daughter would likely one day be a wife and would not be obligated to contribute financially to the family, her smaller share is just and fair because it is, ideally speaking, at her disposal alone. Looked at in this way, Nursi's argument amounts to saying that effectively and in real terms, the daughter's share is not really unequal to the man's share after all because she does not have to share it with anyone. But Nursi goes on to defend the injunction as also merciful and in doing so, underscores the fundamental inequality between the shares. The smaller size of the daughter's share, Nursi argues, ought to make her the beneficiary of greater affection and compassion in the family as a *compensation* for the inequality created by the injunction. To describe the daughter as weak and vulnerable, in need of her father's and brother's protection and love on account of her being financially non-threatening betrays a deeply patriarchal view of sex and gender. Nursi might respond by asserting that his is a more realistic view of the rather limited and imperfect human capacity to exercise compassion even within the family.

Should we read him charitably, we can say that the ideal moral subject as a male (in the roles of father or brother) ought to feel the need to compensate for the smaller (unjust) share of inheritance that the girl would get in some distant future. The ideal male subjects as fathers/brothers ought to treat the daughters/sisters in the family with extra affection and compassion throughout their lives in view of a future smaller, unequal share in the inheritance. Nursi takes the Quran's position to be a more realistic view of the capacity of self-interested and materially-driven and needy humans, to extend affection and compassion to at-risk others, even within a family. In line with Nursi's general view of the value of human existential poverty and weakness, it seems as if he considers the Quran to be creating an inequality so that it becomes the occasion or opportunity for male moral subjects to manifest his names of compassionate and merciful within the sphere of family relations. As well, he does not suggest that this should be the only reason why fathers and brothers would treat women in their families well. The injunction would just take away one possible cause of their possible mistreatment of the womenfolk.

Here I am less interested in arbitrating between variant readings, patriarchal or otherwise, of the Quranic verse and more interested in highlighting how Nursi's larger view of creation, where God's compassion and mercy are manifested through mutual assistance among unequally endowed beings in the universe (e.g., air made to assist beings in need of it to breathe), shapes his view of how asymmetric interhuman relations, even those sanctioned by the Quran itself, ought to be conducted by ideal moral subjects. Moreover, while Nursi justifies the inequality of the inheritance shares in principle, he seems to affirm the values of mercy and protection for daughters/sisters within a traditional family. He uses the inequality to justify greater affection and compassion toward women within the family. We can safely presume, given our discussion of an "ethics of conjunction" above, that Nursi would not encourage the ideal female moral agent to feel indebted to her male family members for their extra, compensatory affection and compassion nor would he allow the father/husband to see themselves as deserving any praise or merit for the compassion they manifest. He would instead ask them to congratulate each other for receiving God's blessings and for serving God by manifesting His names to each other. Surely, Nursi is no feminist thinker and his idea of the ideal moral subject is gendered to a considerable extent. This imposes limits on how much of a Nursian conception of ideal subjectivity contemporary Muslims can uncritically adopt. Still, I do not think the above discussion warrants the conclusion that Nursi thought women were morally or religiously inferior to men in any general sense. I think the discussion above shows the way Nursi, and his ideal moral subject, is shaped by their broader, cosmological view of the universe, a particular way of construing the purpose of asymmetry in the universe at all levels, a commitment to the justice and mercy of God and hence a commitment to finding justice, wisdom and mercy in Quranic injunctions about practical matters.

There is a place in the *Risale* where Nursi addresses women in written form primarily and directly. At that time, he was old, weak and regrets that he is not able to meet them in person, as they had requested, so he wrote a piece addressed specifically to them. In addition to more traditional remarks about the importance of Islamic modest dress, sex within marriage and the importance of family, Nursi takes the interesting position that it is better for a woman to become financially independent and remain single than to marry an impious man for the sake of financial security. For his time, and given his audience, this would have been a counter-cultural and forward-looking advice. He says, "My sisters! I have this to say to you confidentially: rather than entering under the domination of a dissolute, immoral, Westernized husband for the concern of your livelihood, try to economize and work for your own livelihood ... do not try to sell yourselves."[40] He equates marriage for the sake of financial security with selling oneself. But he follows this up with a reminder that if the women do end up having "a husband who is unsuitable for you, be content with your fate and resigned to it. God willing, he will be reformed through your contentment and resignation."[41] Keeping the family intact and concerns about a wretched husband's reform seem to override the well-being of a potentially abused and oppressed woman in a mismatched union. Again, there are other readings possible, if one wanted to be charitable. Perhaps Nursi was aware of the difficulty of being a divorced woman in that context and lack of desirable alternatives for the wife other than remaining married. Perhaps he thought it would be more, rather than less, empowering for such women to think of themselves as teachers, role models, reformers and saviours for their husbands. The reader would have to decide how to interpret such passages in Nursi's writings and how much importance to give them. I am reminded of religious ethicist, Jonathan Schofer, when he describes his rabbinic sources as texts in which the "compelling and disturbing elements are often deeply connected."[42] Nursi's gendered remarks and his innovative vision of a meaning-centered, religio-moral subjectivity are intertwined and we, as religious ethicists, have an obligation to attend to both of those elements.

NURSIAN SUBJECTS BETWEEN POLITICS AND SERVICE

I want to suggest that Nursi is offering a post-identitarian vision of Muslim moral subjectivity. What do I mean by post-identitarian? I think that many widely discussed contemporary accounts of being Muslim are deeply interested in politics and issues of identity—what does it mean or how does it feel to be a particular kind of Muslim in this or that sociopolitical moment or context. Being Muslim is often talked about with attention to how living as a Muslim person (especially as a Muslim woman, woman of color, as a racial or ethnic minority or as a conservative/liberal or a non-binary or an LGBTQ person) poses unique, serious and multiple challenges to Muslims who identify as members of this or that group. Being Muslim then is to be political, the bearer of an identity that is always bigger than the individual's consciousness. I think we can say, perhaps a bit provocatively, that Nursi offers a vision of Muslim moral subjectivity that is post-identitarian and also post-political even as it is deeply Quranic.

As Colin Turner has aptly noted, Nursi thought that constitutionalism, democracy and republicanism were consistent with Quranic teachings but he did not want people to focus on politics. And it is safe to assume, as Turner also points out, that Nursi would be appalled by the idea of a religious elite establishing a theocratic or Islamic state.[43] I think that Nursi understands interest in or engagement in politics, of any kind, to be antithetical to the kind of engagement he wants people to have with the Quran. I think he would have only emphasized his hesitant stance toward direct political involvement more if he had lived to see the contentious and Islamist politics in and beyond the so-called Muslim world. Nursi's focus can be called post-Islamist and post-identitarian insofar as many contemporary Muslim scholars take socioeconomic and sociopolitical forces and realities to be at the center of Islamic ethics, law and theology. Nursi conveys his reasons for making a sharp distinction between his religio-moral vision and religious politics by using an extended parable. In the parable, some people enter a muddy swamp, which represents human beings entering a materialist and naturalist conception of the world. There are a few who are able to travel a safe way (those guided by divine guidance). Those in the swamp are of two kinds, a minority who just don't care and don't want any better and those who do not want to be in the muddy filth they are in but are bewildered and can't find safe passage. It is this bewildered majority (and Nursi thinks Muslims who hold imitative beliefs are among them), trapped in the swamp of naturalism and materialism, that Nursi thinks should make themselves addressees of the Quran. Nursi says that anyone who wants to work to change the conditions of such people (and himself) has two options: to bear the light or to bear the club. By the proverbial club, Nursi is referring to various forms of the exercise of political power. By the proverbial light, he means the belief-centered teachings of the Quran that he explicates in his works. Political Islam, for Nursi, is the equivalent of calling people in the swamp to safe passage while brandishing both the light and the club. He thinks that no matter how much light such a person may carry to the bewildered person, seeing the person bearing "both the club and the light" in their hands does not inspire confidence among the people. People will feel compelled and forced by those bearing clubs and will not appreciate the light. Nursi suggests that choosing the "club of politics" (political engagement) asks us to take sides and become partisans for one or another political ideology. Sooner or later, politics trumps principles. Given Nursi's aim, and the aim he wants Nursian moral agents to have in the world, that is, to free humanity and provide safe passage out of the proverbial swamp of naturalism and atheism, he is firm that politics and service cannot go together and a moral subject must choose one or the other as their primary focus.[44] I do not wish to dwell on the problems and promises of Nursi's seemingly apolitical stance. Clearly, Nursi has been channeled and adopted by many movements of a political nature in Turkey and beyond. I simply wish to suggest that an ideal Nursian moral agent, in my reading, ought to remain politically impartial so as to retain moral credibility in the eyes of the widest possible collection of humanity and, to first and foremost seek to cultivate belief perspectives that Nursi thinks are the main aim of the Quran. Given what religiously motivated Islamist politics has looked like over the twentieth century and into the twenty-first century and the startling violence and divisions it continues to produce among Muslims, I think the time might still be ripe for Muslim students of the Quran to heed Nursi's call and focus attention elsewhere, namely to apolitical projects of religio-moral self-making and perspectival transformations away from a self-injuring naturalism toward a self-elevating witnessing of the beautiful names of God both within the self and without. While many Muslims today continue to engage with politics, post-identitarian Muslim moral subjects can perhaps follow a different path, without making enemies out of (or refusing to express solidarity with) those who may choose peaceful (even if radical) paths of political engagement. The account of Nursian moral subjectivity that I have presented here, does invite us to revisit the implications of trying to bring together identitarian political action and service to others and think deeply about the relationship between these two powerful human orientations to the world.

NOTES

1. Nursi, *The Rays: From the Risale-i Nur Collection*, trans. Sukran Vahide (Istanbul: Sozler Nesriyat, 2002), 243.
2. Nursi, *Rays*, 243.
3. Nursi, *Rays*, 243–244.

4. Interestingly, in this context, it seems like Nursi takes it for granted that one would not be dealing with an abusive father or disloyal spouse or friends. As we noted in the previous chapters, Nursi might put these instances under the context of unrequited injustice that makes the subject invoke belief in life after death. It should be noted that seeking justice is also part of ideal subject's task for Nursi, if the circumstances allow for seeking justice.

5. Nursi's point here echoes for me of Nietzsche's idea of "eternal recurrence." Nursi's point is not an ethical in a traditional, "thou shalt" sense. It is a challenge to form oneself into a subject that could have deep and abiding commitments, such as one of loyalty and love toward one spouse.

6. Nursi, *Flashes*, 269.

7. Nursi, "17th Flash, 13th Note, 4th Point" in *Living the Quran with Joy and Purpose: Selections on Tawhid from Said Nursi's Epistle of Light*, forthcoming, trans. with intro. and notes by Yamina Bouguenaya and Isra Yazicioglu (Piscataway, NJ: Gorgias Press, 2020); also see Nursi, *Flashes*, 183.

8. Nursi, *The Letters: From the Risale-i Nur Collection*, trans. Sukran Vahide (Istanbul: Sozler Nesriyat, 1994), 309.

9. Nursi starts the treatise with the following passage from the Quran "Whether one or both of them attain old age in your life, say not to them a word of contempt, nor repel them, but address them in terms of honour. And out of kindness, lower the wing of humility, and say: 'My Sustainer! Bestow on them Your mercy even as they cherished me in childhood.' Your Sustainer knows best what is in your hearts: if you do deeds of righteousness, indeed he is Most Forgiving to those who turn to Him again and again [in true penitence]" (Q. 17:23–25) in *Letters*, 208.

10. Nursi, *Letters*, 309.

11. Nursi, *Letters*, 309.

12. See recent comprehensive essays by Seyyed Hossein Nasr, Fazlun Khalid, Nawal Ammar and Allison Gray in John Hart, ed., *The Wiley Blackwell Companion to Religion and Ecology* (Hoboken, NJ: Wiley Blackwell, 2017).

13. Nursi, *Flashes*, 189–199.

14. Nursi uses this metaphor of human being as a palace in other contexts as well. For instance, he says "every living being is like a divine palace (*qasr ilāhī*), and human beings are the most beautiful and wondrous of those palaces. Some of the precious stones of this 'human palace' come from the world of spirits, some from 'the world of similitude,' some from the Preserved Tablet (*lawh al-mahfūz*), and others from the realms of air, light, and minerals." Nursi, *Selections on Tawhid*, forthcoming; also see *Flashes*, 184.

15. Nursi, *Flashes*, 190.

16. Vincent J Miller, *Consuming Religion: Christian Faith and Practice in a Consumer Culture* (New York, Continuum: 2003), 108–109.

17. The body and its corporeality in the Islamic tradition (the Persianate Islamic tradition) is the subject of a fascinating study by Shahzad Bashir. See Shahzad Bashir, *Sufi Bodies: Religion and society in Medieval Islam (*New York: Columbia University Press, 2011).

18. Nursi, *Flashes*, 191.

19. Nursi, *Flashes*, 191.

20. Nursi, *Flashes*, 191.

21. Nursi, *Flashes*, 192.

22. Nursi, *Flashes*, 196.

23. Nursi, *The Words: From the Risale-i Nur Collection*, trans. Sukran Vahide (Istanbul: Sozler Publications, 2004), 280.

24. Nursi, *Letters*, 323.

25. For instance, Charles Taylor makes a forceful argument for the necessity of community. See Daniel Bell, "Communitarianism," in *The Stanford Encyclopedia of Philosophy* (Summer 2016), Standord University, 2016–/ Article published with revision March 21, 2016. https://plato.stanford.edu/archives/sum2016/entries/communitarianism/.

26. For an interesting set of essays that challenge the idea that the individual self did not exist in premodern cultures and was somehow discovered in the modern period, see David

Brakke, Michael L. Satlow, Steven Weitzman, ed., *Religion and the Self in Antiquity* (Bloomington: Indiana University Press, 2005).

27. Nursi, *Flashes*, 207. Cf. Richard Rorty's vision of solidarity as "human beings huddling together in the dark." Rorty, *Consequences of Pragmatism* (Minneapolis: University of Minnesota Press, 1982), 150, 153.

28. Nursi, *Flashes*, 202.

29. Nursi, *Flashes*, 206.

30. Nursi, *Flashes*, 207.

31. Nursi, *Flashes*, 208, italics added.

32. Nursi, *Flashes*, 233.

33. Nursi, *Flashes*, 43.

34. Nursi, *Flashes*, 203.

35. Nursi, *Flashes*, 203. In a footnote on the same page, Nursi further encourages cooperation with Christians: "It is even recorded in authentic traditions of the Prophet that at the end of time the truly pious among the Christians will unite with the People of the Qur'an and fight their common enemy, irreligion. And at this time, too, the people of religion and truth need to unite sincerely not only with their own brothers and fellow believers, but also with the truly pious and spiritual ones the Christians, temporarily from the discussion and debate of points of difference in order to combat their joint enemy-aggressive atheism." Ibid.

36. Nursi, *Letters*, 316.

37. For instance, he says "Happy the man who in order not to lose his companion of eternity, copies his righteous wife and so become righteous himself." Nursi, *Flashes*, 263.

38. Nursi, *Letters*, 59. The Quranic verse says, "and for the man a portion equal to that of two women." Quran, 4:176. In the Quranic injunction, however, women do not always inherit half of men, for instance, a deceased person's father and mother gets equal share from the inheritance. On a related note, in the civil law that was adopted in Turkey in place of *sharia* based law, parents do not get any share from the inheritance (if relatives of first degree are present, that is, spouse and children). So, for instance, a mother will not get any from her married son's inheritance. Nursi considers this a major injustice to especially the mother: "This low civilization has caused an injustice by giving daughters more than their due, and it perpetrates an even greater injustice by not giving the mother what is her right." *Letters*, 59.

39. Nursi, *Letters*, 59.

40. Nursi, *Flashes*, 264.

41. Nursi, *Flashes*, 264.

42. Jonathan Schofer, *The Making of a Sage: A Study in Rabbinic Ethics* (Madison: University of Wisconsin Press, 2005), 22.

43. Colin Turner, *The Qur'an Revealed: A Critical Analysis of Said Nursi's Epistles of Light* (Berlin: Gerlach Press, 2013), 545.

44. Nursi, *Flashes*, 143.

Conclusion

Forging Ideal Subjectivities Everyday Over a Lifetime

At the end of her book, *Culture and Redemption*, American studies scholar Tracy Fessenden expresses a wish that "a more dissonant pluralism" emerge on a global stage, one that would allow for modes of religio-moral being presently threatened by what she calls the "reassertion of secular-Protestant identity."[1] She hopes for a "newly energized and contestatory pluralism, where appeals to freedom, values and even faith mean more and otherwise than what the loyalty oaths of our present climate would make of them."[2] I think this book ought to show that reconstructions of Muhasibian and Nursian accounts of ideal subjectivity are germane for thinking about and articulating a "contestatory pluralism," one that moves us beyond fixed and divisive claims about all-too-familiar and problematic formulations of belief, moral agency, freedom and religious identity, especially as these pertain to the Islamic tradition and being Muslim in the world.

This book has taken a curatorial look at Muhasibi's and Nursi's works to recover their accounts of ideal religio-moral Muslim subjectivities and strategies and practices implicated in the formation of an ideal Muslim consciousness in their respective teachings. It has described and analyzed in some depth, their vision of how people could, by means of discursive practices, forge an ideal religious and moral consciousness and subjectivity. Given that their pedagogical projects produce complex, contestatory, fluid and fragile modes of psychic and moral being, the language of subjectivity and subject formation seems to have served us better than the more widely used vocabulary of virtue, character and identity among scholars of Muslim ethics and Muslim anthropology. The ideal subjects they present to us exhibit the kind of "going beyond loyalty oaths" that Fessenden hopes could challenge the dominant secular/Protestant, and I would add identitarian claims, particularly in Western societies.

I hope the book has illustrated how a Foucauldian invitation to think about ethics in the register of self-formation can provide theoretical energy and a new lens for a fresh analysis of familiar Muslim sources and discourses. We have seen how reading complex religious discourses—legal, theological, exegetical and mystical—as discursive practices have allowed us insights into their pedagogical and psychological implications and the power they try to put in the hands of the average Muslim to shape their religio-moral consciousness and subjectivity. And, in the process, I hope the book has reconstructed, however partially, two rich and interesting accounts of what it means to be an ideal Muslim. In concluding the book, I would like to first highlight how incorporating discursive practices into our scholarly toolbox can enrich scholarly analyses of Muslim ethics. Second, I shall reflect briefly on how Muhasibi's and Nursi's particular accounts of subjectivity can offer us insights into religiously grounded, ethical living in the contemporary age.

I hope this book convinces the reader that the study of Muslim ethics stands to benefit by attention to not only Foucault and Hadot but the eclectic and thriving fields of Comparative Religious Ethics (CRE) and moral anthropology. CRE scholarship has been my constant intellectual companion, as I waded into Muhasibi's and Nursi's writings to interrogate their religious ethics. CRE scholarship has helped put the human subject, and its formation and transformation, firmly at the center of ethical inquiry. It has avoided over-theorization and abstraction in favor of thinking about the lived life and moral psychology of lived human beings but without privileging notions of collective identity. It has not shied away from recognizing how theological and philosophical *ideas*, not just embodiment, matter in people's lives and the formative work these ideas do for those who engage in discursive practices built upon and around those ideas. It has raised awareness about the question of human flourishing again, at a time when technology, politics and economics seem united in helping humans forget about their humanity altogether, let alone what may be involved in its fuller and deeper flourishing. In a world where multiple cultures now exist side by side, often in close proximity, and people find themselves confronted with radically different ideals they should aspire for to have meaningful lives, CRE scholarship provide us conceptual and theoretical tools that help us become better, more sophisticated interpreters of the differences and similarities between different worldviews and the implications they have for individual and collective life. It is difficult to specify which particular insights in this book were made possible by my engagement with CRE scholarship but I can safely say that without the pioneering work of scholars like Aaron Stalnaker, Thomas Lewis, Elizabeth Bucar, Talal Asad, Saba Mahmood, Jonathan Schofer,

Charles Matthewes and of course Michel Foucault and Pierre Hadot, a study such as this one would be difficult to conceptualize and execute. Let me now consider Muhasibi and Nursi together and highlight some key lessons we can learn from their accounts as presented in this book.

In both Muhasibi and Nursi, the subject inhabits the world dialectically, dialogically and hence dynamically. It is one reason I have not spoken about the ideal subject in terms of personal virtue and identity. These latter terms connote some level of inner stability and fixity, some kind of fixed character or personality. I think Muhasibian and Nursian subjects are better narrated as people attaining one or another ideal *mode of being*, a particular kind of consciousness which is commensurate with their success, or failure, to engage dialectically and discursively with themselves and the world. For Muhasibi, the dialectic takes the form of introspection: one encounters suggestions and evaluates them, addresses oneself in particular ways to overcome threats to the sincerity of one's actions posed by vicious suggestions such as conceit, hypocrisy, pride and envy. For Nursi, one constantly engages one's affective and intellectual experience of the world, particularly its transient and tragic aspects, addressing oneself with Quranic verses and shifting one's perspective on things, changing the meanings one assigns to the world, both the beautiful and the apparently disturbing, that one finds in it. Both accounts present themselves as grounded in a desire to live and uphold a *tawhidic* perspective, a perspective that takes the oneness of God seriously. Both accounts are, of course, deeply theological. At the same time, how the oneness of God is to be felt and lived by a person, and the subjective standpoints and form of life that one's commitment to God's oneness should take, vary considerably. The emphases are different—fulfilling obligations for Muhasibi and witnessing divine meanings for Nursi—even as both accounts present us with a conception of an unsettled, non-complacent, non-triumphalist, reflective and dynamic subjectivity.

At a time where being Muslim is often seen as a social, even ethnic or political identity, I think it is particularly significant that both Muhasibi and Nursi offer accounts of ideal subjectivity that are not identitarian in their tenor and ends. Their accounts are also non-perfectionist, which is again timely. At a time when political philosophers are warning us about a dangerous impasse between the moral psychology of liberalism (with its psychic commitment to the principle of the revisability of all commitments) and the moral psychology of identarian religious claims (with its fearful rejection of all social and political arrangements that invite adjustments to and revisions of basic value commitments)[3]—Muhasibian and Nursian accounts have the potential to enrich and complicate the impasse and open avenues for discussion and conversation. The ideal subjects they espouse are not expected to attain moral or religious perfection. Instead, ideal subjects engage in processes of thought and interpretation that privilege a person's connection or relation to divine perfection over self-perfection. Perfection (of compassion, wisdom, dutiful observance of rights) is an ideal against which the subject constantly holds itself accountable and toward which it engenders in itself, through discourse, a deep and abiding sense of responsibility, fragility and dependence, a sense of what he might gain by attending to the indicative meanings in the universe.

This brings me to the relationship between conviction or certainty and the possibility of an inclusive and open-minded attitude toward different and even opposed others. Many people today think that the two do not go together. Those who prize open-mindedness tell us that without feeling uncertain about our commitments, we would bring agony and misery to others. We would hurt them by having strong convictions, regardless of the content of those convictions. We will make them feel excluded, weak-minded and inferior. As an act of humility and solidarity, then, we have an ethical duty to hold diluted, ironic and jittery commitments to all truth claims, be they religious or moral. Humility and honesty demand this.

On the other hand, there are those who want us to honor the identity-giving nature of certain commitments, particularly religious ones, and emphasize that certain commitments cannot be diluted or changed without negating one's identity and personhood altogether. In this picture, the person who demonstrates some unshakable commitments signals to others that those commitments are nonnegotiable aspects of their identity and insofar as this nonnegotiability acts as a barrier for deeper social solidarity, one is to simply accept this outcome as the social cost of safeguarding one's worldly or transcendental well-being and a seriousness about living out one's commitments in the face of adversity and opposition.

I think both views are valuable but fail to fully capture the complexities of religious and ethical commitments. Muhasibi and Nursi, in their own way, offer possibilities of a better alternative. Muhasibi and Nursi show us that the theoretical desire to have unshakable convictions may be strong and sincere but actual, lived commitments, as subjectively inhabited, will always be fraught—and productive and beautiful for being so. One is not to imagine that any particular human position or state fully embodies or expresses a sound or unshakable conviction. In other words, truth claims and convictions can be theoretically affirmed as sound and worthy of unshakable commitment but one's relation to those truths is imperfect and revisable. The problem is not always that one needs to dilute one's commitments. What is more important is that one honestly admits that one's ability to inhabit them is neither to be seen as entirely possible nor to be seen, as a matter of honesty, the person's own achievement. Muhasibi teaches, for instance, that a believer in God's unity is to think that the polytheist might be in a better position than himself on account of the latter's misunderstanding or lack of understanding of the truth of God's unity and on account of the believer's misplaced confidence about his own rank with God. Nursi expects the ideal subject to constantly find himself in a state where he would, again, need the healing guidance of the Quran.

There is another aspect to the view that one must be confident and untroubled by questions, doubts and problems in one's life. And this has to do, I think, with the success of the discipline of psychology in the modern world.[4] It seems that being mentally and emotionally troubled by existential or other questions has been thoroughly psychologized and pathologized in our times and many tend to speak about such human states and conditions in the language of psychological disorders and maladies. Anxiety, for many, is a scientific and psychological term, not a fleeting condition of the soul that flags some unmet need, a need that itself conveys some important message from the One who sent it. Not the exploration of self-interpretive possibilities but the pill is often the solution. Similarly, in a religious-identitarian framework, one that operates in a public realm saturated with the language of psychology, troubling uncertainties and anxieties must be overcome once and for all, through a well-administered dose of religious instruction and sacred knowledge. Religion, some feel, would fail if it did not fully cure the psychological problems of modern human beings. To feel unsettled, uneasy, vulnerable and weak is to display a psychologically worrying weakness of mind and will and thus a weakness of faith. Just like triumphalist conceptions of psychology may present it as the solution to all human dilemmas and problems, some religious leaders feel it is their duty to present religion as an alternative, equally total and miraculous, means to fixing everything that is broken, in one fell swoop of faith. Neither religion nor psychology can easily tolerate troubled minds/souls because they take such minds/souls to be signs of their failure. Muhasibi's and Nursi's accounts may show us a different path.

The picture of ideal subjectivity we get from them, I think, invites us to explore how we might be able to practically and reflectively move forward, in solidarity with people with whom we might fundamentally disagree, but without paternalistically asking them—or requiring it of ourselves—to feel uncertain about commitments that we might not actually be uncertain about and about commitments that give, or promise to give, joy and meaning to our lives as individuals and communities. In this sense, Muhasibian and Nursian accounts deserve a hearing and further analysis. This book has, I hope, done enough to open the conversation and invite others to it. I think their accounts of ideal Muslim consciousness may have something to offer those who are looking for resources to meaningfully and authentically reform certain aspects of the Islamic tradition, especially aspects that deal with fundamental reorientations toward oneself, toward one's relationship with the divine and one's relationship with others and the Quran as revelation.[5]

Muhasibian and Nursian subjects, as I have presented them in this book, come across as deeply self-absorbed, engaged in reflective exercises aimed at cultivating particular standpoints, and perceptions. I noted earlier that this personalism cannot be rejected or denied just because it looks to us uncomfortably similar to certain aspects of Protestant piety. In particular, Nursi's emphasis on personal belief and personal engagement with the Quran as divine speech may raise concerns among some who think that the modern, scripturalist attitude among tradition-bashing Muslims breeds a Salafist fundamentalism. But as we have seen, a Nursian subject's approach to the Quran is not a break from the tradition, even though it does introduce new elements and accents.[6] Moreover, a Nursian ideal subject is *not* to be ideologically and politically driven, but focus carefully on existential questions and a stronger sense of other-regard, an ethical other-regard that is simply an extension of self-regard, where the acting subject is acting in God's name, as a mirror to God's beautiful names. One is to manifest the beautiful names of God that one learns to see and perceive from a Quranically-guided perspective on the world, in one's intersubjective relations and encounters with humans and non-humans. It is important to note that Nursi urges ideal subjects to form communities of brotherhood with all believers, not just Muslims. Moreover, even with the opponents of belief, he asks that all and any arguments and disagreements, when they arise, be conducted by the pen and not the sword.[7] In Muhasibi as well, we see a self-absorbed introspective attitude consistent with a sense that one also needs to do right by others, as an obligation to God.

At the same time, we saw that Muhasibi and Nursi consistently warn against the pernicious effects of giving too much importance to the opinions of others, self-avowed identity and membership in a community. Favorable public opinion should never be the motivation or goal of an ideal Muslim subject. One's interest in others' well-being cannot be instrumental in terms of self-other relations in the world. Ideal subjects establish solidarity with others not on identitarian terms or along political and ideological lines. Rather, in the case of Muhasibi, solidarity is established in terms of shared interest in mutual well-being, earthly and transcendental. And, in the case of Nursi, solidarity is based on a shared, existential poverty, weakness and interdependence and thus the need for mutual assistance as a way of witnessing God's names. Nursian solidarity, founded on shared poverty, is not a Rortian "huddling together in the dark," though.[8] Rather, it is a mutual witnessing to God's various names that manifest through those weaknesses, needs and relations of interdependence. Muhasibian and Nursian subjects are asked to fortify their individual consciousness against the powerful forces of traditional and social conformity, that of public approval and censure.

Furthermore, both Muhasibi and Nursi were courageous innovators in their contexts and went against the intellectual currents of their times. In the case of Muhasibi, he went beyond the notion of a self-proclaimed, settled identity, writing at a time where being Muslim had become much easier and more of an inherited identity and communal membership. In the case of

Nursi, the ideal subject transcends ethnic and identitarian divisions and faces the challenges of positivism and scientism in order to see the world—and act in it—in the name of a Just and Compassionate God. Similarly, both teach us, in their own way, how an ideal subject employs a supplicatory agency, to take personal responsibility for making a difference in the world, to make life more beautiful, here and hereafter, for oneself and others.

This last point is important because we find ourselves in a situation where people have become polarized into camps and groups, religiously, morally and politically. The divisions are so deep that hope of reconciliation or mutual understanding and solidarity seems remote. The instruments, legislative powers of the state and public shaming or "canceling," do not seem to be bearing enough fruit. For instance, our governments legislated against racism but could only contain the damage, not heal from the disease. The attempt to solve deeply polarizing issues, from abortion to the environment, through legal means, has been challenging as one group seem entrenched against the opposed other. The hurt, it seems, is quite real on both sides of any polarizing issue today and there are other real difficulties as well; total moral bankruptcy is also a reality that cannot be sidestepped. Nevertheless, legal tools are too blunt to produce the kind of healthy, morally accountable and civil— though not necessarily warm and amicable—intersubjective relations with different and opposed others. In Muhasibian and Nursian accounts of ideal subjectivity, I think we are shown, or reminded of, a different framework for thinking about social relations, a framework that can nurture hope for a better future without asking everyone to just hug each other and forget about commitments to justice or other ethical principles.

I want to reflect about this new possibility that I find implied in these accounts of what it means to be an ideal Muslim subject as a series of "what if" questions, without intending to be rhetorical nor implying to know the full answers: What if people could be trained to feel accountable to their own, inner sense of justice, compassion, truth, mercy and wisdom? What if they felt inwardly moved to manifest compassion in their actions and positions above all other values and labels? What if people realized that what they understood or feel of compassion and wisdom is very tiny compared to the capacities their souls have for manifesting these qualities? What if they could be persuaded to adopt a learning subjectivity, an openness to looking anew at existence and observing the compassion and wisdom with which the cosmos is being managed and sustained? What if they came to realize that looking at the world to notice the compassion and wisdom it indicates is not some regressive theological or metaphysical delusion, but a thoroughly human and spiritually elevating one? What if human beings could reflect about the vastness and depth of compassion manifest in the world, in relations and things, and let those reflections expand their own capacities for love and compassion? What if they could then come to feel the need to express a deep and life-giving compassion for the joy such expression brings to them? What if a commitment to renew and grow in one's capacity to express an observed and felt, divine and subjectively affirmed compassion enabled human beings to act compassionately in situations where they currently feel it is impossible to do so? In all of this, there is no fixed course of action that anyone will be expected to take and so no guarantees of better outcomes can be had. But one can hope that if people could observe the countless instances of compassionate and wise, divine actions in the universe, perhaps their appreciation for those names and their joys of association with those names would lead them to act freely but with an inner sense of responsibility toward the compassion and wisdom they themselves love. This, at any rate, I think, given their accounts of ideal subjectivity I have examined in this book, could be a Muhasibian and Nursian intervention into the bitter and hurtful antagonisms, rivalries and oppressions that so many human communities are facing at so many levels around the globe.

That brings me to my final point. Here is a strange question for you: What do industrially farmed chickens, the internet, Usain Bolt, a professor writing a book and life in the modern world all have in common? I would say its speed. Chickens must grow faster to meet our insatiable need for consuming animal meat, no matter how and what moral cost it is produced. The internet (is it 5G now?) must be faster so we can access more information faster, with little worry whether the information is necessary, reliable or ethical. The professor must finish his book and publish soon or risk losing his job. And all whose lives are structured by the demands of the modern economy must be efficient and accomplish an increasing number of tasks (in multiple roles) in the same amount of time. The examples, demands and perils of fast-paced existence are ubiquitous in our lives. We rightly tell each other to slow down because we sense that our humanity just can't keep up with life lived at the pace we often feel compelled to sustain in order to survive, let alone flourish and be successful.

I think our realization for the need for speed reveals some of our nervousness about the fragility and responsibility that comes with our autonomy and agency.[9] As well, the delayed is anathema to us because it leaves us with an interim that we don't quite know what to do about—the time between starting a task or project and the project's completion. What shall we do with all our energies and capacities to act? Are we wasting them when we are slowing down and not acting fast enough? How do we avoid inaction without getting ourselves or others into trouble with our drive to do something purposeful and meaningful, and fast, with our lives? The anxieties about being late to life, about delays—something should have been but is not—effects the way we think about formations and transformations in the religious and ethical realms (personal, individual and social). In contrast, the discourses of subject formation we looked at in this book suggest that real change happens more slowly, just as winter's ravages take time and so does the gradual return of life in the spring and this may easily escape the rushed gaze. When a Muhasibian subject purifies his intention while helping his neighbor or a Nursian subject relates to the season of fall and winter or to his ageing parent to hear and witness divine names, the changes he himself goes through in acting in those ways and with those goals may not always produce immediate and noticeable external effects. And yet, such inner changes can, in the long run, indeed drive genuine, profound, compassionate and dignified ways of being in the world, both at the individual and social-cultural level. If we insist on seeing the changes fast and seek only major external transformations and changes, we may be missing out on noting and investing in the changes that matter more for human well-being.

On a related note, and in closing, I would like to consider the following striking remarks by a preeminent religious ethicist of our times, Charles Matthewes. Matthewes brings up Osama Bin Laden (mastermind of the 9/11 attacks) while commenting on what he thinks are the psychological underpinnings of contemporary Islamic extremism. Matthewes says,

> Bin Laden offers these young true believers a "pure" version of Islam, by which he means one that is disembodied—stripped of its local saints, customs, and traditions, all traditional to Islamic faith. He offers them an identity, a way to know who they are: righteous members of a global Muslim *umma* to which they can belong despite their diasporic scattering and material entanglement in the *dar al-harb*. And the identity he offers them is quite modern, answering to the unwittingly modern needs of these young men; their faith, he says, is demonstrated not by conformity to a host of external social customs and observances, but rather by a radical act of inner belief. Outward material manifestations are important, but only as signifying that inner "spiritual" belief. For these believers, the *pious intensity of individual faith* is all-important, which is why Bin Laden *can demand a jihadism of all believers*. All of this—the import of the "pure" original (but profoundly innovative) Islamic vision, the concomitant argument that the tradition as developed has demonically misled believers, the insistence on the individual's direct relation with Allah—suggests the distinctive modernity of bin Laden's message. Indeed, in a way it echoes Christian Protestantism. Many voices have called for a "Reformation" of Islam, a Muslim Martin Luther. *Few realize that that Luther may already be out there, but not on our side* [emphasis added].[10]

Even though the overall failure of terrorist organizations in recruiting Muslims has been noted,[11] it is understandable that Matthewes is concerned about the reasons for which Jihadism might appeal to some young Muslims. And, of course, he is also right to note that Bin Laden's "reform" forms a radical break from the classical Islamic tradition and that this reform is not on our side; it is not desirable at all. What is unsettling, however, is the intimate association made between modern Islam's turn to inner spiritual belief and

Bin Laden–style, violent extremism. The accounts of ideal subjectivity offered in this book hopefully help us revisit such baffling associations between a contemporary/modern Muslim interest in a personal, rational, inner, spiritual belief and inhumane and despicable, indiscriminate violence against innocents. The accounts I have presented indeed ask ideal subjects to espouse a purer, inner, spiritual belief and a direct connection with the divine. And those standpoints and forms of life present to us a portrait of ideal Muslim subjectivity quite different from the one that ethicists as well as some Muslims may have come to associate with a belief-focused, personalist approach to piety and scripture.[12]

Muhasibian and Nursian accounts, contrary to lending support to some global violent project, lead us to say that ideal subjects ought to embody a patient hope, through every day, seemingly minor, reflectively and discursively altered standpoints. They ought to spend effort making seemingly inconsequential but crucial perspectival adjustments. There is no need to radically and forcefully restructure the outer world but a need to act self-critically, thoughtfully, justly and compassionately such that more beauty, justice and compassion manifests in the world. Over a lifetime perhaps, through effecting these changes in one's perspective and through constant inner struggles against vicious suggestions, one would find oneself to have lived better, a person who may hope they have fulfilled their obligations toward God and others, as Muhasibi hoped, and more fully manifested God's beautiful names into the world without making any claim to virtue or perfection or piety for themselves, as Nursi suggested. I hope this book allows the reader to appreciate the various nonviolent and ethically salutary discursive practices that Muhasibi and Nursi offer to their Muslim audience for forging an ideal Muslim consciousness through, and not despite, repeatedly turning to personal, inner belief practices over a lifetime.

NOTES

1. Tracy Fessenden, *Culture and Redemption: Religion, the Secular and American Literature* (Princeton, NJ: Princeton University Press, 2007), 214.

2. Fessenden, *Culture and Redemption*, 217.

3. Akeel Bilgrami, "Secular Liberalism and Moral Psychology of Identity," *Economic and Political Weekly* 32, no. 40 (October 1997), 40: 2527–2540. For a more detailed discussion, see his *Secularism, Identity and Enchantment* (Cambridge, MA: Harvard University Press, 2014). Also see Jason A Scorza, "Liberal Citizenship and Civic Friendship," *Political Theory* 32, no. 1 (2004): 85–108.

4. I have benefited from this very interesting reflection on the state of psychology in the modern world written by a psychiatrist: Munawar Butt, *Psychology, Sin and Society: An Essay on the Triumvirate of Psychology, Religion and Democracy* (Lanham, MD: University Press of America, 1992), 125–178.

5. I think, for instance, that emerging work in Muslim theology stands to benefit with a deeper, nontraditional engagement with Muhasibian and Nursian discourses. See Martin Nguy-

en, *Modern Muslim Theology: Engaging God and the World with Faith and Imagination* (Lanham, MD: Rowman & Littlefield Publishers, 2018).

6. Even when Nursi criticizes certain common traditional practices and views or introduces new ideas, he doesn't express it as a break but as a "renewal" project. Tuna, Mustafa. "At the Vanguard of Contemporary Muslim Thought: Reading Said Nursi into the Islamic Tradition," *Journal of Islamic Studies* 28, no. 3 (2017): 311–340. See also Hamid Algar, "The Centennial Renewer: Bediuzzaman Said Nursi and the Tradition of *Tajdīd*." *Journal of Islamic Studies* 12, no. 3 (2001): 291–311.

7. Colin Turner, *The Qur'an Revealed: A Critical Analysis of Said Nursi's Epistles of Light* (Berlin: Gerlach Press, 2013), 565–570.

8. Richard Rorty, *Consequences of Pragmatism* (Minneapolis: University of Minnesota Press, 1982), 150, 153.

9. For a discussion of fragility in relation to moral excellence, see Martha Nussbaum, *The Fragility of Goodness: Luck and Ethics in Greek Tragedy and Philosophy* (New York: Cambridge University Press, 2001).

10. Charles Matthewes, *The Republic of Grace: Augustinian Thoughts for Dark Times* (Grand Rapids, MI: Eerdmans, 2010), 67.

11. See: Charles Kurzman, *The Missing Martyrs: Why Are There So Few Muslim Terrorists?* Second edition (New York: Oxford University Press, 2018).

12. As John Esposito and Dalia Mogahed note, Muslims who support violent means for change do not tend to cite any religious reason but rather a need for a quick political change as justification for violence. See Esposito and Mogahed, *Who Speaks for Islam: What a Billion Muslims Really Think* (New York: Gallup Press, 2007), 72–74.

Bibliography

Ahmad, Shahab. *What is Islam? The Importance of Being Islamic*. Princeton, NJ: Princeton University Press, 2015.
Ahmadi, Nader and Fereshteh Ahmadi. *Iranian Islam: The Concept of the Individual*. London: MacMillan Press, 1998.
Algar, Hamid. "The Centennial Renewer: Bediuzzaman Said Nursi and the Tradition of Tajdīd." *Journal of Islamic Studies* 12, no. 3 (2001): 291–311.
Anscombe, Gertrude Elizabeth Margaret. "Modern Moral Philosophy." *Philosophy* 33, no. 124 (1958): 1–19.
Asad, Muhammad. *The Message of the Qur'an*. Gibraltar, Spain: Dar al-Andalus, 1984.
Asad, Talal. *Genealogies of Religion: Discipline and Reasons of Power in Christianity and Islam*. Baltimore: The Johns Hopkins University Press, 1993.
———. "The Idea of an Anthropology of Islam." *Qui Parle*, 17 no. 2 (2009): 1–30.
Al-Attar, Mariam. *Islamic Ethics: Divine Command Theory in Arabo-Islamic Thought*. New York: Routledge Press, 2010.
Awass, Omer. "Fatwa, Discursivity, and the Art of Ethical Embedding," *Journal of the American Academy of Religion*, 87 (2019) 3: 765–790.
Baker, Judith. "Vulnerabilities of Morality." *Canadian Journal of Philosophy* 141, no. 38 (2008): 141–160.
Bashir, Shahzad. *Sufi Bodies: Religion and Society in Medieval Islam*. New York: Columbia University Press, 2011.
Bell, Daniel. "Communitarianism." In *The Stanford Encyclopedia of Philosophy*. Stanford University, 2016. Article published with revision March 21, 2016. https://plato.stanford.edu/archives/sum2016/entries/communitarianism/.
Bilgrami, Akeel. *Secularism, Identity and Enchantment*. Cambridge, MA: Harvard University Press, 2014.
———. "Secular Liberalism and Moral Psychology of Identity." *Economic and Political Weekly* 32, no. 40 (Oct. 1997): 2527–2540.
Brakke, David., Michael L. Satlow, Steven Weitzman, ed., *Religion and the Self in Antiquity*. Bloomington: Indiana University Press, 2005.
Bucar, Elizabeth M. *Creative Conformity: The Feminist Politics of U.S. Catholic and Iranian Shi'i Women*. Washington, DC: Georgetown University Press, 2011.
———. "Dianomy: Understanding Religious Women's Moral Agency as Creative Conformity." *Journal of the American Academy of Religion* 78, no. 3 (2010): 662–686.
Bucar, Elizabeth M. and Aaron Stalnaker, eds. *Religious Ethics in a Time of Globalism: Shaping a Third Wave of Comparative Analysis*. New York: Palgrave Macmillan, 2012.

Butt, Munawar. *Psychology, Sin and Society: An Essay on the Triumvirate of Psychology, Religion and Democracy*. Lanham, MD: University Press of America, 1992.
Cahill, Lisa Sowle. "Gender and Strategies of Goodness: New Testament and Ethics." *The Journal of Religion* 80, no. 3 (2000), 442–460.
Carney, Frederick. "Some Aspects of Islamic Ethics." *The Journal of Religion* 63, no. 2 (1983): 159–174.
Chan-Malik, Sylvia. *Being Muslim: A Cultural History of Women of Color in American Islam*. New York: NYU Press, 2018.
Chittick, William. *The Sufi Path of Knowledge: Ibn al-Arabi's Metaphysics of Imagination*. State University of New York Press, 1989.
Cillis, Maria De. *Freewill and Predestination in Islamic Thought: Theoretical Compromises in the Works of Avicenna, Al-Ghazālī and Ibn 'Arabī*. New York: Routledge Press, 2014.
Clark, Jane. "Universal Meanings in Ibn 'Arabi's *Fuṣuṣ al-ḥikam*: Some Comments on the Chapter of Moses." *Journal of the Muhyiddin Ibn 'Arabi Society* 38 (2005): 105–129.
Cocking, Dean and Jeanette Kennett. "Friendship and Moral Danger." *Journal of Philosophy* 97 (2000): 278–296.
———. "Friendship and the Self." *Ethics* 108 (1998): 502–527.
Cook, Michael. *Commanding Right and Forbidding Wrong in Islamic Thought*. New York: Cambridge University Press, 2010.
———. *Forbidding Wrong in Islam: An Introduction*. Cambridge University Press, 2003.
Cooperson, Michael. *Classical Arabic Biography: The Heirs of the Prophets in the Age of al-Ma'mūn*. New York: Cambridge University Press, 2000.
Cottine, Cheryl. "Role Modeling in an Early Confucian Context." *Journal of Value Inquiry* 50, no. 4 (2016): 797–819.
Davidson, Arnold I. "Archeology, Genealogy, Ethics." In *Foucault: A Critical Reader*, edited by David C. Hoy, 221–234. New York: Basil Blackwell, 1986.
———. "Introduction." In *Philosophy as a Way of Life: Spiritual Exercises from Socrates to Foucault*, edited by Arnold I. Davidson, 1–45. Malden, MA: Blackwell Publishing, 1995.
Elias, Jamal. *Death before Dying: The Sufi Poems of Sultan Bahu*. University of California Press, 1998.
Esposito, John L. and Dalia Mogahed. *Who Speaks for Islam: What a Billion Muslims Really Think*. New York: Gallup Press, 2007.
Ess, Josef van. *Die Gedankenwelt Des Ḥārith al-Muḥāsibī*. Bonn: Selbstverlag des Orientalischen Seminars der Universität Bonn, 1961.
———. *The Flowering of Muslim Theology*. Translated by Jane Marie Todd. Cambridge: Harvard University Press, 2006.
Faruki, Kemal. "Legal Implications for Today of *al-Aḥkām al-Khamsa* (The Five Values)." In *Ethics in Islam*, edited by Richard G. Hovannisian, 65–72. Malibu, CA: Undena Publications, 1985.
Faubion, James. *An Anthropology of Ethics*. Cambridge: Cambridge University Press, 2011.
Fessenden, Tracy. *Culture and Redemption: Religion, the Secular and American Literature*. Princeton, NJ: Princeton University Press, 2007.
Filiz, Şahin. "The Founder of the Muḥāsaba School of Sufism: Al-Ḥārith ibn Asad al-Muḥāsibī." *Islamic Studies* 45 (2006): 59–81.
Foucault, Michel. "About the Beginnings of the Hermeneutics of the Self: Two Lectures at Dartmouth." *Political Theory* 21, no. 2 (1993): 198–227.
Frank, Richard. "Moral Obligation in Classical Islamic Theology." *Journal of Religious Ethics* 11 (1983): 204–223.
———. "The Structure of Created Causality according to al-Ash'arī." *Studia Islamica* 25 (1966): 13–76.
Frankfurt, Harry G. "Freedom of the Will and the Concept of a Person." *The Journal of Philosophy* 68, no. 1 (1971): 5–20.
Furey, Constance. "Body, Society and Subjectivity in Religious Studies." *Journal of the American Academy of Religion* 80 (March 2012): 7–33.
———. *Poetic Relations: Intimacy and Faith in the English Reformation*. Chicago: University of Chicago Press, 2017.

Gade, Anna. *Perfection Makes Practice: Learning, Emotion, and the Recited Quran in Indonesia*. Honolulu: University of Hawaii Press, 2004.
Geertz, Clifford. "Religion as a Cultural System." In *The Interpretation of Cultures: Selected Essays*, edited by Clifford Geertz, 87–125. London: Fontana Press, 1993.
Ghamari-Tabrizi, Behrooz. *Foucault in Iran Islamic Revolution after the Enlightenment*. Minneapolis: University of Minnesota Press, 2016.
Al-Ghazālī, *Al-Ghazali on the Remembrance of Death and the Afterlife*. Translated by Timothy Winters. Cambridge, UK: Islamic Texts Society, 2016.
Godlas, Alan. "A Religiological Analysis of Nursi's View of Sufism Expressed in the 'Nine Allusions' (*Telvihât-ı Tis'a*) of the Risale-i Nur," *Islam and Christian-Muslim Relations* 19, no. 1 (2008): 39–52.
Hadot, Pierre. *Philosophy as a way of Life: Spiritual Exercises from Socrates to Foucault*. New York: Wiley-Blackwell Press, 1995.
Hallaq, Wael. *The Impossible State: Islamic, Politics and Modernity's Moral Predicament*. New York: Columbia University Press, 2013.
Hart, John. *The Wiley Blackwell Companion to Religion and Ecology*. Hoboken, NJ: John Wiley & Sons, 2017.
Heck, Paul. "Mysticism as Morality: The Case of Sufism." *Journal of Religious Ethics* 34, no. 2 (2006): 253–286.
Hirschkind, Charles. *The Ethical Soundscape: Cassette Sermons and Islamic Counterpublics*. New York: Columbia University Press, 2006.
Hoy, David C., ed. *Foucault: A Critical Reader*. New York: Basil Blackwell, 1986.
Iqbal, Muzaffar. "Scientific Commentary on the Quran." In *The Study Quran: A New Translation and Commentary*, edited by S. Hossein Nasr, Caner Dagli, Marie M. Dakake, Joseph E. B. Lumbard, 1679–1693. New York: Harper One, 2015.
Izutsu, Toshihiko. *Ethico-Religious Concepts in the Quran*. Montreal: McGill-Queens University Press, 2002.
James, William. *The Varieties of Religious Experience: A Study in Human Nature*. London: Longmans, Green, 1910.
Jaques, Robert Kevin. "Belief." In *Key Themes for the Study of Islam*, edited by Jamal Elias. Oxford: Oneworld Publications, 2010, 53–71.
Johansen, Baber. *Contingency in a Sacred Law: Legal and Ethical Norms in the Muslim Fiqh*. Leiden: Brill Press, 1999.
Jong, F. de, Hamid Algar, and C. H. Imber. "Malāmatiyya." In *Encyclopaedia of Islam, Second Edition*. http://dx.doi.org.proxy.library.upenn.edu/10.1163/1573-3912_islam_COM_0643.
Karamustafa, Ahmet. *Sufism: The Formative Period*. Berkeley: University of California Press, 2007.
Kelsay, John. "Islam and the Study of Ethics." *Method and Theory in the Study of Religion* 24, no. 4–5 (2012): 357–370.
———. "Islamic Law and Ethics." *The Journal of Religious Ethics* 22, no. 1 (1994): 93–99.
Knysh, Alexander. *Islamic Mysticism: A Short History*. Leiden: Brill Press, 2010.
Larmore, Charles. *The Practices of the Self*. Translated by Sharon Bowman. Chicago: University of Chicago Press, 2010.
Lear, Jonathan. *Radical Hope: Ethics in the Face of Cultural Devastation*. Cambridge, MA: Harvard University Press, 2008.
Lewis, Thomas A. *Why Philosophy Matters for the Study of Religion—and Vice Versa*. Oxford: Oxford University Press, 2015.
Lewis, Thomas A., Jonathan Schofer, Aaron Stalnaker, and Mark A. Berkson. "Anthropos and Ethics: Categories of Inquiry and Procedures of Comparison." *Journal of Religious Ethics* 33.2 (2005): 177–185.
Librande, L. "Islam and Conservation: The Theologian-Ascetic al-Muḥāsibī." *Arabica* 30 (1983): 125–146.
Lincoln, Bruce. *Authority: Construction and Corrosion*. Chicago: University of Chicago Press, 1994.
MacIntyre, Alasdair. *After Virtue: A Study in Moral Theory*. Notre Dame, IN: University of Notre Dame Press, 1984.

Bibliography

———. *Dependent Rational Animals: Why Human Beings Need the Virtues*. The Paul Carus Lectures. Illinois: Open Court Press, 2001.
Mahmood, Saba. *Politics of Piety: The Islamic Revival and the Feminist Subject*. Princeton: Princeton University Press, 2005.
Martin, Richard, Mark Woodward and Dwi Atmaja. *Defenders of Reason in Islam: Mu'tazilism from Medieval School to Modern Symbol*. Rockport, MA: Oneworld Publications, 1997.
Massignon, Louis. *Essays on the Origins of the Technical Language of Islamic Mysticism*. Translated by Benjamin Clark. Notre Dame, Indiana: University of Notre Dame Press, 1997.
Mathewes, Charles. *The Republic of Grace: Augustinian Thoughts for Dark Times*. Grand Rapids, MI: William B. Eerdmans Publishing Company, 2010.
Mathewes, Charles, Matthew Puffer, and Mark Storslee. *Comparative Religious Ethics: The Major Works*. In 4 Volumes. Editors. New York: Routledge, 2015.
Melchert, Christopher. "Quranic Abrogation across the Ninth Century: Shāfi'ī, Abū 'Ubayd, Muḥāsibī, And Ibn Qutaybah." In *Studies In Islamic Legal Theory*, edited by Bernard G. Weiss, 75–98. Leiden: Brill, 2002.
———. "Transition from Asceticism to Mysticism in the Middle of the 9th Century." *Studia Islamica* 83 (1996): 51–70.
Mermer, Yamina Bougeuenaya. 1996. "Induction, Science and Causation: Some Critical Reflections," *Islamic Studies* 35, no. 3: 243–282.
Mermer, Yamina Bougeuenaya, and Redha Ameur. "Beyond the Modern: Sa'id al-Nursi's View of Science." *Islam and Science* 2 (Winter 2004): 119–160.
Mermer, Yamina Bougeuenaya, and Isra Yazicioglu. "Said Nursi's Qur'anic Hermeneutics," in *The Companion to Said Nursi Studies*. Edited by Ian Markham & Z. Sayilgan, Pickwick Publications, 2017, 51–66.
Miller, Richard B. *Friends and Other Strangers: Studies in Religion, Ethics and Culture*. NY: Columbia Press, 2018.
———. "On Making a Cultural Turn in Religious Ethics." *Journal of Religious Ethics* 33 (2005) 3: 39–74.
Miller, Vincent J. *Consuming Religion: Christian Faith and Practice in a Consumer Culture*. New York, Continuum: 2003.
Moosa, Ebrahim. *Ghazālī and the Poetics of Imagination*. Chapel Hill: The University of North Carolina Press, 2006.
Morad, Suleiman Ali. *Early Islam between Myth and History: al-Ḥasan al-Baṣrī (d. 110H/728 CE) and the Formation of his Legacy in Classical Islamic Scholarship*. Leiden: Brill, 2006.
Al-Muḥāsibī, al-Ḥārith b. Asad. *Bad' man anāba ila Allah wa yalīhi ādāb al-nufūs*. Cairo: Dar al-Islam, 1991.
———. *Kitāb al-ri'āya li ḥuqūq Allāh*. Edited by Margaret Smith. London: Luzac & Co., 1940.
———. *al-Masā'il fī a'māl al-qulūb wa-al-jawāriḥ wa-ma'ahu al-Masā'il fī al-zuhd; wa Kitāb al-Makāsib; wa-Kitāb al-'Aql*. Edited by Khalīl Imran. Bayrūt: Dār al-Kutub al-'Ilmīyah, 2000.
———. *al-Ri'āya li huqūq allah*, ed. Abd al-Halim Mahmud. Cairo: Dar al-Ma'arif, 2003.
———. *Sharḥ al-ma'rifa wa badhal al-naṣīḥa*. Damascus: Dār al-Qalam, 1993.
Nguyen, Martin. *Modern Muslim Theology: Engaging God and the World with Faith and Imagination*. Lanham, MD: Rowman & Littlefield Publishers, 2018.
Norden, Bryan Van. "Virtue Ethics and Confucianism." In *Comparative Approaches to Chinese Philosophy*, edited by Bo Mou. London: Ashgate Publishing, 2003, 99–121.
Nursi, Bediuzzaman Said. *The Flashes: From the Risale-i Nur Collection*. Translated by Sukran Vahide. Istanbul: Sozler Nesriyat, 1995.
———. *The Letters: From the Risale-i Nur Collection*. Translated by Sukran Vahide. Istanbul: Sozler Nesriyat, 1994.
———. *Living the Quran with Joy and Purpose: Selections on Tawhid from Said Nursi's Epistle of Light* (forthcoming). Translated with introduction and notes by Yamina Bouguenaya and Isra Yazicioglu. Piscataway, NJ: Gorgias Press, 2020.
———. *The Rays: From the Risale-i Nur Collection*. Trandlated by. Sukran Vahide. Istanbul: Sozler Nesriyat, 2002.

―――. *The Words: From the Risale-i Nur Collection*. Translated by Sukran Vahide. Istanbul: Sozler Nesriyat, 2004.
Nussbaum, Martha. *The Fragility of Goodness: Luck and Ethics in Greek Tragedy and Philosophy*. New York: Cambridge University Press, 2001.
Picken, Gavin. "Ibn Ḥanbal and al-Muḥāsibī: A Study of Early Conflicting Scholarly Methodologies." *Arabica* 55, no. 3–4 (July 2008): 337–361.
―――. *Spiritual Purification in Islam: The Life and Works of al-Muḥāsibī*. New York: Routledge Press, 2011.
Qadri, Junaid. "Moral Habituation in the Law: Rethinking the Ethics of the Sharīʿa." *Islamic Law and Society* 26, no. 3 (2019):191–226.
Rahman, Fazlur. "The State of the Individual in Islam." *Islamic Studies* 5 (December 1966) 4: 319–330.
Ramli, Harith Bin. "The Predecessors of Ash'arism: Ibn Kullāb, al-Muḥāsibī and al-Qalānisī." In *The Oxford Handbook of Islamic Theology*, edited by Sabine Schmidtke, 215–224. Oxford, UK: Oxford University Press, 2016.
Reinhart, Kevin. "Islamic Law as Islamic Ethics." *Journal of Religious Ethics* 11, no. 2 (1983): 186–203.
Rizvi, Sajjad H. "Philosophy as a Way of life in the World of Islam: Applying Hadot to the study of Mullā Ṣadrā Shīrāzī (d. 1635)." *Bulletin of the School of Oriental and African Studies* 75, no.1 (2012): 33–45.
Rumi, Mawlana Jalal al-din. *Mathnawi*. Book II: 692. (Translated by R. A. Nicholson, Gibb Memorial Trust, 2016, accessed via http://www.masnavi.net/1/25/eng/2/692/).
Rorty, Richard. "The Historiography of Philosophy: Four Genres." In *Philosophy in History: Essays on the Historiography of Philosophy*. Edited by Richard Rorty, J. B. Schneewind and Quentin Skinner. New York: Cambridge University Press, 1984.
Schofer, Jonathan. "Ethical Formation and Subjection." *Numen* 59, vol. 1 (2012): 1–31.
―――. *The Making of a Sage: A Study in Rabbinic Ethics*. Madison: University of Wisconsin Press, 2005.
Schweiker, William. "On The Future Of Religious Ethics: Keeping Religious Ethics, Religious and Ethical." *Journal of the American Academy of Religion* 74, no.1 (2006): 135–156.
Scorza, Jason A. "Liberal Citizenship and Civic Friendship." *Political Theory* 32, no.1 (2004): 85–108.
Sells, Michael. *Early Islamic Mysticism: Sufi, Quran, Miʿrāj, Poetic and Theological Writings*. New York: Paulist Press, 1995.
Sheikh, Faraz. "Encountering Opposed Others and Countering Suggestions [khaṭarāt]: Notes on Religious Tolerance from Ninth Century Arab-Muslim Thought," *Comparative Islamic Studies* 11 (2015) 2: 179–204.
Shulman, David., Guy. S. Stroumsa, ed. *Self and Self-Transformation in the History of Religions*. New York: Oxford University Press, 2002.
Smith, Margaret. *An Early Mystic of Baghdad: A Study of the Life and Teaching of Ḥārith b. Asad al-Muḥāsibī*. London: Sheldon Press, 1935.
―――. "The forerunner of al-Ghazālī." *The Journal of the Royal Asiatic Society of Great Britain and Ireland* (January, 1936): 65–78.
Stalnaker, Aaron. *Overcoming Our Evil: Human Nature and Spiritual Exercises in Xunzi and Augustine*. Washington, DC: Georgetown University Press, 2007.
―――. "Virtue as Mastery in Early Confucianism." *Journal of Religious Ethics* 38, no. 3 (2010): 404–428.
Al-Sulamī, Abū ʿAbd al-Raḥmān. *Kitāb ṭabaqāt al-ṣūfiyya*. Edited by Johannes Pedersen. Leiden: E. J. Brill, 1960.
Sviri, Sara. "Hakim Tirmidhi and the Malamati movement in Early Sufism." In *Classical Persian Sufism from Its Origins to Rumi*, edited by Leonard Lewisohn, 587–92. London: Khaniqahi Nimatullahi Publications, 1993.
―――. "The Self and its Transformation in Sufism: With Special Reference to Early Literature." In *Self and Self-Transformation in the History of Religions*, edited by David Shulman and Guy Stroumsa. New York: Oxford University Press, 2002.
Taylor, Charles. *The Ethics of Authenticity*. Cambridge, MA: Harvard University Press, 1992.

---. *Sources of the Self: The Making of the Modern Identity.* Cambridge, MA: Harvard University Press, 1989.
Tekke, Mustafa and P. J. Watson, "Supplication and the Muslim Personality: Psychological Nature and Functions of Prayer as Interpreted by Said Nursi," *Mental Health, Religion and Culture* 20, no. 2 (2017): 143–153.
Todd, Richard. *The Sufi Doctrine of Man: Ṣadr al-Dīn al-Qūnawī's Metaphysical Anthropology.* Leiden: Brill, 2014.
Tuna, Mustafa. "At the Vanguard of Contemporary Muslim Thought: Reading Said Nursi into the Islamic Tradition." *Journal of Islamic Studies* 28, no. 3 (2017): 311–340.
Turner, Colin. *The Qur'an Revealed: A Critical Analysis of Said Nursi's Epistles of Light.* Berlin: Gerlach Press, 2013.
Vahide, Şükran. *Islam in Modern Turkey: An Intellectual Biography of Bediuzzaman Said Nursi.* Albany: State University of New York Press, 2005.
---. "A Survey of the Main Spiritual Themes of the Risale-i Nur." In *Spiritual Dimensions of Bediuzzaman Nursi's Risale-I Nur,* edited by Ibrahim M. Abu-Rabi. New York: SUNY Press, 2008.
---. "Toward an Intellectual Biography of Said Nursi," In *Islam at the Crossroads: On the Life and Thought of Bediuzzaman Said Nursi,* edited by Ibrahim M. Abu-Rabi, 1–22. Albany: State University of New York Press, 2003.
Vasalou, Sophia. *Moral Agents and Their Deserts: The Character of Mu'tazilite Ethics.* Princeton, NJ: Princeton University Press, 2008.
Yazaki, See Saeko. "Morality in Early Sufi Literature." In *The Cambridge Companion to Sufism,* edited by Lloyd Ridgeon, 74–100. New York: Cambridge University Press, 2015.
Yazicioglu, Isra. "Affliction, Patience and Prayer: Reading Job (p) in the Qur'an." In *The Journal of Scriptural Reasoning,* 4:1, 2004, http://etext.lib.virginia.edu/journals/ssr/issues/volume4/number1/ssr04-01-e01.html.
---. "Engaging with Abraham and His Knife: Interpretation of Abraham's Sacrifice in the Muslim Tradition." In *Interpreting Abraham: Journeys to Moriah,* edited by Bradley Beach and Matthew Powell, 57–86. Minneapolis: Fortress Press, 2014.
---. "A Graceful Reconciliation: Said Nursi on Free Will and Destiny." In *The Companion to Said Nursi Studies,* edited by Ian Markham and Z. Sayilgan, 129–145. Eugene, OR: Pickwick Publications, 2017.
---. "Sa'id Nursi." *The Princeton Encyclopedia of Islamic Political Thought.* Edited by G. Bowering, P. Crone, W. Kadi, D. J. Stewart, M. Q. Zaman, and M. Mirza. Princeton: Princeton University Press, 2011.
---. *Understanding the Qur'anic Miracle Stories in the Modern Age.* University Park: Penn State University Press, 2013.
Yearley, Lee H. *Mencius and Aquinas: Theories of Virtue and Conceptions of Courage.* Albany: State University of New York Press, 1990.
Walbridge, John. *God and Logic in Islam: The Caliphate of Reason.* Cambridge: Cambridge University Press, 2011.
Zargar, Cyrus. *The Polished Mirror: Storytelling and the Pursuit of Virtue in Islamic Philosophy and Sufism.* London, England: Oneworld Academic, 2017.
Zizek, Slavoj. *The Courage of Hopelessness: Chronicles of a Year of Acting Dangerously.* UK: Penguin Press, 2017.

Index

Abdurrahman, 127–129
Abraham, 119–120
abstention (*zuhd*), 55–57
acquisition, 88–89
act analysis (*aḥkām alkhamsa*), 48, 49, 50–53, 61n65
acting: knowledge, reason and deliberation before, 36; publicly, 74, 76, 77
actions: correctness of, 55; good, 77; non-action and, 64
acts of spirituality, 23
advisor-advisee relationship, 71–72
After Virtue (MacIntyre), 17
agency, supplication as, 113–114
aḥkām alkhamsa (act analysis), 48, 49, 50–53, 61n65
Alawis, Sunnis and, 148
analytical space, 20
Anscombe, G., 17
anthropology: ethics and, 20; Islam and, 18, 19, 35; of Muhasibi, 35; philosophical, 15
anxiety, 163
apophatic mirroring, 109
appreciation, 141
Aristotle, 70
arrogance (*kibr*), 89–91
Asad, Talal, 18–20, 49, 60n43
attachment, greed and, 56
al-Attar, 11

avowal: God and, 32; by religious subject, 32
awareness (*taqwa*), 86–87

the bad, the good and, 8
beautiful names of God, 104, 122, 150, 164; indicative meanings and, 101–102, 127; prophets and, 116
beauty, 8, 115–119
being Muslim: juridical and mystical models of, 9–12; Muhasibi and Nursi on, 7–8; politics, identity and, 154
belief: agency and, 114; connection with God through, 107–108; as contemplative perspective, 99; dialectics of, 127–129; faith and, 99; as fluid, 127–129; in the hereafter, subject formation and, 120–125; imitative, 100; as lived practice, 105; Nursi on, 99; in *qadar*, 125–127; reflective, 100; standpoint of, 135; supplication and, 113–114; *tawhid* and, 102–103, 112
belief perspectives, 99–101
Benedictines, 49
Bin Laden, Osama, 167–168
bismillah (in the name of God), 111
blame, praise and, 75–76, 78
blessedness, 135
bodily practices, 35, 87
body, 12
brotherhood, 146–149

care of the self, 23
causality, 103–105, 106, 131n23, 138
Chan-Malik, Sylvia, 95n7
character, 78
children, on the hereafter, 122–123
Christianity: Asad on, 49, 60n43; Islam and, 49; medieval, 49; New England Protestants, 130n2
Cocking, Dean, 70
commitments, 162
comparative religious ethics (CRE), 16, 25n3, 74, 160
compassion, 136–141
concealment, 86–88
conceit (*'ujb*), 89
Confucianism, 74
conjunction, ethics of, 138–141
consciousness (*taqwa*), 86–87
consequential speech, 72
consolations, for the young and the infirm, 122–123
Consuming Religion (Miller, V.), 142
contemplative perspective, belief as, 99
continuity of existence, 124
correctness, of actions, 55
Cottine, Cheryl, 74–75
CRE. *See* comparative religious ethics
criticism, other-regard and, 81–84
Crow Nation, 14–15
Culture and Redemption (Fessenden), 159

Davidson, Arnold I., 17–18, 28n57
death: contemplating, 42–45; Nursi on Abdurrahman, 127–129; transience and, 105–107, 125, 130n5
deliberation, 36
delusion (*ghirra*), 86–88
Dependent Rational Animals (McIntyre), 122
despair, 47
devotional reasoning, 54
diagnostic reasoning, 54
dignity: of beings, 123–125; frugality and, 144; human, 141
discord, 147–149
discourse, Hadot on, 21
discursive practices, 12, 15, 22–23, 37–40, 64, 74
discursive tradition, Islam as, 18

distinct stratum of analysis, 17
diversity, in Islam, 1
Divine Determining, 125–127, 150
divine punishment, reward and, 40–42
divine reward and punishment, 40–42
dying, transience and, 105–107

the elderly, on the hereafter, 123
embarrassment, as moral ideal, 78–80
embodiment, 12
enjoining the good and forbidding the wrong (*ḥisba*), 68
environmental and work ethics, of Nursi, 141–146
envy, health rivalry and, 91–94
eternal bliss, 32–33
ethical-cultural dimension, 14
ethics, 17; of againstness, 64; anthropology and, 20; of causality, 138; of conjunction, 138–141; environmental and work, of Nursi, 141–146; Foucault on, 17–18, 48; of ideal moral subject, 135–136; of listening, 36–37; Muslim, 2, 18, 23, 48, 160; practical, 88–89; religious, 12–14, 23–24; virtue, 17, 23
Ethics, Demonstrated in Geometrical Order (Spinoza), 135
externalization, internalization and, 13–17

faith, 99, 163. *See also* belief
fasting, 140
Faubion, James, 20
favor, of God, 37–40, 75
fear, 40, 66, 88
feeling favored, as discursive practice, 37–40
Fessenden, Tracy, 130n2, 159–160
fiqh (Islamic law), 2, 9, 21, 48
fiṭra (goodness), 126
The Flashes (Nursi), 141
food consumption, 142–143
Foucault, Michel, 17–20; on care of the self, 23; Davidson on, 17–18, 28n57; on ethics, 17–18, 48; Hadot and, 160–161; Muhasabi, Nursi and, 18, 28n57, 160; Muhasibi and, 80; on subjectivation, 20; on technologies of the self, 17, 19, 21

friendship: Aristotle on, 70; ideal moral subjects and, 66–71; mutual direction as, 68–72
frugality: dignity and, 144; generosity and, 143; greed and, 143; Nursian environmental and work ethics and, 141–146; wisdom and, 141–143; work and, 143–146

gendered moral subjects, 151–153
generosity, frugality and, 143
Ghamari-Tabrizi, Behrooz, 23
ghirra (delusion), 86–88
God: as active force in lives, 40; art and beauty of, 115; avowal and, 32; *bismillah*, 111; blessings from, 57, 85–86, 92–94, 139; commands of, 31, 53; compassion of, 140; connection through belief, 107–108; devotional reasoning and, 54; divine reward and punishment, 40–42; embarrassment and, 78–79; favor of, 37–40, 75, 87, 88; fear of, 88; glorifying, 145; gratitude to, 57; heart and, 88; the I and, 108–109, 110, 111, 112; ideal moral subject and, 66–67; ideal subject selling oneself to, 110–113; intelligence, 110; mystical subject and, 10–11; *nafs* and, 34, 39–40, 41–42, 91; names of, 101–102, 104, 111, 113, 116, 122, 127, 150, 164; obedience to, 33, 41–42, 49, 51, 52, 52–53, 59n5, 90–91; obligations to, 49–53, 58n2, 81; protective concealment of, 86–88; punishment of, 40–42, 84; qualities of, 107–108; Quran and, 100; reliance on, 88–89; reward from, 85; Satan and, 45–47, 58; signs of, 102; slaves of, 87–88; as source of good, 93; as *wahdahu*, 112; will of, 49; wisdom, 145–146; worship of, 65–66, 88–89. *See also* beautiful names of God; belief; rights of God
God-awareness, 86–87
God's majesty and dignity (*mutakabbir*), 89
God's oneness. *See tawhid*
God's predetermination (*qadar*), 76, 125–127, 150

good: actions, 77; celebrating, 139; God as source of, 93; ideal religious subject as desirer of, 57–58
the good and the bad, 8
goodness (*fitra*), 126
gratitude, 57, 59n18, 139, 141, 143
greed, 56, 77, 143, 145

habits, 86–88
habitus: bodily practices, ideal Muslim subjectivity and, 35; Foucault, subjectivation and, 17–20
Hadot, Pierre, 21–22, 29n74, 160–161
Hallaq, Wael, 9–10
health rivalry, 91–94
heart: God and, 88; Muhasibi on, 33–34, 63–64
He is the only one (*wahdahu*), 112
the hereafter: belief in, subject formation and, 120–125; consolations for the young and the infirm, 122–123; dignity of beings and, 123–125; unrequited injustices and, 120–122
hisba (enjoining the good and forbidding the wrong), 68
human affliction, 117–119
human capacities, 107–110
human dignity, 141
human self, 108
human will, 127
humility, 89, 162
hypocrisy (*riya*), 73–74, 76–77, 87–88

the I, 16, 108–109, 110, 111, 112
ideal consciousness, 16
ideal Jewish subject, 15–16
ideal moral subjectivity: as discursive, 74; obedience to God in, 90–91. *See also* Muhasibi, on ideal moral subject; Nursi, on ideal moral subject
ideal Muslim subjectivity, 1–3, 4; habitus and bodily practices in, 35; Muhasibi and Nursi on, 16; Muhasibi on, 1, 2–3, 4, 35
ideal Muslim subjects: acts of spirituality in, 23; juridical and mystical accounts of, 2; as juridical subject, 9–10; as mystical subject, 10–12; Quran and, 6

ideal religious subject: on eternal bliss, 32–33; heart of, 33–34; procrastination by, 43; on purpose of life, 32–33. *See also* Muhasibi, on ideal religious subject; Nursi, on ideal religious subject
ideal religious subjectivity, 14, 35, 57–58
ideal standpoints, 14, 146
ideal subject. *See specific topics*
The Idea of an Anthropology of Islam (Asad), 18
identity, 154
idolatry (*shirk*), 73
imitation, influence and, 74–75
imitative belief, 100
indicative meaning: beautiful names of God and, 101–102, 127; nominative meaning and, 101, 102
individualities, multiple, 129
individuality, 146–149
inequality, 151–152
injustices, unrequited, 120–122
inner duties, 33
insincerity, 73
intelligence, 110–111
intention, 75
intentional exchange of greetings, 85–86
internalizations, externalizations and, 13–17
intersubjective receptivity, arrogance and, 89–91
intersubjectivity, 16, 81
in the name of God (*bismillah*), 111
intimacies, 68–72, 81
inwardness, 31, 33
Islam: anthropology and, 18, 19, 35; Christianity and, 49; as discursive tradition, 18; diversity in, 1; humility in, 89; pride in, 89–90; *tawhid* in, 102
Islamic extremism, 167–168
Islamic jurisprudence, 22–23
Islamic law (*fiqh* or *sharia*), 2, 9, 21, 48
Islamic theology, 22–23

James, William, 31
Jesus, 119
Job (prophet), 118
Jonah (prophet), 117–119
juridical and mystical modes, 2, 9–12
juridical subject, 9–10

Kennett, Jeanette, 70
kibr (pride or arrogance), 89–91
knowledge, of Quran, 36

The Language of the Birds (al-Attar), 11
Lear, Jonathan, 14–15
Lewis, Thomas, 12–13, 25n2
Lincoln, Bruce, 71
listening, proper, 36–37
livelihoods, 140
loyalty, 136–137

MacIntyre, Alasdair, 17
Mahmood, Saba, 18, 19–20, 29n68
al-Makāsib (Muhasibi), 88
malāmatiyya, 76
Massignon, Louis, 25n9
McIntyre, Alasdair, 122
meaning, 101–102, 127
medieval Christianity, 49
Miller, Richard, 12, 13–14, 16–17, 71, 81–82; on criticism, 81–82
Miller, Vincent, 142
miracles, 119–120
mirroring: apophatic, 109; the I, God and, 109, 110; positive, 109; responsive, 109
modern civil law, 151
Moosa, Ebrahim, 28n55
moral agency, 136–138
moral authority, 71
Moral Authority and Moral Critique in an Age of Ethnocentric Anxiety (Miller), 81–82
moral philosophers, 17, 18
moral subjectivity, 18, 20, 64, 65; ethics of conjunction and, 138; religious subjectivity and, 13. *See also* Muhasibi, on ideal moral subject; Nursi, on ideal moral subject
moral virtue, 78
Muhammad (prophet), 50, 54, 88–89, 101, 116
al-Muhasibi, al-Harith b. Asad: anthropology of, 35; on arrogance and self-righteousness, 4; on avowal, God and, 32; on deliberation, 36; Foucault and, 80; on the good and the bad, 8; on heart, 33–34, 63–64; on ideal Muslim subjectivity, 1, 2–3, 4, 35; on ideal

religious subjectivity, 35, 57–58; on juridical subject, 10; *al-Makāsib* by, 88; mysticism and Sufism of, 6–7; on *nafs*, 6, 32, 33, 34–35, 36, 39–40, 41–42, 51–52; on *naṣīḥa*, 69, 71, 72; Nursi and, 3–12, 15–17, 18, 20, 23, 28n57, 159–166, 168; Picken on, 4; on pride, 89–90; on purpose of life, 32–33; on self-scrutiny, 65; on worship, 65–66

al-Muhasibi, on ideal moral subject: acting publicly, 74, 76; advisor-advisee relationship, 71–72; arrogance, intersubjective receptivity and, 89–91; criticism, other-regard and, 81–84; delusion habituation, God's protective concealment and, 86–88; embarrassment of, 78–80; envy, healthy rivalry and, 91–94; friendship, mutual direction and, 68–72; friends of, 66–71; God and, 66–67; heart of, 63–64; hypocrisy and, 73–74, 87–88; intentional exchange of greetings, 85–86; intentions of, 75; intimacies of, 68–72; praise, blame and, 75–76; praise and, 73–77; pretense, role modeling and, 73–77; sincerity of, 63, 64; sociality and self-care negotiated by, 65–68; threats discursively negotiated by, 64

al-Muhasibi, on ideal religious subject: *aḥkām alkhamsa* and, 48, 49, 50–53; avowal by, 32; on contemplation of death, 42–45; deliberation and patience of, 36; as desirer of good, 57–58; divine reward and punishment and, 40–42; fear of, 40; God as active force in lives of, 40; God's favor and, 37–40; human psyche and, 35–36; inwardness of, 31, 33; knowledge of Quran and, 36; *nafs* and, 41; obedience to God, 33, 41–42, 49, 51, 52, 52–53; obligations of God, 49–53; proper listening by, 36–37; rationalities of, 53–55; repentance by, 37–40, 42–43; rights of God and, 31, 33, 33–35, 36–37, 42–43; suggestions and self-examinations by, 33–36; *sunna* and, 50–51, 55; wariness of Satan, 45–48; *zuhd* and, 55–57

multiple individualities, 129

mundane social encounters, sacralizing, 85–86
Muslim ethics, 2, 18, 23, 48, 160
Muslim intellectual history, 21
Muslim subjectivity, 2, 20, 21, 23
mutakabbir (God's majesty and dignity), 89
mutual direction, as friendship, 68–72
mystical subject, 10–12; God and, 10–11
mysticism, 6–7, 22–23
mystic piety, 6

nafs (recalcitrant soul): God and, 34, 39–40, 41–42, 91; hypocrisy and, 87–88; inner state of, 63; Muhasibi on, 6, 32, 33, 34–35, 36, 39–40, 41–42, 51–52; Nursi on, 106–107; obedience to God, 53; penitents and, 38; repentance and, 38; self-scrutiny, 79; *taqwa* and, 86–87
naṣīḥa, 69, 71, 72, 81, 83, 96n28
natural causes, Nursi on, 103–105
New England Protestants, 130n2
the New Said, 4–5
Nietzsche, Friedrich, 20
no-god-but-God perspective, 116, 117
nominative meaning, 101, 102
non-action, 64
Nursi, Bediuzzaman Said, 132n29; on beauty of world, 8, 115–119; on belief, 99; on belief perspectives, 99–100; on *bismillah*, 111; on blessedness, 135; on death of Abdurrahman, 127–129; in exile, 5; *The Flashes* by, 141; on human being as antique work of art, 107; on the I, 108–109; on the I, God and, 108–109, 110, 111, 112; on ideal Muslim subjectivity, 1, 2–3; on juridical subject, 10; on livelihoods, 140; Muhasibi and, 3–12, 15–17, 18, 20, 23, 28n57, 159–166, 168; mysticism and Sufism of, 6–7; on *nafs*, 106–107; on natural causes, 103–105; on oneness of God, 103, 104–105; on al-Qarani, 109; on Quran, 5–6, 7, 100–101, 102, 115, 117–118, 119–120, 129, 130n8, 147–148, 151–153, 154–155, 156n9; *Risale-i Nur* by, 5, 7, 138–139, 153; self-narration by, 127;

on standpoints of belief, 135; on studentship of Quran, 101; on Sufism, 130n9; treatise for the sick, 137–138

Nursi, on ideal moral subject: brotherhood, individuality and, 146–149; compassion and, 136–141; discord and, 147–149; eternal life and, 137; ethics, 135–136; ethics of conjunction, 138–141; frugality of, 141–146; gendered, 151–153; generosity, frugality and, 143; hierarchy, indebtedness and, 138–141; politics, service and, 154–155; standpoint of, 146; temporality, relationships and, 136–138; as victim of oppression, 149–151; wisdom, frugality and, 142–143; work, frugality and, 143–146

Nursi, on ideal religious subject: belief in the hereafter, subject formation and, 120–125; belief in *qadar*, 76, 125–127; belief perspective of, 100; connection with God through belief, 107–108; consolations for young and infirm, 122–123; dialectics of belief, 127–129; on dignity of beings, 123–125; dying, transience and, 105–107; Jonah, human affliction and, 117–119; Muhammad and, 116; multiple personalities, 129; on natural causes, 103–105; oneness of God and, 103, 104–105, 107, 108, 110; practices of belief, 99; prophethood, subject formation and, 115–120; prophetic miracles and, 119–120; on prophets as possibility of cherishing beauty, 115–117; Quran, God and, 100; scientific progress and discovery and, 119–120; selling oneself to God, 110–113; supplication as agency, 113–114; *tawhid*, human capacities and, 107–110; *tawhid*, subject formation and, 102–114

obedience, to God, 33, 41–42, 49, 51, 52, 52–53, 59n5, 90–91
obligations: to God, 49–53, 58n2, 81; rights and, 31
oneness, of God. *See tawhid*
oppression, victims of, 149–151
orthodoxy, 31

other-regard, criticism and, 81–84
Ottoman Empire, 4

parrhesia, 23
patience, deliberation and, 36
penitents, 37–38
perfection, 54, 161–162
philosophical anthropology, 15
Picken, Gavin, 4, 26n18
piety, 4, 6
pity, 137–138
pluralism, 159
politics, service and, 154–155
positive mirroring, 109
postponement (*al-taswif*), 42
practical ethics, 88–89
practices of belief: bodily practices, 35, 87; by ideal religious subject, 99; reflective self-scrutiny and, 23
praise, 73–77; blame and, 75–76, 78
praxis, 22
predetermination, of God, 76, 125–127, 150
pretense, role modeling and, 73–77
pride (*kibr*), 89–91
procrastination, 42–43
proper listening, 36–37
prophethood: miracles and, 119–120; as possibility of cherishing beauty, 115–117; subject formation and, 115–120; supplications and, 117–119
prophetic example (*sunna*), 35, 50–51, 55
prophets: beautiful names of God and, 116; Jesus, 119; Job, 118; Jonah, 117–119; Muhammad, 50, 54, 88–89, 101, 116
protective concealment (*satr*), 86–88
purpose of life, 32–33

qadar (God's predetermination), 76, 125–127, 150
al-Qarani, Uways, 109
Quran, 120; on Abraham, 119–120; on *fitra*, 126; God and, 100; ideal Muslim subjects and, 6; on Jesus, 119; Job in, 118; Jonah in, 117, 118; knowledge of, 36; Muhammad and, 101; Nursi on, 5–6, 7, 100–101, 102, 115, 117–118, 119–120, 129, 130n8, 147–148, 151–153, 154–155, 156n9; on perfect

justice and mercy, 151; politics and, 154–155; Satan in, 89; studentship of, 101

Radical Hope (Lear), 14–15
rationalities, 53–55
realization, 114
reason, 36, 53–55
recalcitrant soul. *See nafs*
reflective belief, 100
reflective self-scrutiny, 23
relationships, 136–138
reliance on God, 88–89
religion, orthodoxy and, 31
religious ethics, 12–14, 23–24
religious subject. *See* Muhasibi, on ideal religious subject; Nursi, on ideal religious subject
religious subjectivity, 14; moral subjectivity and, 13; threats to, 63–64
repentance: Muhasibi on, 37–40, 42–43; rights of God and, 37–39
responsive mirroring, 109
resurrection, 106
rights, obligations and, 31
rights of God: contemplation of death and, 44–45; death, transience and, 107; ideal religious subject and, 31; ideal subject and, 33–35, 36–37, 42–43; inwardness and, 33; Muhasibi on, 31, 33, 33–35, 36–37, 42–43; procrastination and, 42–43; proper listening and, 36–37; repentance and, 37–39; self-subjection, 32–33; *zuhd* and, 55–56
Risale-i Nur (Nursi), 5, 7, 138–139, 153
riya (hypocrisy), 73–74, 76–77, 87–88
role modeling, pretense and, 73–77
Rorty, Richard, 21, 29n72

Satan, 150; God and, 45–47, 58; in Quran, 89; wariness of, 45–48
satr (protective concealment), 86–88
Schofer, Jonathan, 15, 16–17, 153
Schweiker, William, 23–24
scientific progress and discovery, 119–120
self-care: Muhasibi and Nursi on, 23; sociality and, 65–68
self-examination, 33–36
self-formation, 19, 20, 23

self-righteousness, 4
self-scrutiny, 23, 36, 65, 79
self-subjection, 32–33
Sells, Michael, 26n24
sense of taste, 143
service, politics and, 154–155
shame, 79, 80
sharia (Islamic law), 2, 9, 21, 48
shaykh (Sufi teacher), 10–11, 101
shirk (idolatry), 73
signs, of God, 102
sincerity, 63, 64
slaves of God, 87–88
sociality, self-care and, 65–68
social media, 81
speed, 166–167
Spinoza, Baruch, 135
spirituality: acts of, 23; reflective self-scrutiny, practices of belief and, 23
standpoint, 20; of belief, 135; of devotional reasoning, 54; God's rights and, 31; of gratitude to God, 57; of the "I", 16; ideal, 14, 146
Stoicism, 23
subject formation: belief in hereafter and, 120–125; prophethood and, 115–120; *tawhid* and, 102–114
subjectivation, 17–20
subjectivity, 12; internalizations, externalization and, 13–17; Muslim, 2, 20, 21, 23. *See also* moral subjectivity; religious subjectivity
subjects, 16; *See also specific topics*
Sufism, 2, 4, 6–7, 11, 22–23, 130n9
Sufi teacher (*Shaykh*), 10–11, 101
suggestions, self-examinations and, 33–36, 36
sunna (prophetic example), 35, 50–51, 55
Sunnis, Alawis and, 148
supplication: as agency, 113–114; prophethood and, 117–119

taqwa (consciousness or awareness), 86–87
al-taswif (postponement), 42
tawhid (God's oneness), 11, 63, 73, 161; belief and, 102–103, 112; human capacities and, 107–110; subject formation and, 102–114

Taylor, Charles, 70, 130n6
technologies of the self, 17, 19, 20, 21
temporality, 136–138
transience, death and, 105–107, 125, 130n5
trial, 64
truth, 23
Turner, Colin, 154

'ujb (conceit), 89
unity and cohesion, of believers, 147
unrequited injustices, 120–122

Vahide, Sukran, 5
virtue ethics, 17, 23

waḥdahu (He is the only one), 112
wariness of Satan, 45–48
wastefulness, 143
Why Philosophy Matters for the Study of Religion—and Vice Versa (Lewis), 12
wisdom, 141–143, 145–146
work, 88–89
work, frugality and, 143–146
work ethics, environmental ethics and, 141–146
worship, 65–66, 88–89

Zargar, Cyrus, 11, 27n37
zuhd (abstention), 55–57

About the Author

Faraz Masood Sheikh is assistant professor of religious ethics in the Department of Religious Studies at William & Mary in Williamsburg, Virginia. His teaching and research focus on the relationship between religious and philosophical ideas and the forms of psychic and cultural life made possible by individual and collective engagements with those ideas in different historical contexts. His research engages with several fields of study in the humanities, including religious studies, comparative religious ethics, anthropology, Islamic studies, Quranic studies and moral philosophy. Faraz also has interests in premodern South Asian Urdu and Punjabi poetry and contemporary social and political ethics in comparative perspective. He is past vice president (2017–2019) of the Society for the Study of Muslim Ethics. He holds a bachelor's in computer science from the Lahore University of Management Sciences. He got his PhD in religious studies from Indiana University Bloomington. His work has been published in the *Journal of Religious Ethics* and *Comparative Islamic Studies* journal. When he is not researching or teaching, he likes to spend time with his family and friends in Philadelphia, and travel to be with family in Istanbul, Karachi, London and Lahore.